the complete

QUICK SHORT

RECIPE COLLECTION

the complete
QUICK SHORT
RECIPE COLLECTION

INDEX

contents

special features

key for symbols

Although all the recipes in this collection have a quick preparation time, our 'super quick' symbol means the combined preparation and cooking time is no more than 25 minutes. 'Low-fat' recipes have a fat content of 10 g or less, and 'vegetarian' recipes are meat-free, but may contain dairy products.

 super quick   **low-fat**   **vegetarian**

Organisation is the key to successful 'quick' cooking. Before you begin, read through the recipe thoroughly, check your pantry and take note of the equipment you will need. As this book will show, it *is* possible to have a recipe that has a short list of ingredients and a relatively short preparation time, yet not be short on flavour.

pantry staples

A well-stocked pantry means fewer hurdles when answering the "What's for dinner?" question, giving you the wherewithal to rustle up a wide range of creative and tasty possibilities. Gone are the days of frustration and disappointment, when, after finally deciding what to prepare, you discover you are missing the vital ingredient.

'Pantry staples' are non-perishable products common to many recipes such as flour, canned tomatoes and dried herbs, and those that make versatile accompaniments (rice, pasta and couscous).

purchase & storage tips

• Store dry ingredients, such as flour, sugar and nuts, in airtight containers as weevils can be a problem in open packets.
• Unopened canned products will last for months provided they are not rusty or damaged.
• Bottles and jars should be stored in the refrigerator once they have been opened.
• Pastes, such as tomato and curry, can be frozen in ice-cube trays. This allows you to keep it for much longer and in convenient small portions for easy use.
• Always check the use-by date of products. Try to have a regular clean-out so you know which basic staples need to be restocked.

pantry staples

pantry staples

beans, canned
breadcrumbs, dry
coconut cream/milk
couscous
curry paste
dried fruits
dried herbs and spices
flour (plain, self-raising)
noodles
nuts (almonds, hazelnuts)
oil (olive, peanut)
rice (arborio, long-grain)
stock (cubes, tetra packs)
pasta
pasta sauce, tomato
sugar (brown, caster)
tomato paste
tomatoes, canned

fresh produce

'Fresh produce' refers to fruit and vegetables, seafood, meat, chicken and dairy products. They should be stored in the refrigerator or freezer with the exception of potatoes, tomatoes and garlic. Fresh produce have a comparatively short shelf life and need to be restocked more frequently than pantry staples.

purchase & storage tips

• Buy fresh fruit and vegetables every few days to gain the best possible texture and flavour. Vegetables keep best in the crisper section of the refrigerator.

• Potatoes and onions are best stored in a cool, dark, dry place. Avoid storing them together as the potatoes will tend to rot. Onions can be kept in the refrigerator—this may also prevent teary eyes.
• Wrap fresh herbs in a damp tea towel or in plastic bags and store in an airtight container. Fresh herbs, when chopped, can also be kept in sealable bags and stored in the freezer.
• Meat and chicken will keep for 2–3 days in the refrigerator. Always put the meat on a plate or tray, cover with plastic wrap or foil, and place on the bottom shelf in the refrigerator to prevent any juice dripping onto other foods.
• When freezing meat or chicken, wrap tightly in foil or plastic wrap and expel any excess air. Label and date the outside.
• Defrost meat or chicken overnight in the refrigerator to keep the meat at a temperature which limits bacterial growth. Never re-freeze meat unless it has been cooked first.
• When selecting meats that are quick to cook, look for boneless cuts. Most butchers can provide a wide range of meats that are pre-trimmed, pre-cut or diced.
• Leftover bread can be made into breadcrumbs and frozen in plastic bags ready for use.
• Products such as margarine, butter, milk, cheese and eggs should be stored in the refrigerator. Wrap block cheese in foil or kitchen paper—avoid using plastic wrap.

With the correct equipment, chopping and cooking can be a breeze. Carefully selected utensils and gadgets, pots and pans, glass and ceramic dishes and electrical appliances can help no end with the preparation of food and, in some cases, take over the job!

types & uses

• Utensils such as egg flips, spatulas, tongs, whisks, ladles, and wooden and metal spoons are part of the most essential and versatile pieces of equipment in the kitchen. They are ideal for mixing cakes, stirring and serving soups, beating egg whites and flipping omelettes.

• Garlic presses, kitchen scissors, graters, zesters, potato mashers and good workable peelers are worth their weight in gold when trying to prepare a meal quickly.

• Measuring cups, spoons and jugs are vital to accurately measure ingredients such as flour and milk, particularly for cakes and desserts. Electronic or manual scales may also be useful for weighing other types of ingredients such as meat and vegetables.

• Good-quality knives made from stainless steel or carbon make slicing and dicing effortless. The most frequently used knives in the kitchen would be the cook's knife and a good paring knife.

• A set of good-quality saucepans can assist with quicker cooking by providing good even heat conduction. This allows fewer opportunities for food to catch on the bottom of the pan.

• Large, non-stick frying pans allow for quick evaporation. This is handy when reducing sauces or liquids.

• Many glass, enamel or ceramic dishes are heatproof, ovenproof and microwave safe. In many cases they are attractive enough to serve in. These dishes come in a range of sizes.

equipment

baking tin
egg flip
food processor
frying pan
garlic press
kitchen scissors
knives
ladle
measuring cups and spoons
metal and wooden spoons
pastry brush
potato masher
saucepans
scales
slotted spoon
spatula
tongs
vegetable peeler
whisk
wok

maintenance

• Wooden utensils such as spoons and pastry brushes are best washed well in hot soapy water. It is important that they are stored dry to help stop bacteria or mould forming when not in use.

• Non-stick tins and pans may be easily scratched if you use metal utensils—use wooden or plastic.

• Line non-stick baking trays with baking paper to prevent baked-on stains accumulating on your tray— this also makes washing up easy.

• Sharpen stainless steel or carbon knives with a steel when not in use. Store knives in a knife block to keep the edges sharp.

electrical

• Electrical appliances such as rice cookers can take over the cooking for you—there's no need to keep a watchful eye on the boiling pot.

• Electric woks are very convenient, but make sure you buy one with the highest wattage possible, otherwise it may not retain the heat throughout cooking. Woks are designed to cook food very quickly at a high temperature and can put a meal on the table in minutes.

• Electric beaters or mix masters are great for preparing smooth batters and cake mixtures, taking the muscle out of beating by hand.

• Food processors and blenders should have a good motor, a strong blade and a bowl large enough to cope with different capacities. They are great for making purées, pesto, mayonnaise and sauces. Small food processors or spice grinders can also grind nuts and spices and make fresh breadcrumbs.

• Handheld blenders are useful for blending soups, sauces and drinks. The advantages of this blender is, obviously, its compact size and its ability to process in any container (glass jug or saucepan), meaning less washing up—which is always a bonus!

• Microwave ovens are commonly used for reheating and defrosting. They also allow you to make great meals in less time, leaving more flavour and nutrients in the food.

• Microwaves are handy for melting chocolate, toasting nuts and drying fresh breadcrumbs in less time than the conventional methods.

You've got the right ingredients and time-saving equipment, but you've only got an hour to whip up a sumptuous meal. With these quick cooking techniques, you'll have that meal on the table with time to spare!

baking

- Preheating your oven is very important when baking, as the oven must reach the required temperature before you are ready to bake.
- When making cakes, always grease and line the tin. This prevents the mixture from sticking to the base and sides.

deep-frying

- Ensure that the saucepan you are using is secure on the stove top, and never leave the hot oil unattended—oil can ignite easily if it is overheated.
- Fill the saucepan one-third full of oil to reduce the possibilities of boiling over. A low to medium heat is sufficient to heat the oil to its required deep-frying temperature.
- Always test the oil before you deep-fry by dropping in a cube of bread. The bread should take 10–35 seconds to brown depending on the temperature required. For example, if the oil is heated to moderate 180°C (350°F) the cube of bread will brown in 15 seconds. The hotter the oil, the less time the bread will take to brown.
- Cook the food in batches to avoid the food sticking together and to provide even cooking. Keep the cooked batch warm in a moderate 180°C (350°F/Gas 4) oven.
- Be careful when lifting the food in and out of the hot oil with tongs or a metal slotted spoon—hot oil will burn you! Drain on several layers of crumpled paper towel.

techniques

techniques
baking
deep-frying
grilling/chargrilling
microwave cooking
steaming
stir-frying

grilling & chargrilling

- Grilling or chargrilling is a fast, healthy way to cook. Preheat the grill or chargrill to hot before adding meats, seafood or vegetables.

microwave cooking

- Cooking in the microwave is quick and fuss-free—cooking times are reduced and you'll often be able to prepare, mix, cook and serve from the same dish.
- All ovenproof glass containers are suitable to use in the microwave, so too are paper or plastic plates. However, metal dishes or dishes with a metal trim are a big no-no as they will damage the microwave.
- When arranging food in a dish always remember that the food on the outer edges of the dish will cook the quickest—place the thickest part of the food at the edge.
- Vegetables should only take a few minutes to cook in the microwave. Keep in mind, microwaves vary in wattage, so cooking times will differ from brand to brand.
- The microwave is a great device for thawing soups and stews or reheating leftovers.

steaming

- Fish and vegetables are great served steamed and take very little time. Fish can be steamed in a covered bamboo steamer over a wok of boiling water or wrapped in foil and cooked in the oven. Steam vegetables in a metal steamer over a saucepan of boiling water. Ensure the bottom of either type of steamer doesn't touch the water.

stir-frying

- Prepare all your ingredients before you heat the wok. Bite-size pieces of meat and vegetables take very little time to cook over high heat and require constant stirring to avoid overcooking or burning. Organise your ingredients in the order that they will be added to speed up the process. Cut the meat across the grain to make it tender.
- Heat the wok before adding the oil. Add the oil and swirl it around to coat. If the oil sizzles when the first ingredient is added, it is ready.
- If there is a large quantity of an ingredient to be added to the wok at one time, such as meat, cook it in batches. This ensures that the meat is cooked quickly, stays tender and doesn't stew.
- Be careful when adding wet ingredients such as washed vegetables and marinated foods to a hot wok, as the oil will spit when the water hits the surface.
- Do not cover the wok during cooking as the food will steam.
- Stir-fries should be served as soon as they have been cooked.

chicken

ingredients

340 g jar marinated
  artichokes in oil
150 g button mushrooms,
  sliced
100 g semi-dried tomatoes
1 red onion, cut into rings
¼ cup (15 g) finely
  shredded fresh basil
1 barbecued chicken
150 g rocket leaves,
  trimmed
200 g feta, cubed

preparation: 10 minutes
cooking: nil
serves: 4–6

1 Place the artichokes and the oil marinade in a large bowl and add the mushrooms, tomato, onion and basil.

2 Remove the skin and bones from the chicken and cut the flesh into bite-sized pieces. Add to the salad and toss well. Season to taste.

3 Arrange the rocket leaves on a serving plate and top with the salad. Scatter the feta over the top and serve with crusty bread.

nutrition per serve (6)
Protein 30 g; Fat 12 g; Carbohydrate 2.5 g; Dietary Fibre 3 g; Cholesterol 87 mg; 960 kJ (230 cal)

handy tip...

Buy semi-dried tomatoes at good supermarkets and delicatessens. If not available, use sun-dried tomatoes. Feta is a salty cheese made from sheep's milk. If the flavour is too strong, use chopped bocconcini. This salad can also be made using 3 thinly sliced smoked chicken breasts.

ingredients

1.5 kg chicken drumsticks
¾ cup (185 ml) buttermilk
1½ tablespoons olive oil
1 cup (150 g) polenta
1 cup (100 g) dry
    breadcrumbs
½ teaspoon chilli powder
    (optional)
2 eggs
40 g unsalted butter,
    melted

preparation: 15 minutes
cooking: 50 minutes
serves: 4–6

1 Preheat the oven to moderate 180°C (350°F/Gas 4). Grease a foil-lined baking tray. Cut two deep incisions into the thickest part of the drumstick (this ensures even cooking). Place the drumsticks in a bowl, add the buttermilk and oil and toss to coat.

2 Place the polenta, breadcrumbs and chilli powder in another bowl. Season to taste, then mix together. Put the eggs in a small bowl and whisk with 1 tablespoon water.

3 Dip the chicken in the egg mixture, then coat with the polenta mixture, pressing with your fingers to make the crumbs stick. Arrange on the prepared tray and drizzle with melted butter. Bake for 45–50 minutes, or until the chicken is crisp and golden. Serve with sweet potato mash and a green salad, if desired.

nutrition per serve (6)
Protein 56 g; Fat 27 g; Carbohydrate 30 g; Dietary Fibre 1.5 g; Cholesterol 287 mg; 2476 kJ (592 cal)

hint

Oven-frying delivers a crisp, crunchy crust with a lot less fat than traditional deep-frying. For an even leaner version, remove the skin from the chicken before coating.
To make the 'fried' chicken really moist, marinate the drumsticks in the buttermilk and oil for up to 8 hours.

ingredients

500 g chicken breast
  fillets, with skin
2 tablespoons peanut or
  vegetable oil
2 spring onions, diced
2 bird's eye chillies, finely
  chopped
2 tablespoons soy sauce
2 tablespoons fish sauce
2 tablespoons grated
  palm sugar
1 cup (30 g) loosely
  packed fresh basil

preparation: 10 minutes
cooking: 12 minutes
serves: 4

1 Cut the chicken breasts into small cubes. Heat the oil in the wok and swirl to coat. Add the chicken in batches and stir-fry over high heat for 5 minutes each batch, or until the chicken is tender.

2 Add the spring onion and chilli and stir-fry for 1 minute. Add the soy sauce, fish sauce and sugar and toss briefly. Stir in the basil and serve with jasmine rice.

nutrition per serve
Protein 30 g; Fat 12 g; Carbohydrate 2.5 g; Dietary Fibre 0.5 g; Cholesterol 62 mg; 1007 kJ (240 cal)

handy tip...

Palm sugar is made from the sap of the coconut palm. It is sold in Asian supermarkets. If unavailable, use brown sugar.
This recipe uses authentic Thai flavour and the chicken may be substituted with fish or tofu.

ingredients

5 cm piece fresh galangal
2 cups (500 ml) coconut
    milk
1 cup (250 ml) chicken
    stock
3 chicken breast fillets,
    cut into thin strips
1–2 teaspoons finely
    chopped red chillies
2 tablespoons fish sauce
1 teaspoon soft brown
    sugar
¼ cup (7 g) fresh
    coriander leaves

preparation: 15 minutes
cooking: 20 minutes
serves: 4

1 Peel the galangal and cut it into thin slices. Place the galangal, coconut milk and stock in a saucepan. Bring to the boil, then reduce the heat to low and simmer for 10 minutes, stirring occasionally.

2 Add the chicken and chilli to the pan and simmer for a further 8 minutes. Stir in the fish sauce and brown sugar.

3 Add the coriander leaves and serve immediately, garnished with extra sprigs of coriander, if desired.

nutrition per serve
Protein 37 g; Fat 30 g; Carbohydrate 6.5 g; Dietary Fibre 2.5 g; Cholesterol 75 mg; 1805 kJ (430 cal)

hint

If fresh galangal is not available, you can use 5 large slices of dried galangal instead. Prepare it by soaking the slices in ½ cup (125 ml) boiling water for 10 minutes before slicing it into small shreds. Add the liquid to the chicken stock to make up 1 cup (250 ml) and use as above.

ingredients

800 g chicken breast
    fillets, cut into
    bite-size cubes
1/2 cup (125 ml) barbecue
    marinade
1 loaf Turkish bread,
    halved lengthways
lettuce leaves, to serve

Salsa
2 large tomatoes, finely
    chopped
1 Lebanese cucumber,
    finely chopped
1 peach or nectarine,
    finely chopped
1/2 cup (25 g) chopped
    fresh coriander leaves

preparation: 15 minutes
cooking: 10 minutes
serves: 4

1 Soak 8 skewers in a bowl of cold water to prevent them from burning while the kebabs are cooking. Preheat a grill or barbecue hot plate.

2 Thread the chicken cubes onto the skewers and place in a shallow dish. Coat with the barbecue marinade, cover and refrigerate until ready to use.

3 To make the salsa, place the tomato, cucumber, peach and coriander in a bowl and mix together well.

4 Remove the kebabs from the marinade (reserving the marinade) and place in a single layer on the hot grill or barbecue hot plate. Cook for 3 minutes, then turn and cook for a further 3 minutes, or until the chicken is cooked through. Baste with the reserved marinade during cooking.

5 Cut the Turkish bread into 8 slices, then cook under a hot grill until golden.

6 Arrange the lettuce leaves on the Turkish bread. Remove the chicken cubes from the skewers and place on top of the lettuce. Serve with the fruity salsa.

nutrition per serve
Protein 54 g; Fat 8 g; Carbohydrate 60 g; Dietary Fibre 4 g; Cholesterol 100 mg; 2159 kJ (516 cal)

handy tip...

You could use mango or pawpaw instead of the peach. Sprinkle the salsa with balsamic vinegar or lemon juice for a more tangy taste.

ingredients

⅓ cup (80 ml) barbecue sauce
1 tablespoon honey
¼ cup (60 g) mayonnaise
2 cloves garlic, crushed
2 teaspoons grated fresh ginger
4 chicken breast fillets (about 200 g each)

preparation: 10 minutes + overnight marinating
cooking: 16 minutes
serves: 4

1 Place the barbecue sauce, honey, mayonnaise, garlic and ginger in a bowl and mix together well. Add the chicken fillets and toss until well coated. Cover and refrigerate for at least 2 hours or preferably overnight.

2 Place the chicken breasts on a cold, lightly oiled grill tray. Cook under a hot grill, brushing occasionally with the remaining marinade, for 5–8 minutes. Turn and cook the other side for 5–8 minutes, or until the chicken is tender and cooked through. Slice the chicken fillets and serve with a crisp mixed green salad, if desired.

nutrition per serve
Protein 46 g; Fat 9.5 g; Carbohydrate 17 g; Dietary Fibre 0.5 g; Cholesterol 105 mg; 1402 kJ (335 cal)

hint

The glaze in this recipe is suitable for other cuts of chicken such as thigh fillets, wings and drumsticks.
Try cooking the chicken on the barbecue instead of grilling.

ingredients

1 tablespoon oil
2 cloves garlic, crushed
4 spring onions, sliced
1 litre chicken stock
500 g broccoli florets
400 g chicken breast
    fillets, cut into thin strips
½ cup (125 g) sour cream

preparation: 15 minutes
cooking: 12 minutes
serves: 4

1 Heat the oil in a saucepan. Add the garlic and spring onion and cook over medium heat for 1–2 minutes, or until softened

2 Add the stock, bring to the boil, then reduce the heat and simmer. Add the broccoli to the stock and cook, covered, over low heat, for 3–5 minutes, or until the broccoli is tender but still green.

3 Transfer the soup to a blender or food processor and blend in batches until completely smooth.

4 Return to the pan and bring to the boil. Add the chicken strips, reduce the heat and simmer for 3–5 minutes, or until the chicken is cooked. Add the sour cream and season with salt and pepper. Reheat gently just before serving.

nutrition per serve
Protein 30 g; Fat 20 g; Carbohydrate 2.5 g; Dietary Fibre 5.5 g; Cholesterol 90 mg; 1290 kJ (310 cal)

handy tip...

If you are not planning to eat this soup straight away, do not add the sour cream until just before serving. Reheating and boiling will split the sour cream and give the soup a curdled appearance.

375 g farfalle pasta
3 chorizo sausages
750 g chicken breast fillets
2 small red chillies,
    seeded and chopped
6 spring onions, sliced
165 g jar sun-dried
    tomato pesto
300 ml cream
¼ cup (25 g) grated
    Parmesan

preparation: 15 minutes
cooking: 20 minutes
serves: 4–6

1 Cook the pasta in a large saucepan of boiling water according to the packet instructions. Drain.

2 Meanwhile, cut the chorizo into 1.5 cm slices and cut the chicken breast fillets into strips.

3 Heat a large frying pan. Add the chorizo and cook, stirring, over high heat for 2 minutes. Add the chicken strips, chilli and spring onion and cook, stirring, for 5 minutes, or until the chicken is lightly browned.

4 Stir in the pesto and cream and simmer for 5 minutes, or until the chicken is tender. Remove from the heat and stir in the Parmesan. Toss with the pasta and serve at once.

nutrition per serve (6)
Protein 40 g; Fat 35 g; Carbohydrate 45 g; Dietary Fibre 4.5 g; Cholesterol 155 mg; 2865 kJ (685 cal)

hint

Chorizo is a spicy pork sausage widely used in Spanish and Mexican cuisine. It is available from good delicatessens. If unavailable, use a spicy salami instead.

ingredients

750 g chicken thigh fillets

Satay sauce
1 tablespoon oil
1 onion, chopped
½ cup (125 g) crunchy
   peanut butter
1 tablespoon soy sauce
½ cup (125 ml) coconut
   cream
2 tablespoons sweet chilli
   sauce

preparation: 15 minutes
cooking: 15 minutes
serves: 4

1 Trim the chicken of excess fat and sinew, then cut into 2.5 cm cubes. Soak 8 wooden skewers in water to prevent them from burning under the grill.

2 To make the satay sauce, heat the oil in a small saucepan. Add the onion and cook over medium heat for 2–3 minutes, or until soft. Add the peanut butter, soy sauce, coconut cream and sweet chilli sauce and cook gently, stirring, until heated through.

3 Thread the chicken cubes onto the skewers, then place on a cold, lightly oiled grill tray. Cook under a hot grill for 5 minutes, turn over and cook for a further 5 minutes, or until tender. Brush with a little sauce during cooking, if desired. Serve with the satay sauce and garnish with fresh coriander.

nutrition per serve
Protein 52 g; Fat 30 g; Carbohydrate 7.5 g; Dietary Fibre 5 g; Cholesterol 95 mg; 2175 kJ (520 cal)

handy tip...

For extra flavour, the cubed chicken can be marinated in the satay sauce overnight, covered, in the refrigerator.

ingredients

600 g chicken thigh fillets
2 tablespoons olive oil
2 tablespoons brandy
½ cup (125 ml) chicken
   stock
300 g mushrooms,
   trimmed and thickly
   sliced *(see hint)*
2 teaspoons fresh thyme
3 tablespoons cream

preparation: 15 minutes
cooking: 15 minutes
serves: 4

1 Cut the chicken into bite-sized pieces. Heat the oil in a frying pan until hot. Add the chicken in batches and cook over high heat for 4 minutes, or until browned. Reheat the pan between batches. Remove the chicken and drain the oil from the pan.

2 Heat the pan until slightly smoking, then pour in the brandy and allow it to bubble until nearly evaporated. Pour in the chicken stock and bring to the boil. Add the mushrooms and thyme. Return the chicken to the pan with any juices and cook for a further 3 minutes, or until the mushrooms are soft. Stir in the cream and season well with salt and freshly ground black pepper. Serve over fettuccine or rice.

nutrition per serve
Protein 35 g; Fat 20 g; Carbohydrate 2 g; Dietary Fibre 2 g; Cholesterol 95 mg; 1395 kJ (335 cal)

hint

Field mushrooms will give the sauce a light-grey colour. For a lighter coloured sauce, use button mushrooms.

nutrition per serve
Protein 33 g; Fat 45 g; Carbohydrate 14 g; Dietary Fibre 4.5 g; Cholesterol 65 mg; 2450 kJ (585 cal)

ingredients

500 g chicken breast fillets
150 g green beans
400 ml coconut cream
1–2 tablespoons green curry paste
400 ml coconut milk
4 kaffir lime leaves
1 tablespoon fish sauce
1 tablespoon brown sugar

preparation: 15 minutes
cooking: 20 minutes
serves: 4

1 Cut the chicken into bite-sized pieces. Top and tail the beans and cut into short lengths.

2 Place the coconut cream in a wok and stir in the curry paste. Bring to the boil, then reduce the heat and simmer for 10 minutes, or until the oil separates from the coconut cream.

3 Add the coconut milk, chicken pieces, green beans and kaffir lime leaves. Bring back to the boil, then reduce the heat and simmer for 10 minutes, or until the chicken is cooked through.

4 Add the fish sauce and brown sugar, stirring until combined. Serve immediately with steamed jasmine rice and garnish with chopped fresh coriander leaves, if desired.

handy tip...

Both coconut milk and cream are extracted from the grated flesh of mature coconuts. The cream is richer and thicker, and comes from the first pressing, while the milk is from the second or third pressing.
Use a good-quality Asian green curry paste.

ingredients

4 small chicken breast
   fillets
2 tablespoons honey
2 tablespoons Dijon
   mustard
1 cup (100 g) pecans
2 tablespoons dry
   breadcrumbs
2 tablespoons plain flour
40 g softened butter
¼ cup (15 g) chopped
   fresh chives

preparation: 15 minutes
cooking: 15 minutes
serves: 4

1 Preheat the oven to hot 220°C (425°F/Gas 7). Trim the chicken of any excess fat. Place the chicken in a 20 x 30 cm shallow baking tin with 2 tablespoons water.

2 Place the honey and mustard in a bowl and mix together well.

3 Place the pecans, breadcrumbs, flour, butter and chives in a food processor. Season with salt and freshly ground black pepper and process very quickly until the mixture is roughly chopped and comes together.

4 Spread the honey mustard mixture over the chicken breasts, then firmly press on the pecan crumbs with your fingers. Bake for 15 minutes, or until the chicken is cooked and the crumbs are golden brown. Serve with a green salad, if desired.

nutrition per serve
Protein 33 g; Fat 30 g; Carbohydrate 20 g; Dietary Fibre 3 g; Cholesterol 88 mg; 1967 kJ (470 cal)

hint

Any nuts may be used in this recipe—walnuts, macadamias, cashews, or a combination. Store nuts in an airtight container in the freezer to stop them from going rancid.

ingredients

500 g linguine
3 smoked chicken breasts
   (about 200 g each)
300 g sour cream
1 tablespoon wholegrain
   mustard
1 tablespoon chopped
   fresh flat-leaf parsley

preparation: 10 minutes
cooking: 15 minutes
serves: 6

1 Cook the linguine in a large saucepan of boiling water according to the packet instructions. Drain the pasta, reserving ½ cup (125 ml) water in case you need to thin the sauce.

2 Meanwhile, cut the smoked chicken breasts into thin slices.

3 Place the sour cream in a frying pan and warm it over low heat until it thins. Do not boil or the sour cream will split. Stir in the mustard and chicken and season with salt and freshly ground black pepper.

4 Toss the linguine into the sauce and mix well. Sprinkle with the parsley and serve immediately.

nutrition per serve
Protein 33 g; Fat 23 g; Carbohydrate 60 g; Dietary Fibre 4.5 g; Cholesterol 116 mg; 2452 kJ (586 cal)

handy tip...

Smoked chicken is usually sold in the deli section at the supermarket. If smoked chicken is not available, use 3 chicken breast fillets, lightly fried in a little olive oil. Allow to cool slightly before slicing.

ingredients

1 tablespoon oil
800 g chicken breast fillets
2 litres chicken stock
3 spring onions, sliced
100 g dried thin egg
   noodles, broken
¾ cup (45 g) chopped
   fresh parsley

preparation: 10 minutes
cooking: 25 minutes
serves: 4

1 Heat the oil in a large frying pan. Add the chicken fillets and cook over medium heat for 15 minutes, or until golden, turning once. Remove from the pan and leave to cool. Shred finely.

2 Place the chicken stock in a large saucepan, bring to the boil, then reduce the heat. Add the chicken, spring onion and noodles and simmer for 5–10 minutes, or until the noodles are just tender. Season to taste with salt and black pepper and stir in the parsley. Divide among four warm bowls and serve immediately.

nutrition per serve
Protein 30 g; Fat 8 g; Carbohydrate 20 g; Dietary Fibre 1 g; Cholesterol 60 mg; 1155 kJ (275 cal)

hint

Any noodles can be used in this recipe. Try replacing the dried egg noodles with fresh Hokkien, Udon or egg noodles. They will only need 5 minutes cooking. Separate them before adding to the saucepan.
This recipe is also delicious with barbecued pork.

ingredients

6 chicken thighs
(about 200 g each),
skin removed
425 ml can apricot nectar
40 g packet French onion
soup mix
425 g can apricot halves
in natural juice, drained
¼ cup (60 g) sour cream

preparation: 10 minutes
cooking: 1 hour
serves: 4–6

1 Preheat the oven to moderate 180°C (350°F/Gas 4). Put the thighs in an ovenproof dish.

2 Place the apricot nectar and soup mix in a bowl and mix together until well combined. Pour the mixture over the chicken.

3 Bake, covered, for 50 minutes, then add the apricot halves and bake, uncovered, for a further 5 minutes. Stir in the sour cream just before serving. Serve with creamy mashed potato or rice to soak up the juices.

nutrition per serve (6)
Protein 23 g; Fat 6 g; Carbohydrate 10 g; Dietary Fibre 0 g; Cholesterol 63 mg; 780 kJ (187 cal)

handy tip...

Any cut of chicken is suitable for this recipe.
Do not allow the sauce to boil after adding the sour cream or it will split and give the dish a curdled appearance.

ingredients

12 chicken drumsticks
2 tablespoons soy sauce
2 tablespoons hoisin
    sauce
¼ cup (60 ml) tomato
    sauce
¼ cup (90 g) honey
1 tablespoon lemon juice
2 tablespoons sesame
    seeds
½ teaspoon five-spice
    powder

preparation: 15 minutes +
    2 hours refrigeration
cooking: 50 minutes
serves: 4–6

1 Pat the chicken drumsticks dry with paper towels.

2 Place the soy sauce, hoisin sauce, tomato sauce, honey, lemon juice, sesame seeds and five-spice in a large bowl and mix together.

3 Add the chicken and mix well to coat. Refrigerate, covered, for at least 2 hours, turning occasionally. Preheat the oven to moderate 180°C (350°F/Gas 4).

4 Drain the chicken and discard the marinade. Place the legs on a rack in a baking dish and bake for 40–50 minutes. Serve warm with rice and steamed or stir-fried vegetables.

nutrition per serve (6)
Protein 40 g; Fat 7 g; Carbohydrate 6 g; Dietary Fibre 1.5 g; Cholesterol 83 mg; 1028 kJ (246 cal)

hint

This recipe is suitable for any cut of chicken.
The longer the chicken is left in the marinade the more developed the flavour will be. These drumsticks can also be grilled or barbecued.

ingredients

1.5 kg whole chicken
2 lemons, roughly
   chopped
4 spring onions, chopped
2 tablespoons chopped
   fresh lemon thyme
2 cloves garlic, crushed
1 tablespoon olive oil
6 sprigs fresh lemon
   thyme
4 thin slices prosciutto

preparation: 15 minutes
cooking: 1 hour 30 minutes
serves: 4

1 Preheat the oven to moderate 180°C (350°F/Gas 4). Trim the chicken of any excess fat and sinew, then rinse the cavity and pat dry with paper towels.

2 Place the lemon, spring onion, lemon thyme, garlic and freshly ground black pepper in a bowl and mix together well. Spoon the mixture into the cavity of the chicken.

3 Bend the chicken wings back and tuck them behind the body. Tie the drumsticks together with string. Place on a wire rack in a baking tin, brush with the oil and top with the sprigs of lemon thyme. Cover the breast with overlapping slices of prosciutto.

4 Cover the chicken with foil and bake for 1 hour 15 minutes, or until cooked through. Remove the foil and cook for a further 15 minutes, or until the chicken is tender and the skin is crispy. Allow the chicken to rest in a warm place for 15 minutes before carving. Discard the stuffing. Serve with roast vegetables, if desired.

nutrition per serve
Protein 65 g; Fat 45 g; Carbohydrate 4.5 g; Dietary Fibre 2 g; Cholesterol 215 mg; 2820 kJ (675 cal)

handy tip...

Prosciutto is the Italian word for ham or salt-cured pork that has been air-dried. If not available, use bacon with excess fat trimmed off.

nutrition per serve
Protein 30 g; Fat 25 g; Carbohydrate
1 g; Dietary Fibre 0 g; Cholesterol
140 mg; 1445 kJ (345 cal)

ingredients

⅓ cup (10 g) chopped fresh flat-leaf parsley

2 cloves garlic, finely chopped

3 teaspoons finely grated lemon rind

4 chicken marylands (chicken quarters)

olive oil, for brushing

preparation: 15 minutes
cooking: 45 minutes
serves: 4

1 Preheat the oven to moderately hot 200°C (400°F/Gas 6).

2 Place the parsley, garlic and rind in a bowl and mix well. Season. Using your fingers, carefully loosen the skin from the chicken and fill with the parsley mixture. Pat the skin back to its original shape.

3 Put the chicken in a baking tin, brush lightly with the oil and bake for 45 minutes, or until the chicken juices run clear when pierced with a skewer. Serve immediately, garnished with lemon wedges.

hint

The gremolata is perfect for whole roast chicken. Simply lift the skin, press the mixture onto the chicken breast, brush with oil and roast until tender.

ingredients

2 sheets ready-rolled
   butter puff pastry,
   thawed
30 g butter
750 g chicken tenderloins,
   finely sliced
2 large leeks, finely
   chopped
4 rashers bacon, finely
   chopped
150 g button mushrooms,
   sliced
1/3 cup (80 ml) chicken
   stock
3/4 cup (185 g) sour cream

preparation: 20 minutes
cooking: 30 minutes
serves: 4

1 Preheat the oven to hot 210°C (415°F/Gas 6–7). Lightly grease four 2-cup (500 ml) ovenproof pie dishes. Cut the pastry into four rounds large enough to cover the tops of the pie dishes.

2 Heat half the butter in a large, deep frying pan and cook the chicken in batches for 3 minutes, or until lightly browned. Remove from the pan.

3 Heat the remaining butter in the same pan over high heat and cook the leek for 2 minutes, or until soft. Add the bacon and mushrooms and cook for 2 minutes. Return the chicken and any juices to the pan and stir. Add the stock and boil for 2 minutes, or until slightly thickened. Reduce the heat, then stir in the sour cream. Season.

4 Spoon the mixture into the pie dishes and top with a pastry round.

Pierce the pastry with a fork. Bake for 15 minutes, or until puffed and golden. Serve immediately with salad or steamed vegetables.

nutrition per serve
Protein 56 g; Fat 37 g; Carbohydrate 40 g; Dietary Fibre 5 g; Cholesterol 235 mg; 2980 kJ (712 cal)

handy tip...

This can be made into one large pie. Use a 23 cm pie dish and roll the sheets of pastry together before placing on top. Pierce a couple of holes in the top of the pastry.

ingredients

1 kg chicken thigh fillets
2 tablespoons lime juice
½ cup (125 ml) sweet chilli
  sauce
3 tablespoons kecap
  manis *(see hint)*

preparation: 15 minutes +
  2 hours refrigeration
cooking: 20 minutes
serves: 6

1 Trim any excess fat and sinew from the chicken thigh fillets and cut them in half. Transfer to a shallow glass or ceramic dish.

2 Place the lime juice, sweet chilli sauce and kecap manis in a bowl and whisk to combine. Pour the marinade over the chicken, cover and refrigerate for 2 hours.

3 Chargrill or bake in a preheated moderately hot 200°C (400°F/ Gas 6) oven for 20 minutes, or until the chicken is tender and cooked through and the marinade has caramelised. Serve with salad greens and garnish with lime wedges.

nutrition per serve
Protein 35 g; Fat 4.5 g; Carbohydrate 4 g; Dietary Fibre 1 g; Cholesterol 85 mg; 880 kJ (210 cal)

hint

Kecap manis (ketjap manis) is a thick Indonesian sauce, similar to—but sweeter than— soy sauce, and is generally flavoured with garlic and star anise. Store in a cool, dry place and refrigerate after opening. If not available, use soy sauce sweetened with a little soft brown sugar.

ingredients

2 chicken breast fillets
(about 200 g each)

2 ripe tomatoes, each cut
into 4 slices

2 slices Swiss cheese

2 tablespoons tomato
relish

2/3 cup (160 g) whole-egg
mayonnaise

4 poppy-seed bagels,
halved

80 g baby English spinach
leaves

120 g semi-dried tomatoes

preparation: 15 minutes
cooking: 15 minutes
serves: 4

1 Lightly spray a non-stick frying pan with oil and heat over medium heat. Cook the chicken for 5–7 minutes on each side, or until cooked through. Remove from the frying pan and keep warm.

2 In the same frying pan, seal the tomato slices on each side.

3 While still hot, cut each chicken breast in half lengthways, through the centre. Place a slice of cheese on two halves, then put the other half of chicken on top to melt the cheese slightly. Cut the chicken breasts in half to give four cheese-filled pieces.

4 Combine the tomato relish and the mayonnaise in a small bowl.

5 To assemble the burgers, spread both halves of each bagel with the tomato relish mayonnaise. Place the baby spinach leaves on the bottom half of the bagel, followed by the chicken breast, tomato slices and semi-dried tomatoes. Put the bagel lid on top and serve immediately.

nutrition per serve
Protein 38 g; Fat 27 g; Carbohydrate 44 g; Dietary Fibre 5 g; Cholesterol 82 mg; 2393 kJ (572 cal)

handy tip...

The tomato relish mayonnaise can be made in advance—a whole batch can be made up and kept in the refrigerator in an airtight container for up to 1 week.

ingredients

1 tablespoon oil
1 carrot, sliced
1 leek, chopped
800 g chicken thigh fillets,
    cut into bite-sized
    pieces
¼ cup (35 g) ditalini pasta
1 litre vegetable stock
2 ripe tomatoes, diced

preparation: 15 minutes
cooking: 15 minutes
serves: 4

1 Heat the oil in a saucepan. Add the carrot and leek and cook over medium heat for 4 minutes, or until softened. Add the chicken and cook for a further 2 minutes, or until the chicken is browned.

3 Add the pasta and the vegetable stock, cover and bring to the boil. Reduce the heat and simmer for 10 minutes, or until the pasta is cooked. Add the tomato halfway through the cooking. Season with salt and freshly ground black pepper. Serve with fresh crusty bread, if desired.

nutrition per serve
Protein 48 g; Fat 10 g; Carbohydrate 9.5 g; Dietary Fibre 2.5 g; Cholesterol 100 mg; 1327 kJ (317 cal)

hint

Ditalini pasta can be replaced with any small soup pasta. Any vegetables may be added to this soup—try mixed frozen vegetables.

sweet potato and spinach chicken salad

Heat 2 tablespoons olive oil in a large frying pan. Cook 500 g thickly sliced (about 1 cm) orange sweet potato in batches for 10 minutes, or until just tender. Set aside. Add 2 leeks cut into thin strips and cook until softened. Add 2 teaspoons brown sugar and cook over low heat for a further 10 minutes, or until caramelised. Remove from the heat. In a small jug, whisk together 2 tablespoons olive oil and 2 tablespoons balsamic vinegar. Remove the skin and bones from a barbecued chicken and chop the flesh into bite-sized pieces. In a bowl, add 150 g baby English spinach leaves, 100 g semi-dried tomatoes, the roasted sweet potato and chicken, then toss gently to combine. Pile the leek on top of the salad, pour the dressing over the top and serve.

serves 4–6

lemon chicken and pancetta pasta

Remove the skin and bones from a barbecued chicken and shred the flesh. Bring a large saucepan of water to the boil. Add 500 g fresh fettuccine to the water and cook until al dente. Drain and keep warm. Heat a large frying pan, add 300 g chopped pancetta and cook for 10 minutes, or until crisp. Add the chicken, 300 ml cream, 1/2 cup (125 ml) lemon juice and 155 g asparagus, cut into 5 cm pieces. Simmer for 5 minutes, or until the sauce thickens slightly. Toss through the pasta with 1/3 cup (35 g) grated Parmesan and 1/4 cup (15 g) shredded fresh basil.

serves 4

chicken wrap

Remove the skin and bones from half a barbecued chicken and shred the flesh. Combine 1/2 cup (125 g) whole-egg mayonnaise with 1 tablespoon lime juice and 1 crushed clove garlic in a small bowl. Spread over 4 rounds of Lebanese bread. Top with some shredded chicken, 200 g thinly sliced chargrilled capsicum and 1/2 diced red onion. Roll up and serve either sliced or wrapped in baking paper.

serves 4

From left to right: Sweet potato and spinach chicken salad; Lemon chicken and pancetta pasta; Chicken wrap; Chicken tacos; Cream of chicken and corn soup; Gourmet chicken pizza.

chicken tacos

Preheat the oven to moderate 180°C (350°F/Gas 4). Remove the skin and bones from a barbecued chicken and shred the flesh. Heat a large frying pan, then add 200 g can mexe beans, including ½ cup (125 ml) of the liquid, and 200 g jar taco sauce. Simmer for 2 minutes, add the shredded chicken and heat through. Combine ²/₃ cup (85 g) grated Cheddar and 2 tablespoons chopped fresh coriander in a bowl. Place 8 taco shells in the oven and bake for 5 minutes, or until heated through and crisp. Spoon some chicken mixture into each taco and top with the grated cheese mixture and 1 tablespoon sour cream. Serve immediately.

serves 4

cream of chicken and corn soup

Remove the skin and bones from half a barbecued chicken and shred the flesh. Heat 40 g butter in a large saucepan and add 6 chopped spring onions. Cook over medium heat, for 2 minutes. Add 420 g creamed corn and stir to combine. Gradually stir in 1 litre chicken stock and ½ cup (125 g) sour cream. Cook gently until the soup thickens, being careful not to boil. Add the chicken and cook until heated through. Stir in ¼ cup (7 g) chopped fresh coriander leaves and season to taste with salt and pepper. Garnish with some finely chopped spring onions and serve with crusty bread.

serves 4

gourmet chicken pizza

Preheat the oven to moderately hot 200°C (400°F/Gas 6). Cut 250 g butternut pumpkin into 2 cm cubes. Heat 1 tablespoon oil in a frying pan, add the pumpkin and cook for 10 minutes, or until tender and golden. Remove the skin and bones from half a barbecued chicken and chop the flesh into bite-sized pieces. Spread a 30 cm pizza base with ¼ cup (70 g) mango chutney. Top with 1 cup (150 g) grated mozzarella cheese, 1 red onion cut into wedges, and the cubed chicken and pumpkin. Bake for 20 minutes, or until the base is golden and crisp. Serve with a dollop of thick yoghurt and garnish with fresh coriander leaves.

serves 4

ingredients

1 tablespoon olive oil
1 red onion, cut into thin
   wedges
25 g butter
800 g chicken breast
   fillets, cut into
   bite-sized pieces
2 teaspoons lemon rind,
   cut into thin strips
2 tablespoons salted
   baby capers, rinsed
   well and drained
⅓ cup (80 ml) lemon juice
¼ cup (15 g) shredded
   fresh basil

preparation: 15 minutes
cooking: 15 minutes
serves: 4

1 Heat a wok until very hot, add 2 teaspoons of the oil and swirl it around to coat the side. Add the onion and stir-fry for 2–3 minutes, or until softened and golden. Remove from the wok and set aside.

2 Reheat the wok, add 1 teaspoon oil and half the butter, and stir-fry the chicken in two batches for 3–5 minutes each batch, or until browned, adding the remaining oil and butter between batches. Return all the chicken to the wok with the onion.

3 Stir in the lemon rind, capers and lemon juice. Toss well and cook until warmed through. Add the shredded basil and season with salt and freshly ground black pepper. Serve with mashed potato.

nutrition per serve
Protein 45 g; Fat 20 g; Carbohydrate 2.5 g; Dietary Fibre 1 g; Cholesterol 115 mg; 1550 kJ (370 cal)

handy tip...

Capers are the flower bud of a shrub native to the Mediterranean region. They are sold in jars in a vinegar brine or sold packed in salt. Salted capers need to be rinsed before adding them to dishes.

4 chicken breast fillets
(about 115 g each)
2 tablespoons oil
4 small zucchini, thinly
sliced
2 leeks, thinly sliced
2 small fresh red chillies,
finely chopped
150 g oyster mushrooms
1 tablespoon lime juice
¼ cup (60 ml) cream

preparation: 15 minutes
cooking: 20 minutes
serves: 4

1 Trim the chicken of any excess fat and sinew. Heat the oil in a frying pan. Add the chicken and cook over medium heat for 5–7 minutes on each side, or until tender. Remove, drain on paper towels and keep warm.

2 Add the zucchini, leek and chilli to the frying pan and cook over high heat for 2 minutes. Add the mushrooms and cook for a further 3 minutes, or until tender.

3 Stir in the lime juice and cream and cook for 2 minutes, or until heated through. Season to taste with salt and pepper. Serve with roasted capsicum and warm crusty rolls or baps, if desired.

nutrition per serve
Protein 12 g; Fat 17 g; Carbohydrate 3.5 g; Dietary Fibre 3 g; Cholesterol 40 mg; 910 kJ (217 cal)

hint

This dish should be served immediately after cooking. If oyster mushrooms are not available, use button or cap mushrooms, sliced. To protect your hands, wear rubber gloves when chopping hot chillies and rinse them afterwards. Avoid touching your face, as the chilli juice can burn your eyes.

ingredients

500 g chicken tenderloins
1 tablespoon sesame oil
150 g snow peas, sliced
   on the diagonal
1/3 cup (50 g) roasted
   unsalted cashews
1 tablespoon honey
2 tablespoons kecap
   manis
1–2 tablespoons chopped
   fresh coriander leaves

preparation: 10 minutes
cooking: 15 minutes
serves: 4

1 Cut the chicken tenderloins into bite-sized pieces.

2 Heat a wok until very hot, add the sesame oil and swirl it around to coat the side. Add the chicken and stir-fry in three batches, tossing, for 1–2 minutes, or until golden brown.

3 Return all the chicken to the wok and add the snow peas. Cook, tossing, for 3 minutes. Add the cashews, honey and kecap manis and cook for 1–2 minutes, or until the chicken is cooked. Scatter with the coriander leaves and serve with rice or noodles, if desired.

nutrition per serve
Protein 33 g; Fat 15 g; Carbohydrate 13 g; Dietary Fibre 3 g; Cholesterol 60 mg; 1285 kJ (307 cal)

handy tip...

To roast the cashews, preheat the oven to 180°C (350°F/ Gas 4). Place the cashews on a baking tray and roast for 5–8 minutes. Keep a close eye on them as they will burn easily.

4 chicken breast fillets
(about 200 g each)
3 tablespoons plain flour
2 tablespoons olive oil
3 teaspoons chopped
fresh lemon thyme
2 teaspoons dry sherry
½ cup (125 ml) cream

preparation: 10 minutes
cooking: 15 minutes
serves: 4

1 Trim the chicken of any excess fat and sinew, then toss the fillets in the flour, shaking off any excess.

2 Heat the oil in a large non-stick frying pan. Cook the chicken fillets for 5 minutes on each side, or until golden brown.

3 Sprinkle on the lemon thyme, then turn the fillets over. Add the sherry, pour on half the cream and boil for 2–3 minutes. Turn the fillets over again and drizzle with the remaining cream. Season to taste. Serve with a salad or vegetables.

nutrition per serve
Protein 45 g; Fat 20 g; Carbohydrate 5 g; Dietary Fibre 0 g; Cholesterol 125 mg; 1670 kJ (395 cal)

hint

This recipe is also suitable for a chargrill pan.
Any herb could be used instead of the thyme. Try tarragon, chervil or basil.

ingredients

1.5 kg chicken pieces
2 tablespoons oil
1.5 kg potatoes, thickly
    sliced
3 large onions, thinly
    sliced
3 cups (750 ml) rich
    chicken stock
60 g butter, melted

preparation: 15 minutes
cooking: 1 hour 50 minutes
serves: 6

1 Trim the chicken pieces of any excess fat. Pat dry with paper towels, then rub with salt and freshly ground black pepper.

2 Heat the oil in a large heatproof casserole dish. Cook the chicken in batches over medium heat until well browned. Remove from the pan.

3 Arrange one quarter of the potatoes over the base of the casserole dish. Top with one quarter of the onions and four pieces of chicken. Repeat the layering process, ending with the onions.

4 Pour the chicken stock and butter over the top and cover with a sheet of greased baking paper and the lid. Bring to the boil, then reduce the heat and simmer, covered, for 1 hour 30 minutes, or until the chicken is tender. Garnish with chopped fresh herbs.

nutrition per serve
Protein 45 g; Fat 19 g; Carbohydrate 37 g; Dietary Fibre 5 g; Cholesterol 109 mg; 2088 kJ (499 cal)

handy tip...

This Scottish dish is sometimes called 'stovies'. It is derived from the French etouffer, to cook in a closed pot, and dates back to the strong link between the Scottish and the French in the 17th century.

4 chicken breast fillets
(about 200 g each)
plain flour, for dusting
2 tablespoons olive oil
125 g button mushrooms,
sliced
3 spring onions, sliced
½ cup (125 ml) cream
1 tablespoon brandy
¾ cup (100 g) grated
Gruyère or Swiss
cheese

preparation: 10 minutes
cooking: 15 minutes
serves: 4

1 Flatten the chicken fillets with the palm of your hand until they are 1 cm thick. Dust the fillets with the flour, shaking off any excess. Heat the oil in a frying pan, add the chicken and cook for 4–5 minutes on each side, or until golden brown. Transfer to a lined baking tray and cover with foil.

2 Add the mushrooms and spring onion to the frying pan and cook for 2 minutes, or until the spring onion is soft. Add the cream and brandy and bring to the boil. Reduce the heat and simmer for 1 minute, or until the sauce reduces slightly. Season with salt and freshly ground black pepper.

3 Spoon the sauce over the chicken and top with the cheese. Place under a hot grill until the cheese melts and begins to brown. Serve with roasted vegetables.

nutrition per serve
Protein 60 g; Fat 35 g; Carbohydrate 6 g; Dietary Fibre 1.5 g; Cholesterol 166 mg; 2379 kJ (568 cal)

hint

Gruyère has a strong distinctive flavour. If you would prefer something a little milder, use Cheddar.

beef & veal

ingredients

4 boneless sirloin steaks or New York cuts (about 200 g each)

1/4 cup (60 ml) soy sauce

1/2 cup (125 ml) teriyaki sauce

2 tablespoons mirin or sweet sherry

2 tablespoons honey

2 cloves garlic, crushed

2 teaspoons grated fresh ginger

spring onions, finely chopped, to garnish

preparation: 15 minutes + overnight refrigeration
cooking: 20 minutes
serves: 4

1 Trim the meat of any excess fat and sinew. Place the soy sauce, teriyaki sauce, mirin, honey, garlic and ginger in a glass or ceramic dish and mix together. Add the steaks and toss well to coat. Cover and refrigerate for at least 2 hours or preferably overnight. Drain the meat and reserve the marinade.

2 Place the steaks in a non-stick frying pan and cook over high heat for 2 minutes on each side to seal. For rare steaks, cook for a further 1 minute on each side. For medium steaks, reduce the heat and cook a further 2–3 minutes on each side. For well-done steaks, cook a further 4–6 minutes on each side.

3 Bring the reserved marinade to the boil in a saucepan. Pour over the steaks during the last few minutes of cooking.

4 Serve the steaks with the marinade drizzled over the top. Garnish with the spring onion.

nutrition per serve
Protein 44 g; Fat 12 g; Carbohydrate 18 g; Dietary Fibre 0.5 g; Cholesterol 100 mg; 1525 kJ (365 cal)

handy tip...

For a different flavour, try a red wine sauce: substitute the soy sauce with balsamic vinegar, the teriyaki sauce with red wine, and the ginger with extra garlic and follow the instructions as above.

ingredients

500 g rump or sirloin steak
1 Lebanese cucumber,
  cut into cubes
4 spring onions, chopped
200 g cherry tomatoes,
  halved

Dressing
2 tablespoons fish sauce
2 tablespoons lime juice
2 tablespoons sweet chilli
  sauce
1 tablespoon chopped
  fresh coriander leaves

preparation: 15 minutes
cooking: 10 minutes
serves: 4

1 Heat a non-stick frying pan. Add the steak and cook over high heat for 4 minutes on each side. Remove from the pan and leave to cool for 5 minutes.

2 To make the dressing, place the fish sauce, lime juice, sweet chilli sauce and chopped coriander leaves in a bowl and mix together.

3 Cut the cooled steak into thin strips and place in a bowl with the cucumber, spring onion and tomato. Toss until well mixed and transfer to a serving dish—line the dish with a few lettuce leaves, if desired. Drizzle with the dressing and serve immediately, garnished with coriander leaves.

nutrition per serve
Protein 30 g; Fat 4 g; Carbohydrate 5 g; Dietary Fibre 2 g; Cholesterol 85 mg; 747 kJ (178 cal)

hint

Steak, lamb or chicken may be used in this recipe.
The meat may be cooked on the barbecue.
Try mint or basil in place of the coriander for a different flavour.

2 tablespoons oil
500 g round steak,
    cut into thin strips
1 onion, sliced
300 g sugar snap peas
2 tablespoons honey
2 tablespoons soy sauce
2 tablespoons oyster
    sauce
3 teaspoons finely
    cracked black pepper

preparation: 15 minutes
cooking: 15 minutes
serves: 4

1 Heat a wok until very hot, then add 1 tablespoon oil and swirl to coat. Stir-fry the beef in batches over high heat for 3–4 minutes each batch, or until browned, then remove and drain on paper towels.

2 Reheat the wok, add the remaining oil and stir-fry the onion and sugar snap peas until softened. Remove from the wok.

3 Add the honey, soy sauce, oyster sauce and pepper to the wok. Bring to the boil, then reduce the heat and simmer for 3–4 minutes, or until the sauce thickens slightly.

4 Increase the heat, return the meat and vegetables to the wok, and toss for 2–3 minutes, or until well combined and heated through. Serve with steamed rice.

nutrition per serve
Protein 30 g; Fat 15 g; Carbohydrate 20 g; Dietary Fibre 4.5 g; Cholesterol 70 mg; 1400 kJ (335 cal)

handy tip...

If sugar snap peas are not available, use snow peas, broccoli or asparagus.
To crush the pepper, place into a pepper or spice grinder, food processor or mortar and pestle, and process until you reach the desired consistency.

ingredients

500 g rump steak, cut into thin strips

3 stems lemon grass, white part only, finely chopped

1 onion, finely chopped

3 cloves garlic, finely chopped

2 tablespoons fish sauce

2 teaspoons sugar

1 tablespoon oil

¼ cup (40 g) chopped roasted peanuts

preparation: 15 minutes + 3–4 hours marinating
cooking: 15 minutes
serves: 4

1 Place the beef strips in a large glass or ceramic bowl. Put the lemon grass, onion, garlic, fish sauce and sugar in a separate bowl and mix together well. Pour the marinade over the meat and toss to coat. Cover and refrigerate for 3–4 hours.

2 Heat the oil in a wok until very hot and stir-fry the beef in batches over high heat for 3 minutes, or until just browned. Toss constantly to make sure the small pieces of onion and lemon grass don't catch on the surface of the wok and burn.

3 Return all the meat to the wok. Add the peanuts and toss quickly until combined. Serve immediately with noodles or rice.

nutrition per serve
Protein 35 g; Fat 8.5 g; Carbohydrate 6 g; Dietary Fibre 2 g; Cholesterol 85 mg; 980 kJ (235 cal)

hint

Lemon grass is an essential flavouring in Thai cooking. Remove the coarse outer layer and use only the white part of the plant. The green parts of the stem can be infused in hot water to make a refreshing tea.

ingredients

2 tablespoons olive oil
60 g sliced prosciutto,
   cut into wide strips
200 g button mushrooms,
   stalks trimmed
4 scotch fillet or
   eye fillet steaks
   (about 200 g each)
2 cloves garlic, crushed
2 tablespoons chopped
   fresh flat-leaf parsley
1/4 cup (60 ml) dry white
   wine
1/2 cup (125 ml) cream

preparation: 15 minutes
cooking: 25 minutes
serves: 4

1 Preheat the oven to moderately hot 200°C (400°F/Gas 6). Heat the oil in a deep ovenproof frying pan (large enough to hold the steaks in one layer without overlapping). Add the prosciutto and mushrooms and toss until the mushrooms start to brown.

2 Arrange the steaks on top of the mushroom mixture, sprinkle with the garlic and parsley, then pour in the wine. Bring to the boil, then remove from the heat. Bake, covered (with a lid or tightly with foil), for 10–15 minutes, or until the steaks are cooked to taste. Remove only the steaks from the pan.

3 Return the pan to the stove top over medium heat. Add the cream and simmer for 3–5 minutes, or until the sauce thickens slightly. Pour the sauce over the steaks and serve immediately with roasted potatoes or steamed vegetables.

nutrition per serve
Protein 27 g; Fat 28 g; Carbohydrate 2 g; Dietary Fibre 1.5 g; Cholesterol 117 mg; 1558 kJ (372 cal)

handy tip...

Flat-leaf parsley is also known as Italian or continental parsley. It has a stronger, more dominant flavour than curly leaf parsley. It is important to bring the wine to the boil to evaporate the alcohol.

ingredients

500 g beef fillet
¼ cup (60 ml) sesame oil
¼ cup (60 ml) soy sauce
2 cloves garlic, crushed
2 tablespoons grated
    fresh ginger
1 tablespoon lemon juice
2 tablespoons chopped
    spring onions
¼ cup (55 g) firmly
    packed soft brown
    sugar

preparation: 15 minutes +
    overnight marinating
cooking: 25 minutes
serves: 4

1 Trim the beef of any excess fat or sinew.

2 Combine the sesame oil, soy sauce, garlic, ginger, lemon juice, spring onion and brown sugar in a glass or ceramic dish. Add the beef and coat well with the marinade. Cover and refrigerate for at least 2 hours, or preferably overnight. Drain and reserve the marinade.

3 Preheat a lightly oiled barbecue grill or flatplate. When very hot, add the beef and brown on all sides to seal the meat. Remove the steak, wrap in foil and cook on the barbecue, turning occasionally, for a further 15–20 minutes, depending on how rare or well done you like your steak. Leave the beef for 10 minutes before slicing.

4 Meanwhile, place the reserved marinade in a small saucepan and boil for 5 minutes. Drizzle over the beef just before serving. Serve with a fresh mixed salad, if desired.

nutrition per serve
Protein 28 g; Fat 20 g; Carbohydrate 15 g; Dietary Fibre 0.5 g; Cholesterol 84 mg; 1442 kJ (345 cal)

hint

If you prefer, individual steaks can be used instead and cooked on the barbecue or in a chargrill pan. However, there is no need to wrap them in foil.

ingredients

1 tablespoon oil
600 g round steak,
    cut into cubes
2 onions, chopped
1 tablespoon madras
    curry paste
2 cups (500 ml) beef stock
    or water
2 tablespoons chopped
    fresh coriander leaves
2 tablespoons chopped
    fresh mint
1/3 cup (80 g) plain yoghurt

preparation: 10 minutes
cooking: 1 hour 45 minutes
serves: 4

1 Heat the oil in a saucepan. Cook the beef over medium heat, in batches, until browned all over. Return all the meat to the pan.

2 Add the onion and stir for 3 minutes, or until golden. Add the curry paste and cook for 1 minute. Pour in the beef stock and bring to the boil. Reduce the heat and simmer, covered, for 1 hour. Check, then cook for up to 30 minutes more (if necessary), or until the meat is tender and the liquid has reduced and thickened slightly. Stir occasionally during cooking.

3 Add the chopped coriander, mint and yoghurt and stir until well combined. Garnish with a sprig of coriander and serve with steamed basmati rice and some curried vegetables, if desired.

nutrition per serve
Protein 33 g; Fat 12 g; Carbohydrate 4 g; Dietary Fibre 1 g; Cholesterol 90 mg; 1070 kJ (255 cal)

handy tip...

This curry can be cooked up to 3 days ahead and stored, covered, in the refrigerator. If you choose to do this, do not add the yoghurt until you reheat the curry, or it will split.
Any curry paste may be used in this recipe.
For a richer curry, add one 400 g can chopped tomatoes.

nutrition per serve (6)
Protein 40 g; Fat 7 g; Carbohydrate
5 g; Dietary Fibre 1 g; Cholesterol
90 mg; 1150 kJ (275 cal)

ingredients

1 kg topside or round
   steak
3 rashers bacon
12 pickling onions
1 cup (250 ml) red wine
2 cups (500 ml) beef
   stock
1 teaspoon dried thyme
200 g button mushrooms
2 bay leaves

preparation: 10 minutes
cooking: 1 hour 45 minutes
serves: 4–6

1 Trim the steak of fat and sinew and cut into 2 cm cubes. Cut the bacon into 2 cm squares.

2 Heat a large saucepan. Add the bacon and quickly cook over medium heat for 3 minutes, or until browned. Remove from the pan. Add the steak, in batches, and cook for 3 minutes each batch, or until browned. Remove from the pan. Add the onions to the pan and cook for 3 minutes, or until golden.

3 Return the bacon and meat to the saucepan with the red wine, stock, thyme, mushrooms and bay leaves. Bring to the boil, then reduce the heat and simmer, covered, for 1 hour 30 minutes, or until the meat is very tender, stirring occasionally. Remove the bay leaves before serving. Serve with mashed potato and steamed green beans, if desired.

hint

This dish can be stored in an airtight container in the refrigerator for up to 3 days. For a richer, slightly sweeter flavour, substitute the red wine for port.
This dish can also be cooked in the oven in a casserole dish. If the sauce is too thin after cooking, remove the lid and boil until reduced slightly.

ingredients

2.5 kg piece roasting beef
2 cloves garlic, crushed
1 tablespoon plain flour
2 tablespoons red wine
1¼ cups (315 ml) beef
   stock

Yorkshire puddings
¾ cup (90 g) plain flour
½ cup (125 ml) milk
2 eggs

preparation: 15 minutes
cooking: 1 hour 45 minutes
serves: 6

1 Preheat the oven to very hot 240°C (475°F/Gas 9). Rub the beef with the garlic and some pepper. Place on a rack in a baking tin, and roast for 15 minutes.

2 Meanwhile, to make the Yorkshire puddings, sift the flour and ½ teaspoon salt into a large bowl, make a well in the centre and whisk in the milk. In a separate bowl, whisk the eggs until fluffy, then add them to the batter and mix well. Add ½ cup (125 ml) water and whisk until large bubbles form on the surface. Cover with plastic wrap and refrigerate for 1 hour.

3 Reduce the oven to moderate 180°C (350°F/Gas 4), and roast the meat for a further 50–60 minutes for a rare result, or a little longer for well done. Cover the meat loosely with foil and leave in a warm place for 10–15 minutes. Increase the oven temperature to hot 220°C (425°F/Gas 7).

4 Pour off all the meat juices into a jug and reserve for making gravy.

Put ½ teaspoon of the juices into twelve ⅓-cup (80 ml) muffin tins. Whisk the batter again until bubbles form on the surface. Pour the batter into each muffin tin to three-quarters full. Bake for 10 minutes, then reduce the oven to moderate 180°C (350°F/Gas 4) and cook for a further 10 minutes, or until puffed and lightly golden.

5 Put the baking tin on the stove, add the reserved meat juices and cook over low heat. Add the flour and stir, scraping the bottom of the tin to release any sediment. Cook over medium heat, stirring constantly, until the flour is browned. Combine the wine and stock, and gradually stir into the flour mixture. Cook, stirring constantly, until the gravy boils and thickens. Simmer for 3 minutes.

6 Serve the roast beef with the gravy, Yorkshire puddings, Brussels sprouts and roast potatoes.

nutrition per serve
Protein 100 g; Fat 16 g; Carbohydrate 14 g; Dietary Fibre 1 g; Cholesterol 267 mg; 2448 kJ (585 cal)

handy tip...

It is important to let the roast stand for up to 15 minutes before slicing. This allows the meat to relax and prevents the juices from spilling out onto the chopping board.

ingredients

500 g minced beef
1 small onion, grated
1 tablespoon light olive oil
4 lettuce leaves
4 buttered hamburger
  buns
4 slices cheese
1 tomato, sliced
1 small red onion,
  finely sliced

preparation: 10 minutes
cooking: 10 minutes
serves: 4

1 Place the beef mince in a large mixing bowl with the grated onion, then season with salt and freshly ground black pepper. With clean hands, gently mix to just combine (too much handling will cause the meat juices to run out and escape during cooking). Form the beef mixture into four patties, shaping the meat quickly and lightly.

2 Heat the olive oil in a wide frying pan and cook the patties over medium heat for 5 minutes on each side, or until cooked through. Drain well on paper towels.

3 Place a lettuce leaf on the bottom half of each bun. Top with a beef patty, slice of cheese, tomato and red onion slices. Season to taste with salt and freshly ground black pepper and top with the other half of the bun. Serve immediately with tomato or barbecue sauce.

nutrition per serve
Protein 35 g; Fat 18 g; Carbohydrate 47 g; Dietary Fibre 5 g; Cholesterol 80 mg; 2072 kJ (495 cal)

hint

Add some chopped fresh herbs such as parsley or rosemary to the mince mixture.
Use a combination of lamb and beef mince for extra flavour.

ingredients

350 g rump steak
12 long sprigs rosemary
12 (60 g) Swiss
    mushrooms, halved
1 tablespoon oil
1 tablespoon honey
1 tablespoon soy sauce

preparation: 15 minutes
cooking: 10 minutes
serves: 4

1 Trim the meat of any excess fat and sinew and cut into 2.5 cm cubes. Trim the leaves from the stems of the rosemary sprigs, leaving 5 cm at one end. Thread the meat alternately with the mushrooms onto the rosemary skewers. Place the oil, honey and soy sauce in a small bowl and mix together well.

2 Place the skewers on a lightly oiled grill tray and brush the meat with the oil and honey mixture. Cook under a hot grill for 10 minutes, or until tender, turning occasionally and brushing with the oil and honey mixture. Serve immediately with a green salad.

nutrition per serve
Protein 20 g; Fat 2.5 g; Carbohydrate 6 g; Dietary Fibre 0.5 g; Cholesterol 60 mg; 545 kJ (130 cal)

handy tip...

Rosemary sprigs make great alternative skewers to wooden or metal skewers. In addition to holding the meat and vegetables, the rosemary aroma permeates throughout the meat and vegetables while cooking.

ingredients

1 tablespoon olive oil
1 onion, chopped
500 g lean minced beef
425 g can crushed
    tomatoes
35 g packet chilli
    seasoning mix
1/2 teaspoon dried oregano
2 tablespoons tomato
    paste
420 g can red kidney
    beans, rinsed and
    drained

preparation: 10 minutes
cooking: 30 minutes
serves: 4

1 Heat the oil in a large saucepan. Add the onion and cook, stirring occasionally, over medium heat for 5 minutes, or until the onion is soft and golden. Add the beef mince and cook over high heat for 5 minutes, or until the meat is brown, breaking up any lumps with the back of a wooden spoon. Drain off any excess liquid.

2 Add the tomato, seasoning mix, oregano, tomato paste and 1/2 cup (125 ml) water, and bring to the boil. Reduce the heat, cover and simmer for 15 minutes, stirring occasionally.

3 Add the red kidney beans and simmer for 3–4 minutes, or until heated through. Season with salt and freshly ground black pepper. Serve hot with corn chips and a dollop of sour cream, or with rice.

nutrition per serve
Protein 28 g; Fat 16 g; Carbohydrate 20 g; Dietary Fibre 9 g; Cholesterol 65 mg; 1423 kJ (340 cal)

hint

The beef mince can be substituted with chicken mince.
If chilli seasoning mix is not available, use 1/2 teaspoon chilli powder or 2 finely chopped red chillies.

ingredients

400 g can coconut cream
1–2 tablespoons red curry
   paste
400 ml can coconut milk
750 g beef strips
6 spring onions,
   cut into 3 cm pieces
200 g green beans,
   cut into 3 cm lengths
1 tablespoon grated palm
   sugar
2 tablespoons fish sauce

preparation: 15 minutes
cooking: 25 minutes
serves: 4–6

1 Heat a wok and add the coconut cream. Bring to the boil, then reduce the heat slightly and simmer rapidly for 10 minutes, or until the oil separates from the coconut cream.

2 tir in the curry paste, then add the coconut milk and beef strips and cook for 5 minutes. Stir in the spring onion, beans, palm sugar and fish sauce and cook for 10 minutes, or until the meat is tender. Serve with jasmine rice and garnish with shredded lime leaves, if desired.

nutrition per serve (6)
Protein 32 g; Fat 40 g; Carbohydrate 14 g; Dietary Fibre 4.5 g; Cholesterol 81 mg; 2258 kJ (540 cal)

handy tip...

If palm sugar is unavailable, use brown sugar. Any vegetables may be added to this dish, including bamboo shoots, baby corn and baby eggplant.
To make a simple mussaman curry, omit the beans, add 2 tablespoons crunchy peanut butter, 8 baby potatoes and 8 baby onions. Serve sprinkled with chopped nuts.

ingredients

800 g minced beef

1 onion, grated

2 cloves garlic, crushed

3 tablespoons fruit
chutney

2 teaspoons chopped
fresh oregano

1 egg, lightly beaten

1½ cups (120 g) fresh
breadcrumbs

8 rashers bacon

preparation: 15 minutes
cooking: 20 minutes
serves: 4

1 Place the mince, onion, garlic, fruit chutney, oregano, egg and breadcrumbs in a large bowl and mix together well (you will find it easier to use your hands for this). Season to taste with salt and freshly ground black pepper. Divide the mixture into eight even portions, forming each into a 9 cm patty shape.

2 Remove the rind from the bacon and cut each rasher in half lengthways. Wrap one length of bacon around the patty and then wrap another length around in the other direction, forming a cross. Secure with a toothpick.

3 Heat a lightly greased frying pan over medium heat and add the patties in batches. Cook for 5 minutes on each side, or until well browned and cooked through. Drain well on paper towels and remove the toothpicks before serving.

nutrition per serve
Protein 80 g; Fat 28 g; Carbohydrate 18 g; Dietary Fibre 1.5 g; Cholesterol 215 mg; 2342 kJ (560 cal)

hint

This mixture can also be made into meatballs or a meatloaf. Finely chop the bacon and fold it through the mince mixture.

nutrition per serve
Protein 80 g; Fat 15 g; Carbohydrate
5.5 g; Dietary Fibre 0.5 g; Cholesterol
205 mg; 1952 kJ (466 cal)

ingredients

1.5 kg beef spareribs
½ cup (125 ml) apricot
   nectar
1 tablespoon soy sauce
1 tablespoon sweet chilli
   sauce
2 cloves garlic, crushed
2 teaspoons grated fresh
   ginger

preparation: 5 minutes
cooking: 30 minutes
serves: 4

1 Preheat the oven to hot 210°C (415°F/Gas 6–7). Arrange the ribs in a single layer in a baking tin.

2 Place the apricot nectar, soy sauce, sweet chilli sauce, garlic and ginger in a bowl and mix together. Pour the glaze mixture over the ribs.

3 Bake for 30 minutes, or until the ribs are tender and well browned. Brush the ribs occasionally with the glaze, turning a couple of times during cooking. Serve immediately with a green salad, if desired.

handy tip...

This dish may also be cooked under the grill or on the barbecue.
The apricot nectar can be replaced with orange juice.

ingredients

500 g rump steak
1 teaspoon olive oil
1 onion, finely diced
1 cinnamon stick
4 cloves
1 bay leaf
2 cups (500 ml) beef stock
8 x 20 cm tortillas

preparation: 15 minutes
cooking: 1 hour 35 minutes
serves: 4

1 Trim the steak of any excess fat and sinew and cut the flesh into 2 cm cubes.

2 Heat the oil in a frying pan. Add the onion and cook over medium heat for 2–3 minutes, or until golden brown.

3 Add the meat, cinnamon stick, cloves, bay leaf and beef stock. Bring to the boil, then reduce the heat and simmer, covered, for 1 hour 30 minutes, or until the meat is soft and the liquid is almost absorbed. Remove the cinnamon stick, cloves and bay leaf.

4 Shred the meat with two forks. Place the meat evenly down the centre of each tortilla. Roll up the burrito. Serve with bottled salsa and red onion, or with green vegetables or a salad, if desired.

hint

The burritos can be cooked in the oven to become enchilladas. Place them in an ovenproof dish, pour on a jar of tomato salsa and sprinkle with grated cheese. Bake in a moderately hot 200°C (400°F/Gas 6) oven for 20 minutes, or until the cheese is golden.

Lemon mustard butter
125 g butter
1 tablespoon French
    mustard
2 teaspoons finely grated
    lemon rind
1 tablespoon finely
    chopped fresh chives

4 fillet steaks
    (about 150 g each)
1 tablespoon olive oil
2 cloves garlic, crushed
1 teaspoon ground
    rosemary

preparation: 10 minutes
cooking: 12 minutes
serves: 4

1 To make the lemon mustard butter, cream the butter with the mustard and rind. Stir in the chives. Shape into a log, wrap in plastic wrap and freeze until required.

2 Trim the meat of any excess fat and sinew.

3 Flatten the steaks to an even thickness and nick the edges to prevent curling. Combine the oil, garlic and rosemary and brush evenly over each steak.

4 Place the meat on a lightly oiled hot grill or flat plate. Cook over high heat for 2 minutes on each side, turning once. For a rare result, cook for a further minute on each side. For medium and well done results, move the meat to a cooler part of the barbecue, cook for a further 2–3 minutes on each side for medium and 4–6 on each side for well done.

5 Serve the steaks with a slice of lemon mustard butter and a wedge of lemon.

nutrition per serve
Protein 33 g; Fat 27 g; Carbohydrate 0.5 g; Dietary Fibre 0.5 g; Cholesterol 154 mg; 1550 kJ (370 cal)

handy tip...

The lemon mustard butter can be prepared a day ahead and refrigerated.
A little sesame or walnut oil added to the mixture rubbed on the steaks will give them a pleasant, slightly nutty taste.

nutrition per serve
Protein 26 g; Fat 24 g; Carbohydrate
2 g; Dietary Fibre 0.5 g; Cholesterol
114 mg; 1370 kJ (327 cal)

ingredients

750 g beef mince

2/3 cup (160 g) sour cream

50 g sachet tomato
soup mix

1 onion, finely chopped

2 cloves garlic, crushed

3 teaspoons ground
paprika

1 teaspoon chopped
red chilli

preparation: 10 minutes
cooking: 1 hour
serves: 6

1 Preheat the oven to moderate 180°C (350°F/Gas 4). Grease a loaf tin (21 x 14 x 7 cm) and line the base and sides with baking paper.

2 Place the mince in a large bowl with the sour cream, soup mix, onion, garlic, paprika and chilli and mix together well.

3 Press the mixture firmly into the prepared tin. Bake for 1 hour, or until well browned and firm—insert a skewer in the centre to check for firmness. Turn out of the tin and serve sliced. Serve with salad, if desired.

hint

Meatloaf may be served hot or cold. If serving hot, cook just before serving. If serving cold, meatloaf can be cooked up to 2 days before required. Store, covered, in the refrigerator.

creamy mustard sauce

Remove the steaks from the frying pan and drain off any excess oil. Add ¼ cup (60 ml) white wine and cook, stirring, to remove any pan juices from the bottom of the frying pan. Boil until the wine has nearly evaporated. Reduce the heat to low and stir in 1 teaspoon honey, 2 tablespoons wholegrain mustard and 300 g sour cream for 5 minutes, or until heated through.

serves 4

From left to right: Creamy mustard sauce; Chunky tomato sauce; Quick herb butter; Rich red wine sauce; Creamy mushroom sauce; Green peppercorn sauce.

chunky tomato sauce

Remove the steaks from the frying pan and drain off any excess oil. Stir in 2 tablespoons tomato chutney, 1 tablespoon balsamic vinegar and 400 g bottled tomato pasta sauce, bring to the boil and cook until thick and pulpy. Sprinkle 1 tablespoon chopped fresh parsley over the sauce on serving.

serves 4

quick herb butter

Remove the steaks from the frying pan and drain off any excess oil. Add 100 g butter, 2 crushed cloves garlic, 1 tablespoon lemon juice and ¼ cup (15 g) chopped fresh mixed herbs (eg. chives, parsley). Stir until the butter melts and turns a nutty brown colour.

serves 4

rich red wine sauce

Remove the steaks from the frying pan and drain off any excess oil. Add 1 cup (250 ml) red wine to the pan and bring to the boil, stirring, to release any pan juices that may be stuck to the bottom of the frying pan. Stir in ½ cup (125 ml) beef stock and 2 tablespoons redcurrant jelly, then simmer for 5 minutes, or until the sauce is reduced by half and becomes syrupy.

serves 4

creamy mushroom sauce

Remove the steaks from the frying pan and drain off any excess oil. Melt 50 g butter and add 2 crushed cloves garlic, 3 sliced spring onions and 100 g thinly sliced button mushrooms. Cook over medium heat until the mushrooms are golden brown. Add 1 tablespoon brandy and 1 cup (250 ml) cream. Bring to the boil, then simmer for 5 minutes, or until the sauce has thickened slightly.

serves 4

green peppercorn sauce

Remove the steaks from the frying pan and drain off any excess oil. Add 1 tablespoon chicken stock, ½ teaspoon Worcestershire sauce, 300 ml cream, 2 tablespoons brandy and 2 tablespoons canned green peppercorns, roughly chopped. Bring to the boil, stirring, to release any pan juices that may be stuck to the bottom of the frying pan. Simmer for 5 minutes, or until the sauce has thickened slightly.

serves 4

3 tablespoons olive oil
60 g butter
8 thin veal steaks
plain flour, for coating
2 tablespoons lemon juice
2 tablespoons finely
    chopped fresh parsley
lemon slices, to garnish

preparation: 15 minutes
cooking: 15 minutes
serves: 4

1 Heat the oil and half the butter in a large frying pan over medium heat. Coat the veal steaks in the flour, shake off any excess and add to the pan, cooking in batches if necessary. Cook for 1 minute, or until lightly browned on one side. Turn over and cook for another minute, or until brown. (Thin veal steaks should only take 1 minute to brown on each side—any longer and it will toughen the meat.) Transfer to a warm plate and season with salt and pepper.

2 To make the lemon sauce, reduce the heat to low and add the lemon juice, parsley and remaining butter to the pan. Stir to combine, then add the veal and turn in the sauce for 1 minute, or until heated through.

3 Serve the veal with the lemon sauce and garnish with lemon slices. Serve with a green salad or vegetables, if desired.

nutrition per serve
Protein 40 g; Fat 30 g; Carbohydrate 4 g; Dietary Fibre 0.5 g; Cholesterol 178 mg; 1855 kJ (443 cal)

handy tip...

For thin veal steaks, cover them with plastic wrap and beat with a rolling pin or meat mallet.
This sauce is delicious with the addition of white wine. Add ½ cup (125 ml) white wine, bring to the boil, then add the lemon juice and remaining ingredients.

ingredients

4 veal loin chops
plain flour, for dusting
2 tablespoons milk
1 egg, beaten
3/4 cup (75 g) dried
    breadcrumbs
1 tablespoon finely
    chopped fresh sage, or
    2 teaspoons dried sage
30 g butter
1 tablespoon olive oil

preparation: 10 minutes
cooking: 10 minutes
serves: 4

1 Trim any excess fat from the veal chops. Curl up the tail on each chop and secure with a toothpick.

2 Dust the chops with the flour. Add the milk to the beaten egg. Combine the breadcrumbs and sage. Brush the chops with the combined egg and milk mixture, then coat in the breadcrumbs.

3 Heat the butter and oil in a large frying pan. Add the chops in a single layer and cook over medium heat for 5 minutes on each side, or until cooked through. Serve with a green salad and garnish with lemon wedges, if desired.

nutrition per serve
Protein 19 g; Fat 13 g; Carbohydrate 15 g; Dietary Fibre 1 g; Cholesterol 80 mg; 1065 kJ (254 cal)

hint

To make your own dried breadcrumbs, place slices of stale bread and crusts on a baking tray. Bake in a preheated slow 150°C (300°F/Gas 2) oven until golden brown, dry and crisp.

nutrition per serve
Protein 21 g; Fat 20 g; Carbohydrate 5 g; Dietary Fibre 0 g; Cholesterol 127 mg; 1227 kJ (293 cal)

ingredients

4 thin veal steaks
2 tablespoons plain flour
90 g butter
1/3 cup (80 ml) Marsala
1/2 cup (125 ml) chicken
    stock

preparation: 10 minutes
cooking: 20 minutes
serves: 4

1 Trim the steaks of any excess fat and flatten to a 5 mm thickness. Pat dry with paper towels.

2 Season the flour with salt and freshly ground black pepper. Toss the veal lightly in the seasoned flour and shake off any excess.

3 Heat 60 g of the butter in a frying pan. Cook the veal over medium heat for 1 minute on each side, turning once. Remove from the pan and keep warm.

4 Add the Marsala and stock to the frying pan and bring to the boil. Boil for 2 minutes, stirring constantly. Return the veal to the pan, reduce the heat and simmer, covered, for 10 minutes, basting the veal occasionally. Transfer the veal to a serving dish.

5 Boil the Marsala sauce rapidly for 2–3 minutes, or until syrupy. Stir in the remaining butter and spoon the sauce over the veal. Serve with pasta and a green salad, if desired.

handy tip...

Marsala is a sweet fortified wine.
To make the sauce richer, add 1/2 cup (125 ml) cream with the Marsala. Bring to the boil, then simmer until the sauce coats the back of a spoon.

ingredients

8 veal chops
1/3 cup (80 ml) olive oil
1 large leek, sliced
3 cloves garlic, crushed
6 fresh sage leaves
2 x 400 g cans cannellini
    beans, rinsed and
    drained
1/2 cup (125 ml) chicken
    stock

preparation: 10 minutes
cooking: 25 minutes
serves: 4–6

1 Trim the chops of any excess fat and sinew.

2 Heat 2 tablespoons of the oil in a large saucepan. Add the leek and cook for 3 minutes, or until softened. Stir in the garlic and sage and add the beans. Pour in the stock and season with salt. Cook, covered, over medium heat for 10 minutes, stirring occasionally, and adding extra stock or water if necessary. Mash a few beans into the liquid to make a thick sauce. Keep warm until ready to serve.

3 Heat the remaining oil in a large non-stick frying pan. Add the steaks and cook over medium heat for 4 minutes each side.

4 Just before serving, season the beans with plenty of salt and freshly ground black pepper. Serve the chops with the beans and a green salad, if desired.

nutrition per serve (6)
Protein 30 g; Fat 15 g; Carbohydrate 15 g; Dietary Fibre 9 g; Cholesterol 78 mg; 1325 kJ (316 cal)

hint

Dried white beans may be used instead of canned, but they will need extra liquid and a much longer cooking time. Chickpeas are a good substitute for the beans.

ingredients

2 tablespoons oil
50 g butter
2 onions, thinly sliced
2 tablespoons plain flour
600 g calves' liver,
    thinly sliced (ask your
    butcher to do this)
½ cup (125 ml) good-
    quality Riesling
1 cup (30 g) finely
    chopped fresh parsley

preparation: 15 minutes
cooking: 20 minutes
serves: 4

1 Heat a wok or frying pan until very hot. Add half the oil with 10 g butter and swirl it around to coat the side. Stir-fry the onion over medium heat for 3–4 minutes, or until soft. Remove from the wok.

2 Season the flour with salt and freshly ground black pepper. Toss the liver in the seasoned flour.

3 Reheat the wok. Add the remaining oil and the remaining butter, and stir-fry the floured liver in four batches for 3 minutes, or until browned. Remove from the wok and keep warm.

4 Reheat the wok, then add the wine and boil until it has reduced by two-thirds. Return the onion and liver to the wok, add the parsley and toss well. Season with salt and freshly ground black pepper. This is delicious served with creamy polenta or mashed potato.

nutrition per serve
Protein 30 g; Fat 35 g; Carbohydrate 10 g; Dietary Fibre 1.5 g; Cholesterol 440 mg; 2025 kJ (485 cal)

handy tip...

It is very important not to overcook the liver or it will be tough and dry.
If you would like this recipe to have a gravy, add 1 cup (250 ml) water with the wine and bring to the boil. Stir until thickened.

ingredients

4 thin slices veal
flour, for coating
1 egg, lightly beaten
dry breadcrumbs,
    for coating
30 g butter
¼ cup (60 ml) oil
⅔ cup (185 g) bottled
    chunky tomato
    pasta sauce
1 cup (150 g) grated
    mozzarella

preparation: 15 minutes +
1 hour refrigeration
cooking: 30 minutes
serves: 4

1 Pat the veal dry with paper towels. Coat the veal in the flour and shake off any excess. Dip in the egg and coat with breadcrumbs. Refrigerate for 1 hour.

2 Preheat the oven to moderate 180°C (350°F/Gas 4). Grease an ovenproof dish large enough to lay the veal slices in a single layer.

3 Heat the butter and oil in a large frying pan. Add the crumbed veal to the frying pan and cook for 2–3 minutes on each side, or until golden. Drain on paper towels.

4 Place in a single layer in the prepared ovenproof dish. Spoon the tomato sauce onto each piece of veal, then sprinkle with the mozzarella. Bake for 20–25 minutes, or until the mozzarella is golden and melted. Serve with a green salad.

nutrition per serve
Protein 32 g; Fat 32 g; Carbohydrate 4 g; Dietary Fibre 0.5 g; Cholesterol 158 mg; 1777 kJ (425 cal)

hint

This recipe may be made up to baking stage several hours ahead and stored, covered, in the refrigerator. Cook just before serving. It may also be frozen, without cheese, for up to 1 month. Sprinkle the cheese on top just before cooking. To make this recipe even quicker, you may purchase already crumbed schnitzels from your butcher.

ingredients

12 thin veal escalopes
12 fresh sage leaves
12 slices leg ham
12 slices mozzarella
plain flour, for coating
80 g butter
1 cup (250 ml) white wine

preparation: 10 minutes
cooking: 30 minutes
serves: 6

1 Flatten the escalopes with a meat mallet to make them as thin as possible.

2 On each escalope, place a sage leaf, a slice of ham and a slice of cheese. Fold the escalopes in two and secure each with a toothpick. Lightly coat in flour.

3 Heat the butter in a frying pan. When foaming, add the escalopes in two batches and cook over medium heat for 5–6 minutes on each side, or until lightly golden. Remove the veal and keep warm.

4 Add the wine to the pan and stir over high heat until reduced by half to form a sauce. Season with salt and freshly ground black pepper. Remove the toothpicks from the escalopes, pour the sauce over the top and serve.

nutrition per serve
Protein 30 g; Fat 15 g; Carbohydrate 0 g; Dietary Fibre 0 g; Cholesterol 132 mg; 1227 kJ (295 cal)

handy tip...

One teaspoon of dried sage sprinkled over each escalope can be used in place of fresh.

ingredients

8 veal cutlets

½ cup (125 ml) chicken
stock

1 lime, cut into wedges

250 g button mushrooms,
finely sliced

200 g sour cream or
fromage fraîs

preparation: 15 minutes
cooking: 1 hour 25 minutes
serves: 4

1 Preheat the oven to slow 150°C (300°F/Gas 2). Trim the veal of any excess fat and sinew.

2 Place the cutlets, chicken stock and lime wedges in a baking tin. Cover and cook in the oven for 1 hour 15 minutes, or until tender.

3 Remove the lime and stir in the sliced mushrooms. Return to the oven and cook, uncovered, for 5 minutes, or until the mushrooms are wilted and heated through, taking care not to cook too long.

4 Transfer the mushrooms and the cutlets to a hot serving dish and keep warm.

5 Place the baking tin with the pan juices over high heat and bring to the boil. Cook for 4–5 minutes, or until the liquid is reduced by half.

6 Whisk the sour cream into the sauce. Pour the sauce over the veal and mushrooms and serve immediately with pasta or rice.

nutrition per serve
Protein 33 g; Fat 22 g; Carbohydrate 2 g; Dietary Fibre 0 g; Cholesterol 180 mg; 1427 kJ (340 cal)

hint

For a thicker sauce, add up to twice the amount of sour cream or fromage fraîs.

lamb

500 g lamb's liver
1 tablespoon olive oil
1 large onion, sliced
125 g bacon, cut into strips
30 g butter
1 tablespoon plain flour
300 ml beef stock
2 tablespoons chopped
   fresh parsley

preparation: 10 minutes
cooking: 10 minutes
serves: 4

1 Remove the membrane and tubes from the liver and slice horizontally into 5 mm slices.

2 Heat the oil in a large frying pan. Cook the onion and bacon until browned, then remove from the pan and keep warm.

3 Increase the heat and add the butter to the frying pan until it sizzles. Quickly cook the liver, in batches, over high heat for 1 minute on each side—do not overcook or it will become tough.

4 Return all the liver to the pan with the bacon and onion. Sprinkle the flour over the top and toss to coat. Gradually add the stock and stir until the sauce boils and thickens. Season. Stir in the parsley and serve with fried tomato slices and mashed potato.

nutrition per serve
Protein 35 g; Fat 22 g; Carbohydrate 7 g; Dietary Fibre 0.5 g; Cholesterol 578 mg; 1526 kJ (364 cal)

handy tip...

Liver is an excellent source of Vitamin A, iron and protein.
This recipe can also be made with beef liver, which is larger, darker and stronger in flavour.

nutrition per serve
Protein 15 g; Fat 9.5 g; Carbohydrate 22 g; Dietary Fibre 0 g; Cholesterol 48 mg; 970 kJ (232 cal)

ingredients

Mint sauce
⅓ cup (90 g) sugar
2 tablespoons malt vinegar
⅓ cup (20 g) finely chopped fresh mint

8 lamb cutlets
1 tablespoon olive oil

preparation: 10 minutes
cooking: 10 minutes
serves: 4

1 To make the mint sauce, combine the sugar and ⅓ cup (80 ml) water in a saucepan. Stir over low heat, without boiling, until the sugar has dissolved. Bring to the boil, then reduce the heat and simmer for 3 minutes. Remove from the heat and pour into a jug. Add the vinegar and mint and mix together well.

2 Trim the excess fat and sinew from each cutlet with a small, sharp knife. Scrape all the sinew from the bone until it is clean.

3 Heat the oil in a frying pan. Cook the cutlets (in batches if necessary) over high heat for 2 minutes on each side, to seal, then for a further 1 minute on each side.

4 Serve the mint sauce at room temperature over the lamb cutlets. This dish is delicious served with boiled new potatoes, squash and zucchini.

hint

To save you time, ask your butcher to "French" (trim) the lamb cutlets for you.
This recipe can also be made using lamb loin chops.

ingredients

2 large tomatoes
1 tablespoon oil
1 onion, finely chopped
2 teaspoons soft brown
    sugar
1 tablespoon red wine
    vinegar
1 tablespoon finely
    chopped fresh mint
8 lamb loin chops
fresh mint sprigs,
    to garnish

preparation: 10 minutes
cooking: 25 minutes
serves: 4

1 To make the salsa, cut a small cross on the bottom of each tomato with a sharp knife. Plunge the tomatoes into boiling water for 30 seconds, then into chilled water for 1 minute. Peel the skin down from the cross, then finely chop the tomatoes.

2 Heat the oil in a small saucepan, then add the onion and cook over low heat for 5 minutes, or until softened. Add the tomato, sugar and vinegar and simmer for 5 minutes, stirring occasionally. Add the chopped mint and stir through.

3 Place the chops on a cold, lightly oiled grill tray and cook under a hot grill for 2 minutes on each side to seal. For a rare result, cook the chops for a further 1 minute on each side. For a medium and well done result, lower the grill tray, or reduce the heat to medium, and cook for a further 2–3 minutes on each side for medium and 4–6 minutes on each side for well done result.

4 Serve the chops immediately with the tomato and mint salsa (the salsa can be served either warm or cold). Garnish with a fresh sprig of mint.

nutrition per serve
Protein 24 g; Fat 9 g; Carbohydrate 4 g; Dietary Fibre 1.5 g; Cholesterol 65 mg; 805 kJ (192 cal)

handy tip...

The salsa can be made up to 2 days before required. Add the mint just before serving. Store, covered, in the refrigerator and reheat just before serving.
This dish is great served with mashed potato and steamed peas or beans.
For a slight variation, use a different cut of lamb, such as leg chops or fillets.

ingredients

12 lamb cutlets
¼ cup (30 g) plain flour
2 eggs, lightly beaten
1½ cups (150 g) dry
    breadcrumbs
¼ cup (60 ml) oil

preparation: 10 minutes +
    30 minutes refrigeration
cooking: 20 minutes
serves: 4

1 Trim the lamb cutlets of any excess fat and sinew.

2 Season the flour on a plate. Toss the cutlets lightly in the seasoned flour and shake off any excess.

3 Dip each flour-coated cutlet into the egg, then quickly coat with the breadcrumbs. Using your fingers, press the breadcrumbs firmly onto the cutlets, then shake off any excess.

4 Place the cutlets in a single layer on a baking tray. Cover and refrigerate for 30 minutes.

5 Heat the oil in a large frying pan (make sure the oil isn't too hot or the crumbs will burn before the meat is cooked through). Add the cutlets in three batches and cook over medium heat for 3 minutes on each side, or until golden and tender. Drain on paper towels.

nutrition per serve
Protein 32 g; Fat 25 g; Carbohydrate 30 g; Dietary Fibre 2 g; Cholesterol 160 mg; 1980 kJ (475 cal)

hint

For a variation to the crumbs, replace the dry breadcrumbs with cornflake crumbs, or stir some chopped fresh mixed herbs and grated lemon rind through the breadcrumbs.

ingredients

4 racks of lamb
   (4 cutlets each)
1 cup (300 g) mint jelly
2 tablespoons white wine
¼ cup (15 g) finely
   chopped fresh chives

preparation: 15 minutes
cooking: 45 minutes
serves: 4

1 Preheat the oven to moderately hot 200°C (400°F/Gas 6). Trim any excess fat from the racks of lamb, leaving a thin layer of fat. Clean any meat or sinew from the bones. Cover the bones with foil and place on a rack in a baking tin.

2 Place the mint jelly and wine in a small saucepan. Cook, stirring, over high heat for 4 minutes, or until the mixture has reduced and thickened. Cool slightly, then add the chives.

3 Brush the racks of lamb with the glaze. Roast for 35 minutes for a rare result, or 40 minutes for medium-rare result, brushing with the glaze every 10 minutes. Remove the foil from the lamb and allow to stand for 5 minutes before serving. Serve with steamed or roast vegetables.

nutrition per serve
Protein 30 g; Fat 9 g; Carbohydrate 0 g; Dietary Fibre 0 g; Cholesterol 95 mg; 900 kJ (215 cal)

handy tip...

For a variation to the mint glaze, substitute the mint jelly with redcurrant jelly or cranberry jelly.

ingredients

1 tablespoon oil
750 g diced lamb
2 cups (500 ml) beef or
    chicken stock
2 small onions, chopped
½ cup (125 g) pitted
    prunes, halved
½ cup (95 g) dried
    apricots, halved
1 teaspoon ground ginger
1 teaspoon ground
    cinnamon

preparation: 15 minutes
cooking: 1 hour 10 minutes
serves: 4

1 Heat the oil in a large saucepan. Add the meat in small batches, and cook over medium heat for 2 minutes, or until well browned. Return all the meat to the pan.

2 Add the stock, onion, prunes, apricots, ginger and cinnamon to the saucepan and season with pepper. Bring to the boil, then reduce the heat and simmer, covered, for 1 hour, or until the meat is tender. Garnish with toasted slivered almonds, if desired, and serve with rice.

nutrition per serve
Protein 44 g; Fat 12 g; Carbohydrate 26 g; Dietary Fibre 5 g; Cholesterol 125 mg; 1617 kJ (386 cal)

hint

This recipe is delicious served with spiced couscous. Place the couscous, a large piece of butter, 1 cinnamon stick and 1 strip of orange rind in a heatproof bowl and cover with boiling water. Allow to stand until the water has been absorbed.

ingredients

1.8 kg leg lamb
2 cloves garlic, sliced
3 large strips lemon rind,
    cut into 1 cm pieces
½ cup (25 g) chopped
    fresh coriander leaves
¼ cup (15 g) chopped
    fresh parsley
2 tablespoons olive oil

preparation: 15 minutes
cooking: 1 hour 20 minutes
serves: 4–6

1 Preheat the oven to moderate 180°C (350°F/Gas 4). Trim the lamb of any excess fat and sinew. Using a sharp knife, make deep cuts in the flesh and place a slice of garlic and a piece of lemon rind into each cut.

2 Place the coriander, parsley, oil and 1 teaspoon freshly ground black pepper in a bowl and mix together well. Coat the lamb with the herb mixture and place on a rack in a baking tin. Pour 1 cup (250 ml) water into the tin.

3 Bake for 1 hour 20 minutes, or until the lamb is cooked to your liking. Add extra water to the baking tin during cooking if it starts to dry out. Allow the lamb to rest for 10 minutes before cutting into slices. Serve with a selection of vegetables, if desired. Drizzle with the pan juices for extra flavour.

nutrition per serve (6)
Protein 46 g; Fat 11 g; Carbohydrate 0 g; Dietary Fibre 0 g; Cholesterol 132 mg; 1178 kJ (282 cal)

handy tip...

Coriander is a pungent, leafy green herb, available at most greengrocers. Do not substitute dried coriander for fresh as they have quite different flavours. Water is added to the baking dish to keep the meat moist and to prevent the juices from burning.

4 large lamb leg chops
(about 175 g each)
1½ tablespoons oil
440 g can cream of
mushroom soup
1 tablespoon
Worcestershire sauce
¾ cup (185 ml) chicken
stock
½ cup (125 ml) dry sherry
250 g button mushrooms,
sliced
2 large onions, sliced

preparation: 15 minutes
cooking: 2 hours 15 minutes
serves: 4

1 Preheat the oven to moderate 180°C (350°F/Gas 4). Trim the chops of any excess fat and sinew. Heat 1 tablespoon oil in a frying pan. Cook the chops for 1 minute on each side, or until well browned. Drain on paper towels.

2 Place the chops in a 2 litre casserole dish. Mix together the mushroom soup, Worcestershire sauce, chicken stock and sherry and pour over the chops. Cover and bake for 1 hour 30 minutes.

3 Heat the remaining oil in the pan and cook the mushrooms for 3 minutes, or until lightly browned. Remove from the pan. Add the onion and cook for 5 minutes, or until soft and golden.

4 Stir the mushrooms into the casserole and top with the onion slices. Return to the oven and cook, uncovered, for 30 minutes, or until the onions are crisp and the lamb is tender. Serve with steamed fresh vegetables, if desired.

nutrition per serve
Protein 40 g; Fat 22 g; Carbohydrate 13 g; Dietary Fibre 4 g; Cholesterol 118 mg; 1868kJ (446 cal)

hint

The sherry can be replaced with white wine. The lamb leg chops can be substituted with lamb neck chops.

ingredients

2 tomatoes
2 teaspoons oil
600 g lamb fillet,
 diagonally sliced
3 cloves garlic, finely
 chopped
1 teaspoon cumin seeds
2 teaspoons finely
 chopped fresh rosemary
2 tablespoons balsamic
 vinegar
300 g can cannellini beans,
 rinsed and drained

preparation: 15 minutes
cooking: 10 minutes
serves: 4

1 Score a cross in the base of each tomato. Cover with boiling water for 30 seconds, then transfer to iced water before peeling them and removing the stalks. Scoop out the seeds and finely chop the flesh into cubes.

2 Heat the wok until very hot, add the oil and swirl it around to coat the side. Stir-fry the lamb in two batches over very high heat for 2–3 minutes, or until browned.

3 Return all the lamb to the wok and add the garlic, cumin seeds and rosemary. Cook for 1 minute. Reduce the heat and add the vinegar. Stir well, scraping any sediment off the base of the wok.

4 Add the tomato and cannellini beans and stir-fry until warmed through. Season with salt and black pepper, then garnish with flat-leaf parsley leaves.

nutrition per serve
Protein 35 g; Fat 6 g; Carbohydrate 3 g; Dietary Fibre 3 g; Cholesterol 100 mg; 890 kJ (210 cal)

handy tip...

Lamb backstrap can be used instead of the lamb fillets. Any beans are suitable for this recipe—try borlotti or lima beans.

ingredients

2 kg leg of lamb
2 cloves garlic, cut into
   thin slivers
2 tablespoons fresh
   rosemary sprigs
2 teaspoons oil

preparation: 15 minutes
cooking: 1 hour 30 minutes
serves: 6

1 Preheat the oven to moderate 180°C (350°F/Gas 4). Using a small sharp knife, cut small slits all over the lamb. Insert the slivers of garlic and sprigs of rosemary into the slits.

2 Brush the lamb with the oil and sprinkle with salt and freshly ground black pepper. Place on a wire rack in a baking tin and pour in ½ cup (125 ml) water.

3 Roast for 1 hour 30 minutes for a medium result, or until cooked as desired, basting often with the pan juices. Keep warm and leave for 10–15 minutes before serving.

nutrition per serve
Protein 75 g; Fat 9 g; Carbohydrate 0 g; Dietary Fibre 0 g; Cholesterol 220 mg; 1625 kJ (390 cal)

hint

Always carve meat across the grain. To ensure even cooking, return the lamb to room temperature before roasting.

ingredients

½ cup (125 ml) olive oil
3 x 250 g lamb backstraps
  (see tip)
½ head red cabbage,
  shredded
1 tablespoon caraway
  seeds
1 tablespoon chopped
  fresh rosemary
2 tablespoons pine nuts,
  lightly toasted

Vinaigrette
1 tablespoon Dijon
  mustard
1 tablespoon white wine
  vinegar

preparation: 10 minutes
cooking: 20 minutes
serves: 6

1 Preheat the oven to moderate 180°C (350°F/Gas 4). Heat 2 tablespoons of the oil in a frying pan. Add the lamb and cook over high heat for 2 minutes on each side. Place the lamb on a wire rack in a baking tin and bake for 5–7 minutes. Remove from the oven and leave for 10 minutes.

2 To make the vinaigrette, whisk together the mustard and vinegar in a bowl. Season with salt and freshly ground black pepper. Gradually whisk in the remaining olive oil until the mixture thickens, then adjust the seasoning to taste.

3 Place the shredded cabbage in a salad bowl, pour on the vinaigrette and mix together well. Add the caraway seeds and rosemary and toss. To serve, place the cabbage on a serving platter. Cut the lamb into 1 cm slices and arrange over the cabbage. Sprinkle with the pine nuts and serve immediately.

nutrition per serve
Protein 29 g; Fat 29 g; Carbohydrate 1 g; Dietary Fibre 1.5 g; Cholesterol 82 mg; 1595 kJ (380 cal)

handy tip...

Lamb backstraps are also known as lamb loin. For best results, turn the meat over halfway during baking for more even heat distribution. When the meat is cooked, remove from the oven and wrap completely in foil. Stand for 10 minutes before carving or slicing.

ingredients

90 g ghee or butter
500 g lamb fillets, cubed
1 onion, sliced
1 carrot, cut into strips
2 cups (400 g) long-grain
   rice
3½ cups (875 ml) boiling
   chicken stock
½ cup (60 g) raisins
fresh parsley, chopped,
   to garnish

preparation: 15 minutes
cooking: 30 minutes
serves: 4

1 Melt the ghee in a frying pan. Add the lamb in batches and cook until lightly browned. Add the onion and carrot and cook for 2 minutes. Season. Stir in the rice until coated.

2 Pour in the boiling stock, then reduce the heat and cook, covered, for 20 minutes, or until the rice is tender and all the liquid has been absorbed. Add the raisins, cover, and leave until plumped. Garnish with the parsley.

nutrition per serve
Protein 35 g; Fat 28 g; Carbohydrate 92 g; Dietary Fibre 4 g; Cholesterol 148 mg; 3182 kJ (760 cal)

hint

Pilaus originated in the Near East and are traditionally cooked, covered, on the stove—pilafs are cooked, covered, in the oven. They are always made with medium- or long-grain rice.

ingredients

1 kg diced lamb
3 leeks, cut into
    5 mm slices
3 carrots, thickly sliced
2 onions, cut into small
    cubes
1 cup (220 g) pearl barley,
    well rinsed
2 cloves garlic, crushed
¼ cup (15 g) chopped
    fresh parsley
parsley sprigs, to garnish

preparation: 15 minutes
cooking: 2 hours
serves: 6–8

1 Place the lamb in a deep saucepan. Add the leek, carrot, onion, barley and 2.5 litres water. Bring to the boil, then reduce the heat and simmer, covered, for 1 hour. Remove any scum as it rises to the surface.

2 Add the garlic and parsley, season with freshly ground pepper and simmer gently, uncovered, for another hour.

3 Season to taste with salt and freshly ground black pepper. Spoon into warm soup bowls and garnish with sprigs of parsley.

nutrition per serve (8)
Protein 30 g; Fat 5.5 g; Carbohydrate 20 g; Dietary Fibre 5 g; Cholesterol 82 mg; 1082 kJ (258 cal)

handy tip...

This is best prepared a day ahead. Refrigerate and remove any fat from the top of the broth. The flavour of the soup will develop on standing.
Diced lamb from the leg is best suited to this recipe.
If you do not have barley, use soup mix.

ingredients

1 kg lamb backstrap
1 green capsicum,
    cut into 2 cm squares
1 red capsicum,
    cut into 2 cm squares
2/3 cup (160 ml) olive oil
1/3 cup (80 ml) lemon juice
2 cloves garlic, crushed
3 teaspoons dried
    oregano leaves
2 bay leaves, crumbled

preparation: 15 minutes +
    overnight refrigeration
cooking: 10 minutes
serves: 4

1 Trim the lamb of any excess fat and sinew and cut into 3 cm cubes.

2 Soak wooden skewers in a bowl of cold water to prevent them from burning during cooking. Thread the meat and capsicum pieces alternately onto the skewers then place in a glass or ceramic dish.

3 Place the oil, lemon juice, garlic, oregano and bay leaves in a jug. Season with salt and freshly ground black pepper and mix together. Pour the marinade over the skewers. Cover with plastic wrap and refrigerate overnight, turning occasionally. Drain and reserve the marinade.

4 Place the skewers on a lightly greased barbecue flat plate or under a hot grill. Cook over medium heat for 10 minutes, or until tender, brushing with the reserved marinade several times during cooking. This is delicious served with warm pita bread, Greek salad and Tzatziki (cucumber yoghurt dip).

nutrition per serve
Protein 56 g; Fat 47 g; Carbohydrate 2.5 g; Dietary Fibre 1 g; Cholesterol 165 mg; 2753 kJ (658 cal)

hint

Uncooked kebabs can be frozen in marinade in an airtight container for up to a month. Thaw the kebabs in the container, then cook as directed.

ingredients

6–8 lamb chump chops
1 lemon
1 teaspoon oil
1 large onion, finely
  chopped
1/3 cup (105 g) redcurrant
  jelly
1 tablespoon barbecue
  sauce
1 tablespoon tomato
  sauce
2 cups (500 ml) chicken
  stock

preparation: 15 minutes
cooking: 1 hour 15 minutes
serves: 4

1 Preheat the oven to warm 170°C (325°F/Gas 3). Trim the meat of any excess fat. Grate 1 teaspoon rind from the lemon and squeeze 1 tablespoon juice.

2 Heat the oil in a large frying pan. Add the chops and cook over medium heat, turning once, for 2–3 minutes, or until well browned. Remove from the pan and place in a casserole dish.

3 Add the onion to the frying pan and cook over medium heat, stirring frequently, for 5 minutes, or until the onion has softened. Add the redcurrant jelly, lemon rind and juice, barbecue and tomato sauces and stock. Stir for 2–3 minutes, or until heated through. Pour the sauce over the chops and stir to coat.

4 Bake, covered, for 1 hour, or until the meat is tender, turning 2–3 times during cooking. Lift the chops out onto a side plate and keep warm.

5 Pour the sauce into a frying pan and boil rapidly for 5 minutes, or until the sauce has thickened and reduced. Return the chops to the sauce before serving.

nutrition per serve
Protein 31 g; Fat 11 g; Carbohydrate 6 g; Dietary Fibre 1.5 g; Cholesterol 96 mg; 1051 kJ (250 cal)

handy tip...

This casserole will keep, covered and refrigerated, for up to 2 days, and is suitable to freeze for up to 1 month.
Other lamb chop cuts can be used instead of chump, if preferred.

ingredients

2 tablespoons oil
500 g lamb backstrap,
    cut into thin strips
2 cloves garlic, crushed
4 spring onions,
    thickly sliced
2 tablespoons soy sauce
1/3 cup (80 ml) dry sherry
2 tablespoons sweet chilli
    sauce
2 teaspoons sesame
    seeds, toasted
    (see hint)

preparation: 15 minutes
cooking: 12 minutes
serves: 4

1 Heat a wok until very hot. Add 1 tablespoon oil and swirl it around to coat the side. Add the lamb strips in two batches and stir-fry over high heat for 3 minutes each batch, or until browned. Remove all the lamb from the wok.

2 Reheat the wok and add the remaining oil. Add the garlic and spring onion and stir-fry for 2 minutes, then remove from the wok. Add the soy sauce, sherry and sweet chilli sauce to the wok. Bring to the boil, then reduce the heat and simmer for 3–4 minutes, or until the sauce thickens slightly.

3 Return the meat, with any juices, and the spring onion to the wok, and toss to coat with the sauce. Serve sprinkled with the toasted sesame seeds.

nutrition per serve
Protein 30 g; Fat 15 g; Carbohydrate 3 g; Dietary Fibre 1 g; Cholesterol 82 mg; 1192 kJ (285 cal)

hint

Lamb fillets can be used instead of the lamb backstrap (loin).
To toast the sesame seeds, place them in a non-stick frying pan and cook over medium heat until golden.

pork

ingredients

4 pork butterfly steaks
1 tablespoon oil
1 teaspoon grated
    fresh ginger
1 cup (250 ml) apple cider
1 teaspoon cornflour
1 tablespoon chopped
    fresh chives

preparation: 10 minutes
cooking: 10 minutes
serves: 4

1 Trim the butterfly steaks of any excess fat and sinew.

2 Heat the oil in a frying pan and add the pork. Cook over medium heat for 2–3 minutes on each side, or until tender, turning once during cooking. Remove and keep warm.

3 Add the ginger to the pan, stirring and scraping with a wooden spoon. Place 1 tablespoon cider in a small bowl, add the cornflour and stir until smooth. Add the remaining cider, mix well, and add to the pan. Bring to the boil, then reduce the heat and simmer, stirring, for 2 minutes, or until the sauce has thickened and reduced. Stir in the chives. Pour the sauce over the steaks and serve with steamed vegetables.

nutrition per serve
Protein 28 g; Fat 6 g; Carbohydrate 7 g; Dietary Fibre 0 g; Cholesterol 62 mg; 812 kJ (194 cal)

handy tip...

Alcoholic or non-alcoholic cider is suitable for this recipe. If you use alcoholic cider, add it to the frying pan before thickening and boil rapidly to evaporate the alcohol. Mix the cornflour with 1 tablespoon water and stir into the cider.

400 g orange sweet
   potato, coarsely grated
2 large potatoes,
   coarsely grated
2 eggs, lightly beaten
1 tablespoon plain flour
2 tablespoons oil
8 rashers bacon
8 thick pork sausages
4 tablespoons fruit
   chutney, to serve

preparation: 15 minutes
cooking: 30 minutes
serves: 4

1 Place the sweet potato, potato, egg and flour in a bowl and mix together well. Season to taste with salt and freshly ground black pepper. Divide into eight portions and, using your hands, form each portion into a 10 cm flat patty.

2 Heat the oil in a non-stick frying pan and cook the rosti in batches for 3–4 minutes on each side, or until golden brown and cooked through. Set aside and keep warm.

3 Wrap a piece of bacon around each sausage and secure with a toothpick.

4 Cook the sausages under a hot grill for 10–15 minutes, or until cooked through, turning often. Remove the toothpick. Divide among the serving plates and top with a dollop of chutney. Serve with the potato rosti and a mixed green salad, if desired.

nutrition per serve
Protein 35 g; Fat 38 g; Carbohydrate 40 g; Dietary Fibre 5 g; Cholesterol 200 mg; 2675 kJ (640 cal)

hint

The sweet potato can be replaced with potato (use a floury potato such as Russet, Idaho or Spunta). Make sure you squeeze the grated potato to remove any excess moisture.

ingredients

500 g spaghetti
8 rashers bacon, cut into
    thin strips
4 eggs
1/2 cup (50 g) freshly
    grated Parmesan
1 1/4 cups (315 ml) cream

preparation: 10 minutes
cooking: 20 minutes
serves: 6

1 Cook the spaghetti in a large saucepan of boiling water according to the packet instructions. Drain well and return the spaghetti to the saucepan.

2 Meanwhile, heat a frying pan. Add the bacon and cook over medium heat until crisp. Remove and drain on paper towels.

3 Place the eggs, Parmesan and cream in a bowl and beat together well. Add the bacon and pour the sauce over the warm pasta. Toss gently until the pasta is well coated.

4 Return the pan to the heat and cook over very low heat for 30–60 seconds, or until slightly thickened. Season with freshly ground black pepper and serve. Garnish with herb sprigs, if desired.

nutrition per serve
Protein 27 g; Fat 30 g; Carbohydrate 60 g; Dietary Fibre 4 g; Cholesterol 225 mg; 2667 kJ (637 cal)

handy tip...

There are two thoughts as to the origin of this dish. Some say it appeared in Rome during the Second World War, when the American GIs combined their rations of bacon and eggs with the local spaghetti. The other possibility suggests it was a quick and easy meal developed by the coal vendors, or *carbonari*.

2 tablespoons olive oil

375 g small mushrooms, quartered

4 rashers bacon, chopped

6 eggs

1/3 cup (80 ml) thick cream

1 tablespoon tomato paste

2 teaspoons chopped fresh basil

1/2 cup (60 g) grated Cheddar

preparation: 10 minutes
cooking: 15 minutes
serves: 4–6

1 Heat the oil in a large frying pan. Add the mushrooms and bacon and stir over medium heat for 5 minutes, or until golden and almost all the liquid is absorbed. Remove the pan from the heat.

2 Place the eggs, cream, tomato paste, basil and Cheddar in a bowl and season to taste. Beat with a whisk until mixed together.

3 Return the frying pan to the heat. Pour the egg mixture over the mushrooms and bacon and stir. Shake the pan to spread the mixture evenly over the base. Cook over medium heat for 5 minutes, or until the omelette has almost set.

Place the pan under a hot grill and cook for 2–3 minutes, or until the top is set. Cut into wedges and serve.

nutrition per serve (6)
Protein 16 g; Fat 22 g; Carbohydrate 2 g; Dietary Fibre 1.5 g; Cholesterol 220 mg; 1107 kJ (265 cal)

hint

Omelettes are great for a late breakfast or light lunch. They are prepared with either savoury (cheese, asparagus, prawns) or sweet (macerated fruit) fillings.

ingredients

4 pork cutlets
1 tablespoon olive oil
15 g butter
1 ripe pear, peeled, cored, sliced into thin wedges
2 spring onions, sliced
1 tablespoon flour
1 cup (250 ml) chicken stock
¼ cup (60 ml) apple juice

preparation: 10 minutes
cooking: 20 minutes
serves: 4

1 Trim the cutlets of any fat. Heat the oil and butter in a frying pan. Add the pear and cook over medium heat until lightly browned, turning occasionally. Remove.

2 Season the pork with salt and pepper. Add to the frying pan and cook over medium heat for 4–5 minutes on each side, or until the pork is cooked through. Remove from the pan and keep warm.

3 Add the spring onion to the frying pan and cook until just soft. Stir in the flour and cook for 2 minutes. Remove from the heat and stir in the combined stock and apple juice. Return the pan to the heat and cook, stirring, until the sauce boils and thickens. Reduce the heat and simmer for 2 minutes. Add any pork juices to the pan.

4 Serve the pork topped with the pear slices and drizzled with the sauce. Serve with baby potatoes and beans. Sprinkle with chopped sage leaves, if desired.

nutrition per serve
Protein 25 g; Fat 10 g; Carbohydrate 9 g; Dietary Fibre 1 g; Cholesterol 58 mg; 935 kJ (225 cal)

handy tip...

If pork cutlets are not available, use pork chops. Apple may be used instead of pear—Golden Delicious or Granny Smith are best for cooking.

ingredients

1 tablespoon oil
1 onion, roughly chopped
4 slices prosciutto, roughly
    chopped
5 small potatoes, cut into
    1 cm cubes
1½ cups (375 ml) chicken
    stock
2 cups (310 g) frozen
    peas
1 tablespoon shredded
    fresh sage leaves

preparation: 10 minutes
cooking: 25 minutes
serves: 4

1 Heat the oil in a saucepan and add the onion and prosciutto. Cook; stirring constantly, over high heat for 2–3 minutes, or until the onion is golden. Add the potato and cook for another minute.

2 Pour in the stock and 2½ cups (625 ml) water. Cook over medium heat for 15 minutes. Add the peas and cook for a further 5 minutes. Stir in the sage and season to taste with salt and freshly ground black pepper.

3 Divide the soup among four warm serving bowls. Serve with crusty bread and butter.

nutrition per serve
Protein 7 g; Fat 5.5 g; Carbohydrate 15 g; Dietary Fibre 6 g; Cholesterol 1.5 mg; 550 kJ (130 cal)

hint

Trimmed rashers of bacon can be used instead of prosciutto, and minted or fresh peas are a nice alternative to frozen peas. For a richer soup, replace the water with more stock, but don't be tempted to use stock powder—the soup will be too salty.

1 tablespoon oil
4 pork loin chops
1 cup (250 ml) white
   wine
⅓ cup (105 g) redcurrant
   jelly

preparation: 5 minutes
cooking: 25 minutes
serves: 4

1 Heat the oil in a frying pan. Add the chops and cook over medium heat for 8 minutes on each side, or until tender and browned. Remove from the pan and keep the chops warm.

2 Add the wine and jelly to the pan and stir until blended with the pan juices. Bring the sauce to the boil, then reduce the heat and simmer for 10 minutes, or until reduced by half. Divide the chops among the serving plates and pour the sauce over the chops. Serve with a green salad, if desired.

nutrition per serve
Protein 23 g; Fat 6.5 g; Carbohydrate 0 g; Dietary Fibre 0 g; Cholesterol 45 mg; 815 kJ (195 cal)

handy tip...

Orange or lime-and-ginger marmalade can be used instead of the redcurrant jelly. The sauce will thicken as it boils and reduces.
Pork cutlets can be used instead of pork chops.

nutrition per serve
Protein 25 g; Fat 23 g; Carbohydrate
36 g; Dietary Fibre 2.5 g; Cholesterol
70 mg; 1950 kJ (465 cal)

ingredients

30 cm purchased pizza
base

½ cup (125 g) purchased
pizza sauce

1 cup (150 g) grated
mozzarella or Cheddar

80 g pepperoni, thinly
sliced

50 g salami, thinly sliced

40 g mortadella, cut into
quarters

preparation: 15 minutes
cooking: 20 minutes
serves: 4

1 Preheat the oven to hot 210°C (415°F/Gas 6–7). Place the pizza base on a lightly oiled pizza tray.

2 Spread the sauce evenly over the pizza base. Sprinkle ¾ cup (110 g) of the mozzarella over the sauce, then arrange the pepperoni, salami and mortadella on top. Sprinkle with the remaining mozzarella.

3 Bake for 20 minutes, or until the cheese has melted and the base is crunchy and golden. Cut into wedges and serve with a green salad and garlic bread, if desired.

hint

Other meats, such as pancetta, prosciutto or any hot or spicy salami can also be used.
If you prefer a really spicy pizza, use a hot salami such as Hungarian.

ingredients

2 tablespoons olive oil
4 pork leg steaks
1 onion, sliced into rings
2 cloves garlic, crushed
1/2 cup (125 ml) white wine
1 cup (250 ml) cream
2 tablespoons wholegrain
    mustard
2 tablespoons chopped
    fresh parsley

preparation: 10 minutes
cooking: 25 minutes
serves: 4

1 Heat the oil in a large frying pan. Add the pork steaks and cook for 3–4 minutes on each side, or until golden. Remove from the pan.

2 Reduce the heat and add the onion. Cook for 3 minutes, or until golden. Add the garlic and cook for 1 minute more. Add the wine, bring to the boil and cook until the liquid is reduced by half.

3 Stir in the cream and mustard and simmer gently for 5 minutes. Add the pork and simmer for a further 5 minutes. Stir in the parsley and season. Divide the steaks among the serving plates. Spoon the sauce over the pork and serve immediately.

nutrition per serve
Protein 30 g; Fat 38 g; Carbohydrate 4 g; Dietary Fibre 1 g; Cholesterol 150 mg; 2051 kJ (490 cal)

handy tip...

To make a quick mustard sauce, omit the wine and cream and stir in 1 1/2 cups (375 g) sour cream. Gently heat, but do not boil.

ingredients

1/3 cup (115 ml) honey
1/3 cup (80 ml) plum sauce
1/3 cup (80 ml) cold,
    strong tea
2 tablespoons soy sauce
1 tablespoon grated fresh
    ginger
2 cloves garlic, crushed
1/2 teaspoon five-spice
    powder
1.5 kg pork ribs

preparation: 10 minutes +
    overnight marinating
cooking: 45 minutes
serves: 4

1 Place the honey, plum sauce, tea, soy sauce, ginger, garlic and five-spice powder in a jug and mix together well.

2 Place the pork ribs in a shallow glass or ceramic dish. Pour on the marinade and brush over the ribs to coat thoroughly. Cover and refrigerate for 2 hours or preferably overnight.

3 Preheat the oven to moderate 180°C (350°F/Gas 4). Drain the ribs and reserve the marinade. Place the ribs on a rack in a large baking tin and bake for 45 minutes, or until tender and golden. Turn the pork occasionally and brush with the reserved marinade during cooking. Garnish with strips of spring onion, if desired, and serve immediately.

nutrition per serve
Protein 60 g; Fat 7.5 g; Carbohydrate 25 g; Dietary Fibre 0.5 g; Cholesterol 130 mg; 1695 kJ (405 cal)

hint

There are two cuts of pork ribs: 'Spare ribs' contain no bone, while 'American-style ribs' are on the bone—this is what Americans refer to as 'ribs'.

ingredients

4 kg leg of pork
oil, to rub on pork
salt, to rub on pork

Gravy
1 tablespoon brandy or
   Calvados
2 tablespoons plain flour
1½ cups (375 ml) chicken
   stock
½ cup (125 ml)
   unsweetened apple
   juice

preparation: 15 minutes
cooking: 3 hours 15 minutes
serves: 6–8

1 Preheat the oven to very hot 250°C (500°F/Gas 10). Score the rind of the pork with a sharp knife at 2 cm intervals. Rub in some oil and salt to ensure a crisp crackling.

2 Place the pork, rind-side up, on a rack in a large baking tin, then add a little water to the tin. Roast for 30 minutes, or until the rind begins to crackle and bubble. Reduce the heat to moderate 180°C (350°F/Gas 4), then roast for 2 hours 40 minutes (20 minutes per 500 g). The pork is cooked if the juices run clear when the flesh is pierced with a fork. Do not cover the pork or the crackling will soften. Leave in a warm place for 10 minutes.

3 To make the gravy, drain off all except 2 tablespoons of the pan juices from the baking tin. Place on top of the stove over medium heat, add the brandy and stir quickly to lift the sediment from the bottom of the tin. Cook for 1 minute. Remove from the heat, stir in the flour and mix well. Return the tin to the heat and cook for 2 minutes, stirring constantly. Gradually add the stock and apple juice, and cook, stirring constantly, until the gravy boils and thickens. Season to taste with salt and freshly ground black pepper. Slice the pork and serve with the crackling and gravy. May also be served with apple sauce and baked apple wedges, if desired.

nutrition per serve (8)
Protein 120 g; Fat 4 g; Carbohydrate 0 g; Dietary Fibre 0 g; Cholesterol 230 mg; 2145 kJ (515 cal)

handy tip...

To produce delicious crisp crackling it is essential to score the pork skin and rub it with a generous amount of oil and salt. For 4 kg you will need approximately 3 tablespoons oil and 3–4 tablespoons salt. Do not turn the pork over or the crackling will go soft.

ingredients

2 sheets frozen shortcrust
  pastry, thawed
20 g butter
1 onion, chopped
4 rashers bacon, cut into
  thin strips
2 tablespoons chopped
  chives
2 eggs
1 cup (250 ml) cream
100 g Swiss cheese,
  grated

preparation: 15 minutes +
  20 minutes refrigeration
cooking: 1 hour 5 minutes
serves: 4–6

1 Line a shallow, loose-based, round, 25 cm flan tin with two sheets of pastry, pressing it well into the base and side. Trim off any excess pastry by using a sharp knife or by rolling a rolling pin across the top of the tin. Place the pastry-lined flan tin in the refrigerator for 20 minutes. Preheat the oven to moderately hot 190°C (375°F/Gas 5).

2 Cover the pastry shell with baking paper and fill evenly with baking beads or rice. Bake for 15 minutes. Remove the paper and beads and bake for a further 10 minutes, or until the pastry is golden. Remove from the oven, then reduce the temperature to moderate 180°C (350°F/Gas 4).

3 To make the filling, heat the butter in a frying pan. Add the onion and bacon and cook, stirring frequently for 10 minutes, or until the onion is soft and the bacon is cooked. Stir in the chives, then leave to cool.

4 Place the eggs and cream in a jug and whisk until well combined. Season with pepper.

5 Spread the onion and bacon mixture evenly over the base of the pastry shell. Pour the egg mixture over the top, then sprinkle with the cheese. Bake for 30 minutes, or until the filling has set and the top is golden.

nutrition per serve (6)
Protein 16 g; Fat 44 g; Carbohydrate 27 g; Dietary Fibre 1.5 g; Cholesterol 170 mg; 2344 kJ (560 cal)

hint

If the flavour of Swiss cheese is too strong, use Cheddar.
If bacon is not available, try ham.
The quiche originated in Lorraine, on the French-German border and was originally made with bread dough—Quiche Lorraine, with its filling of egg and bacon or ham, is a speciality of the region.

quick snacks with ham

crispy bacon, egg, bocconcini and tomato salad

Grill 4 rashers bacon until crisp, allow to cool, then break into large pieces. Hard boil 4 eggs, peel and cut in half. Arrange 150 g baby English spinach leaves in a large flat salad bowl. Top with the egg, 150 g sliced baby bocconcini and 200 g halved mixed cherry and teardrop tomatoes. Make a simple dressing by combining 100 g plain yoghurt with 2 tablespoons orange juice and 2 teaspoons wholegrain mustard. Drizzle over the salad and serve immediately.

serves 4

blt

Grill 8 rashers bacon until crisp. Cut 4 pieces of Turkish bread or wholemeal baps in half and spread both sides with whole-egg mayonnaise. Top one half with a few lettuce leaves, slices of tomato and 2 rashers of crispy bacon. Drizzle with a little tomato sauce and top with the remaining half of bread.

serves 4

fried ham, cheese and mustard sandwiches

Divide 250 g sliced leg ham among 4 thick slices white bread and top each piece of bread with a slice of Swiss cheese. Spread another 4 slices of bread with Dijon mustard, and place them mustard-side-down on the cheese. Butter the outside of the bread. Heat a frying pan and cook the sandwiches, in batches, over medium heat until the outside is crisp and golden brown and the cheese has melted.

serves 4

chicken skewers wrapped in ham

Cut 4 chicken breast fillets into 3 cm cubes and place in a bowl with ½ cup (125 ml) classic French dressing. Cover and refrigerate for 20 minutes. Wrap each cube in a piece of sliced leg ham—you will need 6–8 slices in total. Thread the chicken pieces onto bamboo skewers, which have been soaked in water, alternating with cherry tomatoes and bay leaves. Cook under a hot grill, brushing lightly with the reserved dressing and turning frequently, for 5 minutes, or until cooked through.

serves 4–6

From left to right: Crispy bacon, egg, bocconcini and tomato salad; BLT; Fried ham, cheese and mustard sandwiches; Chicken skewers wrapped in ham; Eggs on toast with bacon and cheese; Chicken cordon bleu.

eggs on toast with bacon and cheese

Place 100 g grated mature Cheddar, 30 g butter, ½ teaspoon mustard powder and a pinch paprika in a small saucepan and cook over low heat for 2 minutes, or until the cheese has melted. Remove from the heat. Poach 4 eggs until cooked to your liking and grill 8 rashers bacon until crisp. Toast 4 thickly cut slices of wholegrain bread. Place the bacon onto the toast, top with the egg, pour the sauce over the egg and grill until bubbling. Serve immediately.

serves 4

chicken cordon bleu

Cut a pocket into the side of 4 chicken breasts and fill each pocket with 1 slice of Swiss cheese and 1 slice of smoked leg ham, then skewer with a toothpick. Heat 1 tablespoon oil in a large frying pan and cook the chicken in batches until golden brown on both sides. Transfer to a baking tray and bake for 15 minutes, or until cooked through.

serves 4

2 tablespoons oil
2 cloves garlic, chopped
1 large onion, cut into
　　wedges
500 g pork loin, cut into
　　thin slices
2 tablespoons cornflour
¼ cup (60 g) plum sauce
1 tablespoon soy sauce
2 teaspoons hoisin sauce

preparation: 15 minutes
cooking: 15 minutes
serves: 4

1 Heat half the oil in a wok and swirl around to coat the side. Add the garlic and onion and stir-fry over medium heat for 2 minutes, or until softened. Remove.

2 Coat the pork lightly in the cornflour and season well with salt and pepper. Add the remaining oil to the wok and when it is extremely hot, stir-fry the pork in two batches for 5–6 minutes, or until dark golden brown. Set aside with the garlic and onion.

3 Add the plum, soy and hoisin sauces to the wok. Return the garlic, onion and pork to the wok. Toss well to coat the meat and serve immediately with rice.

nutrition per serve
Protein 30 g; Fat 15 g; Carbohydrate 20 g; Dietary Fibre 1 g; Cholesterol 60 mg; 1445 kJ (345 cal)

handy tip...

The cornflour is added to thicken the sauce. For a thinner sauce, simply omit the cornflour.

ingredients

2 tablespoons oil
30 g butter
140 g fennel bulb, thinly
   sliced
600 g pork fillet,
   cut into thin strips
1 tablespoon lemon juice
¼ cup (60 ml) chicken or
   vegetable stock
2 tablespoons baby
   capers, drained and
   rinsed

preparation: 15 minutes
cooking: 15 minutes
serves: 4

1 Heat the wok until very hot, add half the oil and half the butter, and swirl it around to coat the side. When the butter begins to sizzle, add the fennel and stir-fry for 3–5 minutes, or until golden and tender. Remove and keep warm.

2 Reheat the wok and add the remaining oil and remaining butter. Stir-fry the pork in two batches until browned.

3 Return the pork and fennel to the wok. Add the lemon juice, stock and capers and stir through the pork mixture, scraping any sediment from the wok. Season with salt and freshly ground pepper. For a slight Italian twist, garnish with shaved Parmesan.

nutrition per serve
Protein 40 g; Fat 20 g; Carbohydrate 2 g; Dietary Fibre 1 g; Cholesterol 105 mg; 1525 kJ (365 cal)

hint

Be sure to trim the tough base and outer leaves from the fennel.
Fennel has a mild aniseed flavour. If it is not available, use 1 leek instead.

ingredients

7 kg leg ham
cloves, to garnish

Glaze
2/3 cup (125 g) soft brown
    sugar
1/4 cup (90 g) honey
1 tablespoon English
    mustard

preparation: 20 minutes
cooking: 65 minutes
serves: 20

1 Preheat the oven to moderate 180°C (350°F/Gas 4). Using a sharp knife, cut through the rind 6 cm from the shank end. To remove the rind from the ham, run a thumb around the edge, under the rind, and carefully pull back. Using a sharp knife, remove and discard the excess fat from the ham.

2 Using a sharp knife, score the fat with cuts crossways and then diagonally to form a diamond pattern. Do not cut all the way through to the ham or the fat will fall off during cooking. Press a clove into the centre of each diamond.

3 To make the glaze, place the sugar, honey and mustard in a bowl and mix together. Spread carefully over the ham with a palette knife or the back of a spoon.

4 Place the ham on a rack in a deep baking tin. Add 2 cups (500 ml) water to the dish. Cover the ham and tin securely with foil, and cook for 45 minutes. Increase the heat to hot 210°C (415°F/Gas 6–7) and bake for 20 minutes, or until the surface is slightly caramelised. Rest for 15 minutes before carving.

nutrition per serve
Protein 53 g; Fat 10 g; Carbohydrate 10 g; Dietary Fibre 0 g; Cholesterol 144 mg; 1439 kJ (345 cal)

handy tip...

It may not be that often that you get to cater for 20 people, however do not let that deter you from trying this recipe. Leftovers are great for quick soups, pies, quiches, toasted sandwiches and salads. Leftover ham can be stored in the refrigerator, wrapped in a damp tea towel, for up to 10 days.

ingredients

2 bunches Chinese
  broccoli, trimmed,
  cut into 5 cm lengths
1 tablespoon peanut oil
2 cm piece fresh ginger,
  julienned
2 cloves garlic, crushed
500 g Chinese barbecued
  pork, thinly sliced
¼ cup (60 ml) chicken or
  vegetable stock
¼ cup (60 ml) oyster
  sauce
1 tablespoon kecap manis

preparation: 10 minutes
cooking: 10 minutes
serves: 4

1 Place the broccoli in a steamer over a saucepan of simmering water and cook for 5 minutes, or until just tender but still crisp. Set aside.

2 Heat a wok until very hot, add the oil and swirl around to coat the side. Add the ginger and garlic and stir-fry for 30 seconds, or until fragrant. Add the broccoli and barbecued pork and toss through.

3 Place the stock, oyster sauce and kecap manis in a small bowl and mix together well. Add to the wok and stir-fry until heated through. Serve with steamed rice or noodles.

nutrition per serve
Protein 50 g; Fat 10 g; Carbohydrate 5 g; Dietary Fibre 5.5 g; Cholesterol 116 mg; 1307 kJ (312 cal)

hint

If Chinese broccoli is not available, try choy sum. Some Asian vegetables are available at supermarkets. If not, try an Asian supermarket.

seafood

ingredients

12 taco shells

2 x 185 g cans tuna in brine, drained

½ cup (125 g) sour cream

½ small red onion, finely chopped

300 g can cannellini or butter beans, rinsed and drained

2 cups (90 g) shredded lettuce

3 tomatoes, finely sliced

preparation: 15 minutes
cooking: 10 minutes
serves: 6

1 Preheat the oven to moderate 180°C (350°F/Gas 4). Warm the taco shells for 5–10 minutes while preparing the filling.

2 Place the tuna in a large bowl and flake with a fork. Add the sour cream, red onion and beans and mix together well. Season with salt and freshly ground black pepper.

3 Place some of the lettuce and a couple of slices of tomato in each taco, then fill with the tuna and bean mixture. Serve immediately.

nutrition per serve
Protein 20 g; Fat 15 g; Carbohydrate 8 g; Dietary Fibre 4.5 g; Cholesterol 60 mg; 1306 kJ (297 cal)

handy tip...

The filling for the tacos also makes a good lunch box salad. Put it in an airtight container and serve the tacos or corn chips on the side. Salmon can be used instead of the tuna.

4 boneless white fish fillets
(about 180 g each)

3 tablespoons plain
yoghurt

1½ teaspoons garam
masala

1 clove garlic, crushed

½ teaspoon chilli flakes

preparation: 10 minutes +
20 minutes marinating
cooking: 6 minutes
serves: 4

1 Arrange the fish fillets in a large glass or ceramic dish.

2 Place the yoghurt, garam masala, garlic and chilli flakes in a small bowl, season to taste with salt and mix together well. Spread the marinade evenly over the fillets, cover, and refrigerate for 20 minutes.

3 Drain the fish fillets and place on a lightly oiled grill tray. Cook under a hot grill for 2–3 minutes on each side, or until the flesh can be flaked easily with the point of a knife. Serve immediately with steamed white rice.

nutrition per serve
Protein 38 g; Fat 5.5 g; Carbohydrate
1 g; Dietary Fibre 0 g; Cholesterol
130 mg; 872 kJ (210 cal)

hint

To make tandoori fish fillets, simply add 2 tablespoons of bottled tandoori paste to the yoghurt.

ingredients

500 g squid tubes
1 tablespoon finely
    chopped fresh ginger
2–3 teaspoons finely
    chopped red chilli
3 cloves garlic, finely
    chopped
¼ cup (60 ml) oil
2 onions, thinly sliced
500 g baby bok choy,
    roughly chopped

preparation: 10 minutes +
    2–3 hours marinating
cooking: 15 minutes
serves: 4

1 Wash the squid well and dry with paper towels. Cut into 1 cm rings and place in a shallow glass or ceramic bowl.

2 Place the ginger, chilli, garlic and oil in a bowl and mix together. Pour the mixture over the squid and toss well. Cover and refrigerate for 2–3 hours.

3 Heat the wok until very hot. Stir-fry the squid over high heat in three batches for 1–2 minutes each batch, reserving the marinade. Remove from the wok as soon as the squid turns white. Do not overcook or the squid will be rubbery. Remove all the squid from the wok.

4 Pour the reserved marinade into the wok and bring to the boil. Add the onion and cook over medium heat for 3–4 minutes, or until it is slightly softened. Add the bok choy and steam, covered, for 2 minutes, or until it has wilted slightly.

5 Return the squid to the wok and toss until well combined. Season with salt and freshly ground black pepper. Remove from the wok and serve immediately. Serve with rice or noodles, if desired.

nutrition per serve
Protein 25 g; Fat 15 g; Carbohydrate 7 g; Dietary Fibre 2 g; Cholesterol 250 mg; 1105 kJ (265 cal)

handy tip...

Reheat the wok in between the batches of squid—if it is not hot enough, the squid will become tough.

4 thick ocean trout or
salmon fillets
(about 155 g each)
45 g melted butter

Leek and caper sauce
50 g butter, melted
1 leek, chopped
1 cup (250 ml) white wine
(Riesling or chardonnay)
2 tablespoons capers,
drained
1 tablespoon chopped
fresh flat-leaf parsley

preparation: 10 minutes
cooking: 20 minutes
serves: 4

1 Lightly grease a shallow baking tray and arrange the salmon fillets in a single layer. Brush each fillet with the melted butter and cook under a medium grill, without turning, for 10 minutes, or until the fillets are just cooked. Remove and cover loosely with foil to keep the fillets warm while making the sauce.

2 To make the leek and caper sauce, melt the butter in a saucepan. Add the leek and cook gently for 5 minutes, or until soft, but not brown. Add the wine and boil for 3–4 minutes. Add the capers and parsley and season to taste with salt and freshly ground black pepper. Remove the pan from the heat.

3 Spoon the hot sauce over the fish fillets and serve immediately with steamed potatoes.

nutrition per serve
Protein 70 g; Fat 29 g; Carbohydrate 1 g; Dietary Fibre 0.7 g; Cholesterol 182 mg; 1937 kJ (463 cal)

hint

The trout or salmon may be pan-fried, baked or barbecued instead of grilled.
Use only the white part of the leek and cut it in half and rinse well to remove any dirt before chopping.

ingredients

18 baby octopus
2 teaspoons finely grated
   lemon rind
¼ cup (60 ml) lemon juice
¼ cup (60 ml) olive oil
2 cloves garlic, crushed
¼ cup (15 g) chopped
   fresh parsley
1 tablespoon ground
   sweet paprika

preparation: 15 minutes +
   3 hours marinating
cooking: 6 minutes
serves: 4–6

1 To clean the octopus, use a small sharp knife and remove the gut by either cutting off the head entirely or by slitting open the head and removing the gut.

2 Pick up the body and use your index finger to push the beak up. Remove, then clean the octopus thoroughly. Remove the eyes and cut the sac into two or three pieces.

3 Place the lemon rind and juice, olive oil, garlic, parsley and paprika in a large bowl and mix together well. Add the prepared octopus, cover with plastic wrap and marinate for 2–3 hours.

4 Lightly oil a grill tray and arrange the octopus evenly over the surface. Cook under a hot grill for 3 minutes on each side, or until tender, basting with the marinade during cooking. Serve immediately with a green salad, if desired.

nutrition per serve (6)
Protein 28 g; Fat 12 g; Carbohydrate
0.5 g; Dietary Fibre 0 g; Cholesterol
332 mg; 915 kJ (220 cal)

handy tip...

Look for small octopus with curly tentacles. This means they have been tenderised at the markets and your octopus is less likely to be chewy.
This recipe is also suitable to barbecue.

ingredients

4 salmon cutlets
   (about 200 g each)
120 g unsalted butter
2 spring onions, chopped
1 cup (250 ml) cream
1 tablespoon lemon juice
8 fresh sorrel leaves

preparation: 10 minutes
cooking: 20 minutes
serves: 4

1 Season the salmon cutlets with freshly ground black pepper. Heat half the butter in a frying pan and quickly cook the salmon cutlets in batches for 3–4 minutes on each side, or until golden. This will vary depending on the thickness of the cutlets. Test by gently prying the flesh apart—if it pulls away easily, the cutlet is cooked. Be careful not to overcook.

2 To prepare the sauce, melt the remaining butter in a saucepan and cook the spring onion over low heat for 1 minute, or until softened. Add the cream and lemon juice. Bring to the boil, then reduce the heat and simmer gently for 1 minute. Remove the stems from the sorrel and slice the leaves into strips. Add to the pan and cook for 2 minutes. Season to taste.

3 Place the salmon cutlets on a serving dish. Spoon on the warm sauce and serve immediately with a green salad, if desired.

nutrition per serve
Protein 37.5 g; Fat 60 g; Carbohydrate 2.5 g; Dietary Fibre 0 g; Cholesterol 160 mg; 3500 kJ (833 cal)

hint

If salmon cutlets are not readily available, use fresh trout fillets. As an alternative to frying, steam the salmon cutlets on a bed of sorrel leaves over simmering water.

ingredients

2 cups (250 g) self-raising
　flour
¾ cup (185 ml) beer
light olive oil,
　for deep-frying
750 g potatoes, cut into
　thick finger shapes
4 white fish fillets
　(about 160 g each),
　skinned and boned

preparation: 15 minutes +
　20 minutes standing
cooking: 25 minutes
serves: 4

1 Sift the flour and ½ teaspoon salt into a large bowl. Make a well in the centre and gradually add the beer and ¾ cup (185 ml) cold water, whisking to form a smooth batter. Cover and leave to stand for 20 minutes.

2 Fill a deep heavy-based saucepan one third full of oil. Heat the oil to 160°C (315°F), or until a bread cube dropped into the oil browns in 30–35 seconds. Add the potato, in two or more batches if necessary, and deep-fry until tender, but pale in colour. Drain on paper towels.

3 Heat the same oil to 180°C (350°F), or until a bread cube browns in 15 seconds. Cut each fillet in half diagonally and pat dry with paper towels. Dip the fish in the batter, gently shaking off the excess. Deep-fry for 3–4 minutes, depending on the thickness, or until crisp, golden and cooked through. Drain on paper towels.

4 Reheat the oil to 180°C (350°F) and gently return the chips to the pan. Cook for 1–2 minutes, or until crisp and golden. Drain on paper towels and serve with the fish.

nutrition per serve
Protein 26 g; Fat 13 g; Carbohydrate 25 g; Dietary Fibre 3 g; Cholesterol 72 mg; 1398 kJ (334 cal)

handy tip...

For best results, the fish fillets should have moist, resilient flesh with no discolouration or dryness and should not be waterlogged.

ingredients

750 g raw prawns

1 cup (250 ml) white wine

400 g scallops

8 spring onions, finely chopped

2 cloves garlic, crushed

2 tablespoons chopped fresh dill

125 g chilled butter, chopped

1/3 cup (80 ml) thick cream

preparation: 15 minutes
cooking: 8 minutes
serves: 4

1 Peel the prawns, leaving the tails intact. Gently pull out the vein from the tail, starting at the head.

2 Place the wine in a saucepan and bring to the boil. Add the prawns and scallops and simmer for 1 minute, or until the prawns and scallops are just cooked through. Remove the seafood with a slotted spoon.

3 Add the spring onion, garlic and dill to the wine and bring to the boil. Cook for 5 minutes, or until the sauce has reduced by half.

4 Reduce the heat to low. Add the butter gradually, whisking after each addition until it has melted. Add the cream and seafood and stir until heated through. Season to taste with salt and freshly ground black pepper. Garnish with a sprig of fresh dill and serve with rice or steamed vegetables, if desired.

nutrition per serve
Protein 50 g; Fat 36 g; Carbohydrate 3 g; Dietary Fibre 1 g; Cholesterol 420 mg; 2420 kJ (578 cal)

hint

Remove the black muscle from the outside of the scallop before cooking.
This recipe can also be made using a good marinara mix from your local fishmonger.
This dish is delicious served with boiled rice or pasta.

ingredients

700 g fresh tuna,
  finely chopped
3 spring onions,
  finely chopped
1 tablespoon mirin
1 teaspoon soy sauce
1 tablespoon lime juice

preparation: 15 minutes +
  2 hours refrigeration
cooking: 10 minutes
serves: 4

1 Place the tuna, spring onion, mirin, soy sauce and lime juice in a bowl and mix together. Divide into four portions and shape into patties. Cover and refrigerate for 2 hours.

2 Cook the patties on a preheated chargrill pan or barbecue grill or flatplate for 4–5 minutes on each side, or until cooked through. Serve hot or cold with lime wedges, your favourite relish and salad leaves.

nutrition per serve
Protein 35 g; Fat 5.5 g; Carbohydrate 0 g; Dietary Fibre 0 g; Cholesterol 67.5 mg; 860 kJ (205 cal)

handy tip...

To make tuna meatballs, shape heaped tablespoons of the mince mixture into balls and refrigerate for 2 hours. Preheat the oven to moderate 180°C (350°F/Gas 4). Add a little oil to a frying pan and cook in batches for 3 minutes, or until just brown. Place the meatballs on a baking tray and bake for 5 minutes.

nutrition per serve
Protein 32 g; Fat 16 g; Carbohydrate 27 g; Dietary Fibre 2 g; Cholesterol 90 mg; 1603 kJ (382 cal)

ingredients

1 cup (60 g) chopped mixed fresh herbs *(see hint)*
8 slices day-old bread, crusts removed
1 egg
2 tablespoons milk
4 tuna steaks
2 tablespoons olive oil

preparation: 15 minutes + 15 minutes refrigeration
cooking: 6 minutes
serves: 4

1 Place the mixed herbs and bread in a food processor and process for 30 seconds, or until the bread forms very fine crumbs.

2 Place the egg and milk together in a small bowl and whisk together well. Dip each tuna steak in the egg mixture, then coat evenly with the herb breadcrumbs, pressing firmly with your fingers. Refrigerate for 15 minutes.

3 Heat the oil in a frying pan, add the tuna and cook over medium heat for 2–3 minutes on each side, or until tender. Serve immediately with a green salad, if desired.

hint

Try to avoid using strong-flavoured herbs such as rosemary, tarragon and oregano as they will overpower the fish. Try parsley, basil and thyme. This recipe is suitable for any thick fish steaks or fillets. Try salmon, blue eye, swordfish or marlin.

30 g butter

1 tablespoon plain flour

2/3 cup (170 ml) milk

1/3 cup (40 g) finely grated Cheddar

24 fresh oysters in half shells

2 tablespoons shredded fresh Parmesan

preparation: 10 minutes
cooking: 7 minutes
serves: 4

1 Heat the butter in a small saucepan and stir in the flour. Cook over medium heat for 1 minute, or until golden. Take the pan off the heat and add the milk. Stir until smooth then return to the heat. Stir constantly until the sauce boils and thickens. Simmer for 1 minute, then add the Cheddar. Stir until the cheese melts.

2 Place the oysters on a grill tray. Spoon a level tablespoon of the sauce onto each oyster and sprinkle with the Parmesan. Grill under a hot grill for 2–3 minutes, or until the sauce is hot and the cheese is lightly golden. Serve immediately.

nutrition per serve
Protein 10 g; Fat 14 g; Carbohydrate 4.5 g; Dietary Fibre 0 g; Cholesterol 63 mg; 740 kJ (177 cal)

handy tip...

Oysters vary in flavour depending on their size and where they are grown. As a general rule, smaller oysters tend to be milder than larger ones.
Oysters Kilpatrick is another popular way to serve oysters. Melt 30 g butter in a small saucepan. Add 2 tablespoons Worcestershire sauce and 1 tablespoon tomato sauce, season with pepper and cook for 1 minute. Place 24 fresh oysters in half shells on a grill tray. Sprinkle 3 rashers finely chopped thin bacon over the oysters, then spoon on the butter mixture. Grill for 2–3 minutes, or until the bacon is cooked. Garnish with freshly chopped parsley and serve immediately

ingredients

4 skinless and boneless
white fish fillets
(about 200 g each)
75 g butter, melted
3 cloves garlic, crushed
2 cups (160 g) fresh white
breadcrumbs (made
from Italian bread)
1 tablespoon finely
chopped fresh parsley
lemon wedges, to serve

preparation: 15 minutes
cooking: 15 minutes
serves: 4

1 Preheat the oven to moderately hot 200°C (400°F/Gas 6). Grease an ovenproof dish and arrange the fish fillets in a single layer.

2 Mix together the melted butter and garlic in a bowl and set aside. Place the breadcrumbs and parsley in a bowl and mix together well. Scatter the breadcrumb mixture in a thick layer over the fillets, then drizzle with the garlic butter.

3 Bake for 10–15 minutes, or until the fish is white and flakes easily, and the breadcrumbs are golden brown. If the breadcrumbs are not golden but the fish is cooked, flash under a hot grill for a couple of minutes, or until golden—don't take your eyes off it as it can burn very quickly. Garnish with lemon wedges and, if desired, serve with steamed vegetables or a salad.

nutrition per serve
Protein 16 g; Fat 18 g; Carbohydrate 27 g; Dietary Fibre 2 g; Cholesterol 83 mg; 1402 kJ (335 cal)

hint

Fresh breadcrumbs are very simple to make. Remove the crusts from slightly stale (at least one-day old) slices of bread. Put the bread in a food processor and mix until crumbs form. Use ordinary bread or, as in this recipe, Italian bread.

ingredients

1 cup (250 ml) vegetable oil

60 g butter, chopped

8 cloves garlic, finely chopped

2 small red chillies, seeded and finely chopped

20 raw medium king prawns, peeled and deveined, with tails intact

¼ cup (15 g) finely chopped fresh parsley

preparation: 15 minutes
cooking: 5 minutes
serves: 4

1 Heat the oil and butter in a large, deep, frying pan. When very hot, but not smoking, carefully add the garlic, chilli and prawns all at once. Cook, stirring, for 3 minutes, or until the prawns turn pink. Take care not to overcook the prawns.

2 Using a large spoon, quickly transfer the prawns into four hot individual serving dishes and drizzle with some of the garlic butter. Sprinkle with the parsley and serve with crusty bread to soak up the juices.

nutrition per serve
Protein 20 g; Fat 43 g; Carbohydrate 1 g; Dietary Fibre 1.5 g; Cholesterol 180 mg; 1939 kJ (463 cal)

handy tip...

This recipe is traditionally cooked in small cast-iron pots (available from kitchenware shops). Preheat the oven to very hot 250°C (500°F/Gas 10). Place the oil and butter in the pots and heat in the oven for 5–10 minutes, or until hot. Add the prawns, return to the oven and bake for 5 minutes, or until cooked. Stir through the garlic and serve immediately. Although there appears to be a high amount of fat used, not all is generally consumed. The nutritional analysis is based on half the oil being eaten.

ingredients

White sauce
3 cups (750 ml) milk
1 onion, peeled and
    halved
1 clove
1 bay leaf
60 g butter
1/3 cup (40 g) plain flour
1/3 cup (20 g) chopped
    fresh chives or parsley

1 kg smoked cod or
    haddock fillets

preparation: 15 minutes
cooking: 30 minutes
serves: 6

1 Preheat the oven to moderate 180°C (350°F/Gas 4).

2 To make the white sauce, place the milk in a saucepan with the onion, clove and bay leaf, then heat slowly to a simmer. Remove from the heat. Allow to stand for 3 minutes, then strain into a jug.

3 Melt the butter in a saucepan, then add the flour. Stir constantly over low heat for 2–3 minutes, or until lightly golden. Gradually add the strained milk to the pan, stirring until the mixture is smooth. Stir constantly over medium heat for 8–10 minutes, or until the sauce boils and thickens. Reduce the heat, and simmer for another minute. Remove from the heat. Season lightly with salt and pepper and stir in the chives.

4 Grease an ovenproof dish. Cut the fillets into serving-sized pieces and arrange in the prepared dish. Pour the white sauce over the fish and bake for 10–15 minutes, or until the fish is tender and the flesh flakes at the thickest part. Serve with the white sauce and garnish with snipped fresh chives, if desired.

nutrition per serve
Protein 37 g; Fat 15 g; Carbohydrate 11 g; Dietary Fibre 0.5 g; Cholesterol 125 mg; 1345 kJ (322 cal)

hint

Smoked fish is often very salty. If you want to make it less so, combine 1/2 cup (125 ml) milk and 1/2 cup (125 ml) water in a bowl. Add the fish and soak for several hours before cooking. Discard the soaking liquid. Instead of baking the fish, poach the fillets in 1/2 cup (125 ml) milk and 1/2 cup (125 ml) water, in a pan, until tender and flaking at the thickest part. Transfer to heated plates and pour the white sauce over the fish.

ingredients

4 salmon cutlets
(about 150 g each)
1 tablespoon finely
shredded fresh ginger
2 spring onions, finely
sliced on the diagonal
1 tablespoon soy sauce
½ teaspoon sesame oil

preparation: 5 minutes
cooking: 15 minutes
serves: 4

1 Preheat the oven to moderately hot 190°C (375°F/Gas 5). Cut out four 30 cm squares from foil and four from baking paper. Place the baking paper on top of the foil and put one cutlet on each square. Scatter the shredded ginger and spring onion over the cutlets.

2 Place the soy sauce, sesame oil and 2 tablespoons water in a small bowl and mix together well. Spoon over the salmon and seal the foil to make parcels. Place the parcels on a shallow baking tray.

3 Bake for 15 minutes, or until the fish flakes easily. Open the parcels and serve the fish immediately with rice or noodles and steamed Asian greens.

nutrition per serve
Protein 27.5 g; Fat 18.5 g; Carbohydrate 0.5 g; Dietary Fibre 0 g; Cholesterol 105 mg; 1140 kJ (270 cal)

handy tip...

This recipe may also be cooked in a bamboo steamer over simmering water in a wok.
Any cutlet of fish is suitable for this recipe—try blue eye, tuna or snapper.

ingredients

Herbed butter
60 g butter, softened
3 teaspoons lemon juice
2 tablespoons chopped
    fresh mixed herbs
    (parsley, chives and
    tarragon or dill)

4 firm white fish fillets
    (about 160 g each)
½ cup (125 ml) dry
    white wine
2 slices lemon
lemon wedges, to garnish

preparation: 10 minutes +
    refrigeration
cooking: 10 minutes
serves: 4

1 To make the herbed butter, place the butter, lemon juice and mixed herbs in a small bowl and mix together well. Season to taste with salt and freshly ground black pepper. Form the butter into a log shape, wrap in plastic wrap and freeze until firm.

2 Place the fish in a large shallow frying pan. Add the wine, lemon slices and enough water to just cover the fish. Bring to the boil, then reduce the heat and simmer for 5 minutes, or until the fish is tender, and the thickest part of the fish flakes when tested with a fork. Drain the fish on paper towels.

3 Serve on warm plates, topped with slices of the herbed butter and garnished with lemon wedges.

nutrition per serve
Protein 8.5 g; Fat 13 g; Carbohydrate 0.5 g; Dietary Fibre 0 g; Cholesterol 66 mg; 737 kJ (176 cal)

hint

This recipe also works well with caper and lime herb butter. Add 1 tablespoon chopped, drained capers and 1 teaspoon lime zest to the butter. Stir through 2 tablespoons chopped fresh parsley. Wrap and chill.

ingredients

500 g raw prawns

1 tablespoon oil

2–3 tablespoons laksa
  paste

2 cups (500 ml) coconut
  milk

8 ready-made fried fish
  balls, sliced

400 g fresh rice spaghetti
  (laksa noodles)

100 g bean sprouts,
  trimmed

½ cup (10 g) Vietnamese
  mint leaves or coriander

preparation: 15 minutes
cooking: 1 hour 15 minutes
serves: 4

1 Set aside four prawns. Peel the rest, and place the heads, shells, tails and legs in a deep saucepan, without any oil. Cook over medium heat, shaking the pan occasionally, for about 10 minutes, or until the shells are aromatic and a bright, dark orange.

2 Stir in 1 cup (250 ml) water. When it has almost evaporated, stir in another cup of water and bring to the boil. Add 1 litre water. (Adding the water gradually will produce a rich, dark, flavoursome stock.)

3 Bring the stock to the boil, then reduce the heat and simmer gently for 30 minutes. Add the four reserved prawns and cook until pink. Remove from the pan. Strain the stock and discard the peelings. You should have between 2–3 cups (500–750 ml) stock.

4 Heat the oil in a wok, add the laksa paste and cook, stirring constantly, over low heat for 4 minutes, or until aromatic. Stir in the prawn stock and coconut milk. Bring to the boil, then reduce the heat and simmer for 5 minutes. Add the shelled prawns and fish ball slices and simmer until the prawns turn pink.

5 Separate the noodles and cook in boiling water for 30 seconds (they will fall apart if overcooked). Drain well and divide among four deep soup bowls.

6 Ladle the soup over the noodles. Garnish with bean sprouts, mint and a whole prawn. Serve at once.

nutrition per serve
Protein 35 g; Fat 35 g; Carbohydrate 30 g; Dietary Fibre 4 g; Cholesterol 200 mg; 2220 kJ (530 cal)

handy tip...

It's worth investing in a good-quality laksa paste, available at Asian supermarkets. If rice spaghetti is not available, use dried rice vermicelli and soak it in boiling water for 15 minutes, or until tender. Drain before adding to the soup.

ingredients

750 g raw medium prawns

1/3 cup (50 g) sun-dried tomatoes in oil

4 spring onions, finely chopped

1 cup (250 ml) chicken stock

1/2 cup (125 ml) dry white wine

1 cup (250 ml) thick cream

2 tablespoons finely chopped fresh basil

preparation: 15 minutes
cooking: 15 minutes
serves: 4

1 Peel the prawns, leaving the tails intact, and gently pull out the vein. Drain the oil from the sun-dried tomatoes and reserve 2 teaspoons. Cut the tomatoes into strips.

2 Heat the oil in a wok or frying pan over high heat, and swirl it around to coat the side. Add the prawns and spring onion in batches and stir-fry for 5 minutes, or until the prawns are pink and cooked. Remove from the wok.

3 Add the sun-dried tomatoes, stock, wine and cream to the wok and bring to the boil. Reduce the heat and simmer for 7 minutes, or until the sauce has thickened and reduced.

4 Return the prawns to the wok with the basil. Stir-fry over high heat for 1 minute, or until heated through. Serve with pasta.

nutrition per serve
Protein 40 g; Fat 28 g; Carbohydrate 3 g; Dietary Fibre 0.5 g; Cholesterol 364 mg; 1856 kJ (443 cal)

hint

This recipe is also delicious using scallops or a seafood marinara mix.

ingredients

1 tablespoon vegetable oil
1 tablespoon Thai red
curry paste
2 cups (500 ml) coconut
milk
2 tablespoons fish sauce
2 tablespoons soft brown
sugar
3 fresh kaffir lime leaves,
finely shredded
750 g firm white fish fillets,
cut into 2 cm pieces
1/3 cup (10 g) fresh
coriander leaves

preparation: 10 minutes
cooking: 15 minutes
serves: 4

1 Heat the oil in a wok or frying pan and swirl it around to coat the side. Add the curry paste and cook over medium heat for 2 minutes, or until fragrant.

2 Stir in the coconut milk, fish sauce, sugar and lime leaves and bring to the boil. Reduce the heat and simmer for 5 minutes.

3 Add the fish and simmer, covered, for 5 minutes, or until the fish is cooked. Stir in the coriander leaves and serve over steamed rice. Garnish with finely sliced spring onion and lime wedges, if desired.

nutrition per serve
Protein 42 g; Fat 36 g; Carbohydrate 15 g; Dietary Fibre 2.5 g; Cholesterol 132 mg; 2290 kJ (547 cal)

handy tip...

To make a green fish curry, substitute the red curry paste for green curry paste. For a mild flavour, use 1 tablespoon curry paste—increase it to 2–3 tablespoons, if you like your curries with a bit more heat.
Always use a good-quality Asian brand of paste, available from Asian supermarkets.

ingredients

8 flathead fillets, boned
  and skinned
plain flour, to coat
1 egg, lightly beaten
dry breadcrumbs, to coat
2 tablespoons oil
100 g butter
grated rind and juice from
  4 limes (see hint)
¼ cup (15 g) chopped
  fresh parsley

preparation: 15 minutes +
  20 minutes refrigeration
cooking: 10 minutes
serves: 4

1 Pat the fillets dry with paper towels. Coat in the flour, shaking off any excess. Dip in the egg, then coat in the breadcrumbs. Cover and refrigerate for 20 minutes.

2 Heat the oil in a frying pan over medium heat. Add the fillets and cook for 3 minutes, then turn over and cook for a further 2 minutes, or until cooked through. Drain on paper towels, then place on warm serving plates. Wipe out the frying pan with paper towels to remove any burnt crumbs.

3 Add the butter, lime rind and juice to the clean frying pan. Stir over low heat until the butter has melted. Stir in the parsley. Spoon the sauce over the fillets and serve immediately.

nutrition per serve
Protein 30 g; Fat 35 g; Carbohydrate 9 g; Dietary Fibre 0.5 g; Cholesterol 200 mg; 1975 kJ (472 cal)

hint

You should be able to get 1 tablespoon grated rind and ¼ cup (60 ml) juice from 4 limes.
Most skinless and boneless fish fillets are suited to this recipe—try John Dory, snapper, rainbow trout or bream.

smoked salmon bagel

Cut 4 bagels in half. Combine 125 g spreadable cream cheese, 2 finely chopped gherkins and 1 tablespoon chopped fresh dill. Spread evenly over the base of each bagel. Divide 200 g smoked salmon and 1 tablespoon baby capers among the bagel bases, and season with cracked black pepper. Cover each with the remaining bagel half and serve.

serves 4

From left to right: Smoked salmon bagel; Creamy salmon herb pasta; Avocado and salmon salad.

creamy salmon herb pasta

Cook 500 g spaghetti in boiling water until *al dente*. Place 300 ml sour cream, 1 teaspoon lime rind, 3 teaspoons lime juice, 1/2 cup (125 ml) milk, 2 chopped spring onions and 2 tablespoons snipped fresh chives in a large bowl and whisk together well. Season to taste with salt and pepper. Drain the pasta then toss through 200 g thinly sliced smoked salmon and the cream mixture.

serves 4

avocado and salmon salad

Place 150 g baby English spinach leaves, 1 avocado cut into large pieces, 100 g sliced Camembert, 100 g thinly sliced smoked salmon and 200 g fresh raspberries in a large salad bowl and toss together well. Place 1 tablespoon honey mustard, 1 tablespoon lemon juice and 1/3 cup (80 ml) olive oil in a small bowl and whisk together. Pour the dressing over the salad and serve.

serves 4

smoked salmon puff pastry rounds

Preheat the oven to 200°C (400°F/Gas 6). Cut out 5 cm rounds with a fluted cutter from 2 sheets thawed ready-rolled puff pastry. Place onto non-stick baking trays, brush lightly with milk and bake for 10 minutes, or until crisp and golden. Allow to cool. Place 100 g fromage fraîs and 2 teaspoons chopped fresh dill in a small bowl and mix together well. Spoon 1 teaspoonful of the mixture onto each pastry round. Cut 100 g smoked salmon into strips and place on top of the fromage fraîs. Garnish with a sprig of dill.

makes 32

mini smoked salmon frittatas

Preheat the oven to moderate 180°C (350°F/Gas 4). Place 12 eggs, 1 cup (250 ml) cream, 50 g chopped smoked salmon, 3 sliced spring onions and 2 tablespoons chopped fresh parsley in a bowl and whisk together well. Divide the mixture among twelve ½-cup (125 ml) muffin holes and bake for 20 minutes, or until set.

makes 12

From left to right: Smoked salmon puff pastry rounds; Mini smoked salmon frittatas; Quick smoked salmon benedict.

quick smoked salmon benedict

Melt 85 g butter in a saucepan. Process 2 teaspoons tarragon vinegar and 2 egg yolks in a food processor until combined. With the motor running, gradually add the melted butter and process until the sauce is thick enough to coat the back of a spoon. Cut 4 English muffins in half and toast under a hot grill until golden. Butter and keep warm. Poach 8 eggs, in batches, in warm water until cooked to your liking. Divide 100 g smoked salmon among the English muffins and top with the poached eggs and sauce. Garnish with chopped fresh chives.

serves 4

creamy lemon prawn sandwiches

Peel and devein 600 g cooked king prawns, then roughly chop. Place the prawns, 3–4 tablespoons lemon juice, 2 tablespoons whole-egg mayonnaise, 2 tablespoons seafood sauce and 2 tablespoons chopped fresh coriander leaves in a bowl and mix together well. Serve sandwiched between thick slices of buttered sourdough bread.

serves 6

prawn cocktail

Cut 2 avocados in half and remove the stones. Peel and devein 300 g cooked king prawns and arrange the prawns in the hole of each avocado. Place 2 teaspoons lime juice cordial, 2 tablespoons plain yoghurt and 2 tablespoons whole-egg mayonnaise in a bowl and mix together well. Spoon the dressing over the prawns, season with ground pepper and a squeeze of fresh lime juice.

serves 4

mediterranean prawn salad

Peel and devein 300 g cooked king prawns. Place 1 chopped red capsicum, 1 sliced red onion, 100 g marinated Kalamata olives, 200 g feta broken into large pieces and 150 g rocket leaves in a salad bowl. Place 2 tablespoons extra virgin olive oil and 1 tablespoon balsamic vinegar in a small bowl and mix together well. Drizzle the dressing over the salad and toss gently before serving.

serves 2–4

spicy prawn pasta

Cook 500 g pasta in a large saucepan of boiling water until *al dente*. Drain and keep warm. Peel and devein 500 g cooked king prawns. Heat 1 tablespoon oil in a frying pan, add 1 thinly sliced onion and cook over medium heat for 3 minutes, or until golden. Add the prawns, 300 g bottled tomato salsa and 300 g sour cream, then reduce the heat to low and stir until heated through. Stir in 2 tablespoons chopped fresh basil. Toss the sauce through the pasta and serve.

serves 4–6

From left to right: Creamy lemon prawn sandwiches; Prawn cocktail; Mediterranean prawn salad; Spicy prawn pasta; Cajun prawn burritos; Pappadam prawn cups with mango yoghurt.

cajun prawn burritos

Preheat the oven to moderate 180°C (350°F/Gas 4). Place 4 flour tortillas on a baking tray, cover with foil, and bake for 10 minutes, or until heated through. Peel and devein 500 g cooked king prawns, then halve lengthways. Heat 1 tablespoon oil in a frying pan. Add 3 thinly sliced spring onions, 1 tablespoon cajun seasoning, 1 tablespoon lemon juice and the prawns. Cook, stirring gently to coat the prawns in the seasoning, for 3 minutes, or until heated through. Divide the prawn mixture among the tortillas. Serve with shredded lettuce, chopped tomato and grated cheese. Dollop with sour cream and taco sauce, if desired.

serves 4

pappadam prawn cups with mango yoghurt

Cut 8 chilli pappadams into quarters with a sharp knife or scissors. Cook, according to the packet instructions. Place 100 g plain yoghurt, 1 tablespoon mango chutney and 2 teaspoons chopped fresh mint in a bowl and mix together well. Divide the yoghurt mixture among the pappadams and top with 150 g cooked peeled small prawns. Garnish with a wedge of lime and a sprig of mint.

makes 32

creamy salmon pie

Preheat the oven to hot 220°C (425°F/Gas 7). Heat 1 tablespoon oil in a frying pan, add 1 thinly sliced leek and cook over medium heat for 5 minutes, or until golden. Add 2 tablespoons flour and cook, stirring, for 1 minute. Gradually pour in 1½ cups (375 ml) milk and bring to the boil, stirring constantly, until the mixture boils and thickens. Add 1 cup (125 g) grated Cheddar, 415 g can pink salmon, drained and bones removed, 1 tablespoon lemon juice, 1 teaspoon lemon rind and 2 tablespoons chopped fresh dill. Season. Spoon the mixture into a 23 cm pie plate and allow to cool slightly before covering with 1 sheet of thawed ready-rolled puff pastry. Brush lightly with milk and bake for 20 minutes, or until golden.

serves 6

simple low-fat niçoise

Place the torn leaves of 1 cos lettuce, 250 g halved cherry tomatoes, 1 cup (185 g) Kalamata olives, 200 g chopped 78% fat-free feta, 200 g blanched green beans, 4 peeled and quartered hard-boiled eggs and 425 g can salmon in brine, drained and broken into bite-sized chunks, in a serving bowl. Drizzle with your favourite oil-free dressing and toss.

serves 6

salmon salad on crispy french bread

Drain a 415 g can pink salmon, then flake in a bowl. Add 3 chopped spring onions, ¼ cup (60 g) sour cream, ¼ cup (60 ml) thousand island dressing and 2 tablespoons chopped fresh chives. Season with freshly ground black pepper and mix together well. Serve on a baguette with rocket leaves.

serves 4

From left to right: Creamy salmon pie; Simple low-fat niçoise; Salmon salad on crispy French bread.

tuna pasta bake

Preheat the oven to moderately hot 200°C (400°F/Gas 6). Boil 400 g macaroni until *al dente*, then drain well. Combine 3 chopped spring onions, 425 g can tuna in brine, drained and flaked, 400 g can drained asparagus pieces, 420 g creamy chicken soup, 300 g sour cream, ¼ cup (60 ml) milk and 1 cup (125 g) grated Cheddar in a bowl, then stir in the macaroni. Spoon into four 2½-cup (625 ml) greased ovenproof dishes and sprinkle with an extra ½ cup (60 g) grated Cheddar. Bake for 20 minutes, or until crisp and golden.

serves 4

tuna patties

Place 650 g floury potatoes, cooked and mashed, 425 g can drained tuna, 2 tablespoons sweet chilli sauce, 1–2 tablespoons lemon juice, 1 lightly beaten egg, 2 finely chopped spring onions and 2 tablespoons chopped fresh parsley in a large bowl and mix well. Shape into 8 patties and roll in 1–2 cups (100–200 g) dry breadcrumbs. Shallow-fry in batches in a large frying pan for 3–5 minutes on each side, or until crisp and golden.

serves 4

salmon and brie turnovers

Preheat the oven to hot 220°C (425°F/Gas 7). Cut 2 sheets thawed ready-rolled puff pastry into four squares on each sheet. Divide 415 g can drained pink salmon among the pastry squares—in a triangle shape, in the bottom corner—top with 100 g thinly sliced Brie, 2 teaspoons grated lemon rind and a large sprig of dill. Fold into a triangle and press to seal the edges with the tip of a teaspoon. Place the triangles on a non-stick baking tray and brush lightly with a beaten egg. Bake for 20 minutes, or until crisp and golden brown.

serves 4

From left to right: Tuna pasta bake; Tuna patties; Salmon and brie turnovers.

noodles, grains, pasta & rice

quick orange and raisin couscous

ingredients

1 cup (250 ml) orange juice
1½ cups (375 ml) vegetable stock
2¼ cups (415 g) instant couscous
2 cloves garlic, crushed
¼ cup (30 g) raisins
60 g butter
2 tablespoons orange rind

preparation: 10 minutes
cooking: 10 minutes
serves: 4

1 Place the orange juice in a saucepan with the stock and bring to the boil. Stir in the couscous, garlic and raisins. Reduce the heat to low, and simmer, covered, for 5 minutes, stirring occasionally.

2 Remove the pan from the heat and add the butter and orange rind. Mix together well, then cover and set aside for 5 minutes. Separate the grains with a fork before serving.

nutrition per serve
Protein 6 g; Fat 13 g; Carbohydrate 55 g; Dietary Fibre 3 g; Cholesterol 40 mg; 1470 kJ (350 cal)

handy tip...

Couscous is a cereal made from semolina and wheat flour pressed into tiny bead-like grains. It is traditionally served hot as an accompaniment to vegetable tagine.

ingredients

2 cloves garlic, crushed
1 cup (150 g) instant
    polenta
1/2 cup (125 ml) cream
40 g butter, chopped
1/3 cup (35 g) freshly
    grated Parmesan
1/4 teaspoon paprika, and
    extra to garnish
shaved Parmesan,
    to garnish

preparation: 10 minutes
cooking: 10 minutes
serves: 4

1 Place 3 1/2 cups (875 ml) water in a large saucepan and bring to the boil. Add the garlic and 1 teaspoon salt. Stir in the polenta with a wooden spoon, breaking up any lumps. Cook, stirring frequently, over medium heat for 4–5 minutes, or until smooth.

2 Add half the cream and cook for 2–3 minutes, or until the polenta is thick and comes away from the pan. Stir in the butter. Remove from the heat and stir in the Parmesan, paprika and remaining cream. Transfer to a warm serving bowl and sprinkle with paprika. Garnish with the shaved Parmesan and serve at once. This dish is a delicious accompaniment to chilli beans.

nutrition per serve
Protein 7 g; Fat 25 g; Carbohydrate 30 g; Dietary Fibre 1 g; Cholesterol 80 mg; 1510 kJ (360 cal)

hint

Instant polenta cooks in half the time of regular polenta. If it is not available, your polenta will take about 20 minutes to cook. Polenta must be served hot to keep its creamy, light consistency. Use a vegetable peeler to peel cheese shavings from a block of Parmesan.

ingredients

60 g butter

3 onions, sliced

2 cloves garlic, crushed

2 cups (400 g) basmati rice

1.25 litres vegetable stock

1½ cups (235 g) shelled peas

½ cup (50 g) grated Parmesan

½ cup (30 g) chopped fresh parsley

preparation: 10 minutes
cooking: 20 minutes
serves: 6

1 Melt the butter in a large saucepan over low heat. Add the onion and garlic and stir for 5 minutes, or until soft and golden.

2 Add the rice and stock, then bring to the boil, stirring once. Reduce the heat and simmer for 5 minutes, or until almost all the liquid has been absorbed.

3 Stir in the peas and cook, covered, over very low heat for 10 minutes, or until the rice is tender. Stir in the Parmesan and parsley and serve immediately.

nutrition per serve
Protein 11 g; Fat 12 g; Carbohydrate 60 g; Dietary Fibre 5 g; Cholesterol 34 mg; 1612 kJ (385 cal)

handy tip...

Basmati is a creamy long-grain rice meaning 'fragrant' and is grown in the foothills of the Himalayas. The grains separate when cooked and have a sweet, nutty, dusky flavour and aroma.

ingredients

1 cup (200 g) basmati rice
1 cup (250 g) red lentils
3 tablespoons ghee
2 onions, sliced
2 teaspoons garam
   masala

preparation: 10 minutes
cooking: 50 minutes
serves: 4–6

1 Wash the rice two or three times, and then drain. Wash the lentils and drain. Heat 2 tablespoons ghee in a large saucepan, add half the onion and cook, stirring frequently, over low heat for 10 minutes, or until golden.

2 Add the rice and lentils and stir over low heat for 2–3 minutes. Add the garam masala and 1 teaspoon salt and stir for 1 minute, then slowly add 3½ cups (875 ml) hot water. Bring to the boil, stirring, then reduce the heat to very low and cover with a tight-fitting lid. Cook for 20–25 minutes, checking after about 20 minutes.

3 Heat the remaining ghee in a small frying pan. Add the remaining onion and cook over moderate heat for 15 minutes, or until golden and caramelised. Drain on paper towels. Serve the kitchri immediately, garnished with the caramelised onion.

nutrition per serve (6)
Protein 13 g; Fat 9.5 g; Carbohydrate 43 g; Dietary Fibre 7 g; Cholesterol 25 mg; 1300 kJ (311 cal)

hint

Also known as clarified butter, ghee is the result of removing the milk solids from unsalted butter. Once the milk solids have been removed, butter will keep longer without becoming rancid. It also has a high smoke point and can be heated to higher temperatures than ordinary butter without the risk of burning. This means it is ideal for sautéing and frying.

Pesto
2 cups (100 g) firmly
  packed fresh basil
¼ cup (40 g) pine nuts,
  lightly toasted
2 large cloves garlic,
  chopped
⅓ cup (80 ml) extra virgin
  olive oil
½ cup (50 g) grated
  Parmesan

1 clove garlic, crushed
300 ml cream
500 g fresh potato gnocchi

preparation: 15 minutes
cooking: 10 minutes
serves: 4

1 To make the pesto, place the basil, pine nuts and garlic in a blender or food processor. Process until smooth. Reserve 2 teaspoons of the oil. With the motor running, slowly pour in the remaining oil. Add the Parmesan and process until smooth.

2 Heat the reserved oil in a small saucepan. Add the garlic and cook over medium heat for 1 minute. Add the cream and 3 tablespoons of the pesto and bring to the boil. Be careful as it will boil over easily. Reduce the heat to low and simmer for 3 minutes.

3 Meanwhile, cook the gnocchi in a large saucepan of boiling water according to the packet instructions. Drain and place the gnocchi in a large bowl. Pour on the sauce and toss thoroughly. Season. Transfer to a serving bowl. Garnish with basil and serve with lemon wedges.

nutrition per serve
Protein 4 g; Fat 22 g; Carbohydrate 8 g; Dietary Fibre 1 g; Cholesterol 42 mg; 953 kJ (230 cal)

handy tip...

Store the remaining pesto in an airtight container and cover the surface with a thin layer of extra virgin olive oil. Seal and refrigerate for up to 7 days.
Fresh gnocchi is available from supermarkets and delicatessens.

ingredients

500 g fresh potato
    gnocchi
2 tablespoons oil
1 leek, sliced
1 cup (250 g) bottled
    tomato pasta sauce
²/₃ cup (160 ml) vegetable
    stock
¹/₃ cup (50 g) chopped
    black olives
6 anchovies, chopped

preparation: 10 minutes
cooking: 10 minutes
serves: 4

1 Cook the gnocchi in a large saucepan of boiling water according to the packet instructions. Drain.

2 Meanwhile, heat the oil in a saucepan and add the leek. Cook over medium heat for 5 minutes, or until golden. Add the tomato sauce, stock, olives and anchovies. Stir the mixture for 5 minutes, or until heated through. Pour over the gnocchi and serve.

nutrition per serve
Protein 6 g; Fat 11 g; Carbohydrate 24 g; Dietary Fibre 4 g; Cholesterol 3.5 mg; 919 kJ (219 cal)

hint

The sauce can be cooked a day ahead and stored, covered, in the refrigerator. Reheat just before serving.
Purchase good-quality fresh gnocchi or make your own. Use any other dried or fresh pasta, if preferred.

ingredients

500 g fresh mixed
  tagliatelle
  (spinach and plain)
1 tablespoon olive oil
1 cup (155 g) pine nuts
300 g rocket
2 cups (40 g) fresh mint
½ cup (125 ml) olive oil

preparation: 10 minutes
cooking: 10 minutes
serves: 6

1 Preheat the oven to moderate 180°C (350°F/Gas 4). Cook the tagliatelle in a large saucepan of boiling water according to the packet instructions. Drain, toss with oil and keep warm. Scatter the pine nuts on a baking tray and bake for 5 minutes, or until golden.

2 Place the rocket and mint in a food processor or blender and process for 10 seconds. Add the pine nuts and oil and process a further 20 seconds, or until the mixture is finely chopped and well combined. Season to taste.

3 Place the pasta on a serving platter and top with the pesto. Serve with shaved Parmesan, if desired.

nutrition per serve
Protein 13 g; Fat 40 g; Carbohydrate 60 g; Dietary Fibre 6 g; Cholesterol 0 mg; 2775 kJ (665 cal)

handy tip...

Rocket is a salad green with a peppery mustard flavour.

ingredients

300 g pasta spirals
150 g sun-dried tomatoes
   in olive oil, drained
1/2 cup (15 g) fresh basil
1/3 cup (50 g) pine nuts
1/2 cup (50 g) finely grated
   Parmesan
1/3 cup (80 ml) oil

preparation: 15 minutes
cooking: 15 minutes
serves: 6

1 Cook the pasta spirals in a large saucepan of boiling water according to the packet instructions.

2 Meanwhile, place the sun-dried tomatoes in a food processor with the basil, pine nuts and Parmesan. Using the pulse action, process for 1 minute, or until finely chopped. With the motor running, pour in the oil in a steady stream.

3 Drain the pasta well and place in a large serving bowl. Add the sun-dried tomato pesto and toss to combine well. Serve immediately.

nutrition per serve
Protein 10 g; Fat 22 g; Carbohydrate 36 g; Dietary Fibre 3 g; Cholesterol 8 mg; 1592 kJ (380 cal)

hint

This dish can be made 1 hour ahead and served at room temperature.
Sun-dried tomato pesto can be made up to one day in advance and stored in an airtight container in the refrigerator.

ingredients

1 litre vegetable stock
20 g butter
1 large onion, chopped
2 cloves garlic, crushed
2 cups (440 g) arborio or
    short-grain rice
2 x 400 g cans chopped
    tomatoes
½ cup (60 g) grated
    Cheddar
½ cup (30 g) chopped
    fresh herbs
    (oregano, basil,
    parsley and chives)

preparation: 15 minutes
cooking: 35 minutes
serves: 4

1 Heat the stock in a saucepan and bring to the boil. Reduce the heat and keep at a low simmer.

2 Melt the butter in a saucepan. Add the onion and garlic and cook over medium heat for 1–2 minutes, or until soft. Add the rice and stir for 1 minute, or until well coated.

3 Add ½ cup (125 ml) stock, stirring constantly, and cook over medium heat until all the stock is absorbed. Continue adding the stock, ½ cup (125 ml) at a time, stirring constantly over low heat for 20–25 minutes, allowing the stock to be completely absorbed after each addition.

4 When all the stock has been absorbed and the rice is almost cooked, stir in the tomato. Cook for a further 2–3 minutes, or until the rice is tender and creamy in texture. Stir in the cheese and herbs and season with salt and freshly ground black pepper. Serve immediately with grated Parmesan or extra Cheddar, if desired.

nutrition per serve
Protein 15 g; Fat 10 g; Carbohydrate 90 g; Dietary Fibre 6 g; Cholesterol 30 mg; 2130 kJ (510 cal)

handy tip...

It is important to make sure that the stock is really hot before gradually adding to the rice—this allows it to be absorbed faster and will not cool the risotto down. Leftover, cold risotto can be shaped into patties, coated with egg and breadcrumbs and fried in oil.

ingredients

2 litres vegetable stock
90 g butter
1 onion, finely chopped
250 g pumpkin,
    cut into cubes
2 carrots, cut into cubes
2 cups (440 g) arborio rice
¾ cup (90 g) freshly
    grated Romano cheese
¼ teaspoon ground
    nutmeg

preparation: 15 minutes
cooking: 40 minutes
serves: 4

1 Heat the vegetable stock in a saucepan and bring to the boil. Reduce the heat and keep at a low simmer.

2 Heat 60 g of the butter in a large saucepan. Add the onion and cook for 3–5 minutes, or until soft. Add the pumpkin and carrot and cook for 10 minutes, or until tender.

3 Add the rice to the vegetables and cook for 1 minute, stirring constantly. Add enough hot stock to cover the rice and stir well. Reduce the heat and add more stock as it is absorbed, stirring constantly. Continue, adding the stock ½ cup (125 ml) at a time, cooking for 25 minutes, or until the rice is tender and creamy in texture. (You may not need to use all the stock.)

4 Remove from the heat. Add the cheese, nutmeg and remaining butter. Season to taste with salt and freshly ground black pepper. Cover and leave for 5 minutes before serving.

nutrition per serve
Protein 18 g; Fat 9.5 g; Carbohydrate 93 g; Dietary Fibre 6.5 g; Cholesterol 20 mg; 2218 kJ (530 cal)

hint

Romano is a hard, grating cheese similar to Parmesan. For a creamier risotto, mash the carrot and pumpkin before adding the rice.

ingredients

¼ cup (60 ml) peanut oil

2 eggs, beaten

1½ cups (220 g) finely
   diced ham

100 g cooked prawns,
   finely chopped

4 cups (740 g) cold
   cooked rice

¼ cup (40 g) frozen peas

¼ cup (60 ml) light soy
   sauce

6 spring onions, thinly
   sliced on the diagonal

preparation: 10 minutes
cooking: 5 minutes
serves: 4–6

1 Heat a wok until very hot, add 1 tablespoon of the peanut oil and swirl to coat the side. Add the egg and start to scramble. When almost cooked, remove from the wok and set aside. Heat the remaining oil in the wok, then add the ham and prawns, tossing to heat through evenly.

2 Add the rice and peas, toss and stir-fry for 3 minutes, or until the rice grains separate. Add the scrambled egg, sprinkle with the soy sauce and toss to coat the rice. Add the spring onion, stir-fry for 2 minutes and serve.

nutrition per serve (6)
Protein 17 g; Fat 14 g; Carbohydrate 41 g; Dietary Fibre 2.5 g; Cholesterol 105 mg; 1497 kJ (358 cal)

handy tip...

Cook the rice in a large saucepan of boiling water for 10–15 minutes, or until tender. Drain well, then cover and refrigerate until ready to use. This recipe is great for using up leftover cooked rice.

ingredients

650 g pumpkin, peeled
2 tablespoons olive oil
500 g ricotta
⅓ cup (50 g) pine nuts, toasted
¾ cup (35 g) firmly packed fresh basil
⅓ cup (35 g) finely grated Parmesan
125 g fresh lasagne sheets *(see hint)*
1¼ cups (185 g) grated mozzarella

preparation: 15 minutes
cooking: 1 hour 25 minutes
serves: 4

1 Preheat the oven to moderate 180°C (350°F/Gas 4). Lightly grease a baking tray. Cut the pumpkin into 1 cm slices and arrange in a single layer on the tray. Brush with oil and cook for 1 hour, or until softened, turning halfway through cooking.

2 Place the ricotta, pine nuts, basil and Parmesan in a bowl and mix together well.

3 Lightly grease a square 20 cm ovenproof dish. Cook the lasagne sheets according to the packet instructions, or until tender. Cover the base of the dish with a single layer of the pasta sheets. Spread with a layer of the ricotta mixture and top with another layer of pasta.

4 Arrange the pumpkin evenly over the pasta sheets with as few gaps as possible. Season to taste with salt and freshly ground black pepper and top with a final layer of pasta sheets. Sprinkle with the grated Mozzarella and bake for 20–25 minutes, or until the cheese is golden. Stand for 10 minutes, then cut into squares and serve.

nutrition per serve
Protein 37 g; Fat 46 g; Carbohydrate 35 g; Dietary Fibre 4.5 g; Cholesterol 97 mg; 2935 kJ (700 cal)

hint

If the pasta has no cooking instructions, cook the sheets one at a time in a large saucepan of boiling water for 3 minutes, or until tender. If fresh lasagne sheets are not available, use dried sheets and adjust the cooking time accordingly.

blue cheese sauce

Place 200 g crumbled creamy blue cheese (or to taste) in a large frying pan with 300 ml cream. Stir over low heat until the cheese melts, then bring to the boil. Boil for 5 minutes, or until the sauce is thick enough to coat the back of a wooden spoon.

serves 4

From left to right: Blue cheese sauce; Speedy bolognese; Simple browned butter and herb sauce; Rich capsicum, olive and tomato sauce; White wine and mushroom sauce; Creamy bacon and mushroom sauce.

speedy bolognese

Heat 1 tablespoon oil in a large frying pan. Add 1 finely chopped onion and 2 crushed cloves garlic, and cook over medium heat for 3 minutes, or until golden. Add 500 g minced beef and cook for 10 minutes, or until browned. Break up any lumps with a wooden spoon. Drain off any excess fat, then add 400 g bottled pasta sauce, ½ cup (125 ml) red wine, 1 tablespoon balsamic vinegar and 1 teaspoon dried mixed herbs. Bring to the boil, then reduce the heat and simmer for 10 minutes, or until the sauce is slightly thickened.

serves 4

simple browned butter and herb sauce

Melt 200 g butter in a large frying pan and cook over medium heat for 3 minutes, or until the butter turns a nutty brown colour. Be careful—if done too quickly the butter will burn and become bitter. Add 3 tablespoons chopped fresh mixed herbs (sage, chives, parsley) and stir gently.

serves 4

rich capsicum, olive and tomato sauce

Heat 1 tablespoon oil in a frying pan. Add 1 crushed clove garlic and 1 finely chopped onion and cook over medium heat for 3 minutes, or until golden. Add 200 g chopped marinated chargrilled capsicum and cook for 2 minutes. Stir in 400 g pomodoro sauce and 100 g Kalamata olives, then bring to the boil. Cook for 10 minutes, or until the sauce reduces and thickens slightly. Stir in 2 tablespoons finely shredded basil and season with salt and freshly ground black pepper before serving.

serves 4

white wine and mushroom sauce

Heat 1 tablespoon oil and 30 g butter in a frying pan, add 2 crushed cloves garlic and cook over medium heat for 1 minute. Add 500 g mixed mushrooms (enoki, oyster, Swiss brown, button) and fry until golden brown. Stir in 1 tablespoon tomato paste and ½ cup (125 ml) white wine. Bring to the boil, then reduce the heat and simmer for 3 minutes. Stir in 1 tablespoon chopped fresh parsley before serving.

serves 4

creamy bacon and mushroom sauce

Heat 1 tablespoon oil in a large frying pan. Add 4 rashers chopped bacon, 2 crushed cloves garlic and 3 chopped spring onions and cook over medium heat for 2 minutes, or until golden. Add 300 g sliced button mushrooms and cook for 5 minutes, or until soft and browned. Stir in 1 tablespoon brandy and 500 ml cream, bring to the boil and cook for 9 minutes, or until the sauce is thick enough to coat the back of a spoon.

serves 4

ingredients

500 g rissoni
30 g butter
3 tablespoons olive oil
4 onions, sliced
100 g mascarpone
185 g blue cheese
2 cups (130 g) shredded
   English spinach leaves

preparation: 15 minutes
cooking: 35 minutes
serves: 4

1 Cook the rissoni in a large saucepan of boiling water according to the packet instructions. Drain and return to the pan.

2 Meanwhile, heat the butter and olive oil in a large frying pan. Add the sliced onion and cook over low heat for 20–30 minutes, or until golden brown and caramelised. Remove from the pan with a slotted spoon and drain on paper towels.

3 Place the mascarpone, blue cheese and onion in a bowl and mix together well.

4 Add the spinach and the cheese and onion mixture to the rissoni and toss through. Season to taste with salt and freshly ground black pepper before serving.

nutrition per serve
Protein 30 g; Fat 45 g; Carbohydrate 95 g; Dietary Fibre 9 g; Cholesterol 90 mg; 3755 kJ (895 cal)

handy tip...

Blue vein is a soft cheese made from cow's milk, with veins of blue-green mould culture criss-crossing the interior. It is a sharp and strong-flavoured cheese with a crumbly texture. Varieties include Gorgonzola and Stilton.

ingredients

500 g linguine
2 cups (500 ml) cream
1⅓ cups (200 g) frozen
    peas
1 clove garlic, crushed
pinch of nutmeg
½ barbecued chicken
200 g sliced ham,
    cut into strips
¾ cup (15 g) loosely
    packed fresh flat-leaf
    parsley, finely chopped

preparation: 15 minutes
cooking: 15 minutes
serves: 4

1 Cook the linguine in a large saucepan of boiling water according to the packet instructions. Drain and keep warm.

2 Meanwhile, pour the cream into a large frying pan and bring to the boil. Reduce the heat, add the peas, garlic and nutmeg and simmer for 3 minutes. Season to taste.

3 Remove the skin and bones from the chicken and cut the flesh into bite-sized pieces. Add the chicken, ham and parsley to the cream and bring to the boil. Reduce the heat and simmer until the sauce has thickened slightly.

4 Add the linguine to the cream sauce. Toss to coat, then transfer to a serving bowl. Top with grated Parmesan, if desired, and serve with a fresh green salad.

nutrition per serve
Protein 50 g; Fat 65 g; Carbohydrate 70 g; Dietary Fibre 7.5 g; Cholesterol 320 mg; 4410 kJ (1055 cal)

hint

Linguine is a long flat pasta that is about the width of spaghetti. Other types of flat pasta can be used in this recipe—try fettuccine, pappardelle or tagliatelle.

ingredients

500 g fresh tortellini
60 g butter
200 g small mushrooms,
    finely sliced
1 clove garlic, crushed
300 ml cream
pinch of nutmeg
2 teaspoons finely grated
    lemon rind
3 tablespoons grated
    Parmesan

preparation: 10 minutes
cooking: 10 minutes
serves: 4

1 Cook the tortellini in a large saucepan of boiling water according to the packet instructions. Drain and keep warm.

2 Meanwhile, melt the butter in a saucepan. Add the mushrooms and cook over medium heat for 5 minutes, or until browned and tender.

3 Add the garlic, cream, nutmeg, lemon rind and freshly ground black pepper. Bring to the boil and cook until the sauce is thick enough to coat the back of a spoon. Stir in the Parmesan and cook gently for 3 minutes.

4 Place the cooked tortellini in a warm serving dish. Add the sauce and stir gently to combine well. Serve immediately.

nutrition per serve
Protein 17 g; Fat 16 g; Carbohydrate 88 g; Dietary Fibre 7 g; Cholesterol 45 mg; 2405 kJ (575 cal)

handy tip...

Tortellini are small rings of pasta, usually stuffed with finely chopped seasoned meat—they can also be filled with spinach and ricotta for a complete vegetarian meal. Tortellini is often served with a cream or tomato sauce.

ingredients

500 g fresh egg noodles

3 tablespoons olive oil

1 clove garlic, crushed

4 spring onions, sliced

750 g raw prawns, peeled and deveined

1 cup (30 g) fresh coriander leaves

2 tablespoons finely chopped preserved lemon *(see hint)*

1 teaspoon harissa

preparation: 15 minutes
cooking: 10 minutes
serves: 4

1 Cook the egg noodles in a large saucepan of boiling water according to the packet instructions. Drain and keep warm.

2 Heat the oil in a wok or large frying pan over high heat. When hot, add the garlic, spring onion and prawns. Stir-fry until the prawns just turn pink.

3 Add the cooked egg noodles, coriander leaves, preserved lemon and harissa, and stir-fry until the noodles are hot. Serve at once.

nutrition per serve
Protein 50 g; Fat 15 g; Carbohydrate 35 g; Dietary Fibre 5 g; Cholesterol 280 mg; 2025 kJ (480 cal)

hint

To use preserved lemons, wash well under cold water. Remove the flesh and only use the rind.
Harissa is a fiery condiment for meats, couscous and soups. It's also used as a marinade for chicken, lamb or fish.

nutrition per serve
Protein 32 g; Fat 64 g; Carbohydrate
73 g; Dietary Fibre 5 g; Cholesterol
182 mg; 4160 kJ (995 cal)

ingredients

400 g pappardelle
50 g unsalted butter
300 ml cream
200 g fresh Parmesan,
    grated
1 tablespoon olive oil
1 small red chilli,
    cut into fine shreds
2–3 drops chilli oil
1/2 teaspoon paprika

preparation: 10 minutes
cooking: 12 minutes
serves: 4

1 Cook the pappardelle in a large saucepan of boiling water according to the packet instructions. Drain.

2 Melt the butter in a saucepan (do not allow it to brown). Add the cream and Parmesan and heat gently for 4–5 minutes.

3 In another saucepan, heat the olive oil. Add the chilli, chilli oil and paprika. Cook for 1–2 minutes. Add the pasta and toss well.

4 Place the pasta onto a heated serving dish. Pour on the cream sauce and serve immediately.

handy tip...

It is advisable to protect your hands with plastic gloves when preparing chillies. Try using scissors to chop, instead of a knife—it makes the job much easier.

ingredients

250 g fresh thick egg noodles

2 red capsicums, seeded, cut into quarters

2 green capsicums, seeded, cut into quarters

1 large carrot, cut into fine strips

3 spring onions, chopped

⅓ cup (80 ml) olive oil

2 tablespoons lemon juice

1 tablespoon finely chopped fresh mint

preparation: 15 minutes + 10 minutes standing + overnight refrigeration
cooking: 20 minutes
serves: 4

1 Cook the noodles in a large saucepan of boiling water according to the packet instructions. Drain and cool.

2 Place the capsicum on a foil-lined tray, skin-side up. Cook under a medium grill for 20 minutes, or until the skin blackens and blisters. Remove from the grill, cover with a clean damp tea towel and leave for 10 minutes.

3 Carefully remove the skins from the capsicum and cut the flesh into 1 cm wide strips. Place the capsicum in a bowl with the noodles, carrot and spring onion and toss together well.

4 Place the oil, lemon juice and mint in a small jug and whisk together. Pour over the salad and mix well. Cover and refrigerate for several hours or overnight. Toss again just before serving.

nutrition per serve
Protein 10 g; Fat 20 g; Carbohydrate 50 g; Dietary Fibre 3.5 g; Cholesterol 11 mg; 1770 kJ (425 cal)

hint

Drained, canned pimientos may be used in this recipe if desired, but the full roasted flavour will not be obtained.

vegetables & salads

ingredients

6 Roma tomatoes
5 bocconcini
2/3 cup (20 g) loosely
    packed fresh basil

Dressing
1/4 cup (60 ml) extra virgin
    olive oil
2 tablespoons balsamic
    vinegar

preparation: 15 minutes
cooking: nil
serves: 4

1 Cut the tomatoes lengthways into 3–4 slices, discarding the thin outside slices, which won't lie flat. Slice the bocconcini lengthways into 3–4 slices.

2 Arrange some tomato slices on a serving plate, place a bocconcini slice on top of each tomato and scatter with some of the basil leaves. Repeat the layers until all the tomato, bocconcini and basil have been used. Season with salt and freshly ground black pepper.

3 To make the dressing, place the oil and vinegar in a small bowl and whisk together well. Drizzle over the salad.

nutrition per serve
Protein 10 g; Fat 25 g; Carbohydrate 3 g; Dietary Fibre 2 g; Cholesterol 25 mg; 1080 kJ (255 cal)

handy tip...

Try this salad with a pesto dressing: Process 1/2 cup (25 g) firmly packed fresh basil, 1 tablespoon pine nuts, 1/4 cup (25 g) grated Parmesan and 1 crushed garlic clove in a food processor until finely chopped. With the motor running, add 1/4 cup (60 ml) olive oil and 1 tablespoon lemon juice in a steady stream and process until smooth.

ingredients

½ cup (125 g) plain yoghurt
½ cup (125 g) whole-egg mayonnaise
75 g creamy or mild blue cheese
2 tablespoons cream
500 g button mushrooms
2 celery sticks, sliced
1 cup (35 g) firmly packed rocket leaves
2 tablespoons chopped walnuts

preparation: 15 minutes
cooking: nil
serves: 4

1 To make the dressing, place the yoghurt, mayonnaise, cheese and cream in a food processor and process until smooth. Season.

2 Wipe the mushrooms with a damp paper towel, cut in half and place in a large bowl with the celery. Add the dressing and toss gently to combine.

3 Arrange the rocket leaves in a large serving dish and spoon in the mushroom and celery mixture. Sprinkle with the chopped walnuts.

nutrition per serve
Protein 10 g; Fat 25 g; Carbohydrate 10 g; Dietary Fibre 4 g; Cholesterol 45 mg; 1295 kJ (310 cal)

hint

If you would like to marinate some mushrooms, try these marinated garlic mushrooms. Place 500 g button mushrooms, 3 crushed cloves garlic, 1 tablespoon Dijon mustard, 1 tablespoon lemon juice and 1 cup (250 ml) olive oil in a bowl and mix to combine. Allow to marinate for 3 hours before serving.

ingredients

6 tomatoes, cut into thin wedges

1 red onion, cut into thin rings

2 Lebanese cucumbers, sliced

1 cup (185 g) Kalamata olives

200 g feta cheese

¼ cup (60 ml) extra virgin olive oil

dried oregano, to sprinkle

preparation: 15 minutes
cooking: nil
serves: 6–8

1 Place the tomato, onion rings, sliced cucumber and Kalamata olives in a large bowl and mix together. Season with salt and freshly ground black pepper.

2 Break the feta up into large pieces with your fingers and scatter over the top of the salad. Drizzle with the olive oil and sprinkle with some dried oregano.

nutrition per serve (8)
Protein 6.5 g; Fat 14 g; Carbohydrate 4 g; Dietary Fibre 2.5 g; Cholesterol 17 mg; 710 kJ (170 cal)

handy tip...

Feta is a sheep's milk cheese with a sharp salty flavour. There are many different varieties available.
If you are looking to add a little more flavour to the salad, use marinated feta and use the oil that it has been marinating in for the dressing.

ingredients

100 g baby English
   spinach leaves
1 oak leaf lettuce
2 avocados, thinly sliced
¼ cup (60 ml) olive oil
2 tablespoons sesame
   seeds
1 tablespoon lemon juice
2 teaspoons wholegrain
   mustard

preparation: 15 minutes
cooking: 2 minutes
serves: 8

1 Wash and dry the spinach and lettuce. Tear into bite-sized pieces and place in a serving bowl. Scatter the avocado over the leaves.

2 Heat 1 tablespoon oil in a small saucepan. Add the sesame seeds and cook over low heat until they just start to turn golden. Remove from the heat immediately. Set aside and cool for a minute or so.

3 Add the lemon juice to the saucepan, with the mustard and remaining oil and stir to warm through. Pour over the salad and toss gently.

nutrition per serve
Protein 2.5 g; Fat 26 g; Carbohydrate 0.5 g; Dietary Fibre 1.7 g; Cholesterol 0 mg; 1014 kJ (242 cal)

hint

This dish is best prepared just before serving.
You can replace the sesame seeds with pumpkin or sunflower seeds or a mix of both. You could also try roasted pine nuts or chopped peanuts.

ingredients

1 cup (175 g) burghul
½ cup (125 ml) olive oil
1 cup (30 g) chopped
  fresh flat-leaf parsley
1 cup (50 g) chopped
  fresh mint
¾ cup (90 g) finely
  chopped spring onions
4 Roma tomatoes,
  chopped
½ cup (125 ml) lemon
  juice
2 cloves garlic, crushed

preparation: 15 minutes +
  30 minutes refrigeration
cooking: nil
serves: 8

1 Place the burghul in a bowl and pour in 1 cup (250 ml) boiling water. Mix in 2 teaspoons of the oil, then set aside for 10 minutes. Stir again and cool.

2 Add the parsley, mint, spring onion and tomato to the burghul and mix well. Place the lemon juice, garlic and remaining oil in a small bowl and whisk together well. Add to the burghul and mix gently. Season to taste with salt and freshly ground black pepper. Cover and chill for 30 minutes before serving.

nutrition per serve
Protein 3 g; Fat 15 g; Carbohydrate 15 g; Dietary Fibre 5 g; Cholesterol 0 mg; 880 kJ (210 cal)

handy tip...

Burghul is also sold as bulgur or cracked wheat. For a different taste, couscous can be used instead of burghul in this recipe.

ingredients

300 g orange sweet
potato, peeled
2 slender eggplant
(about 350 g each)
oil, for deep-frying
¼ teaspoon ground chilli
powder
1 teaspoon chicken salt
¼ teaspoon ground
coriander

preparation: 5 minutes
cooking: 10 minutes
serves: 4–6

1 Cut the sweet potato and the eggplants lengthways into long, thin strips, similar in size. Place the vegetables into a large bowl.

2 Fill a deep heavy-based saucepan one third full of oil. Heat the oil to moderately hot 190°C (375°F), or until a cube of bread dropped in the oil browns in 10 seconds. Cook the sweet potato and eggplant in batches over high heat for 5 minutes, or until golden and crisp. Carefully remove the crisps from the oil with tongs or a slotted spoon. Drain on paper towels.

3 Place the chilli powder, chicken salt and coriander in a small bowl and mix well. Sprinkle the mixture over the hot crisps, toss until well coated and serve immediately.

nutrition per serve (6)
Protein 1.5 g; Fat 6.5 g; Carbohydrate 8.5 g; Dietary Fibre 2 g; Cholesterol 0 mg; 413 kJ (100 cal)

hint

Cook the crisps just before serving.
Try using other vegetables such as beetroot, carrot, potato and zucchini.

ingredients

Dressing
1/3 cup (80 ml) olive oil
2 tablespoons balsamic
   vinegar
2 tablespoons chopped
   fresh rosemary
3 cloves garlic, crushed

2 large red capsicums
2 large orange sweet
   potatoes, cut into slices
6 zucchini, halved
4 large cap mushrooms

preparation: 15 minutes
cooking: 15 minutes
serves: 4

1 To make the dressing, place the oil, balsamic vinegar, rosemary and garlic in a small bowl. Season with salt and freshly ground black pepper and whisk together well.

2 Remove the seeds and membrane from the capsicum, then cut the flesh into thick strips. Place with the sweet potato, zucchini and mushrooms on a cold, lightly oiled grill tray and brush with the dressing. Cook under a hot grill for 15 minutes, turning occasionally, or until all the vegetables are tender and lightly golden. Brush the remaining dressing over the vegetables during cooking. Serve warm with mashed potato, if desired.

nutrition per serve
Protein 3 g; Fat 20 g; Carbohydrate 13 g; Dietary Fibre 3 g; Cholesterol 0 mg; 1005 kJ (240 cal)

handy tip...

For a faster version of this recipe, use your favourite bottled dressing to brush on the vegetables instead of making your own.

ingredients

2 large potatoes, cubed
5 large parsnips, cubed
30 g butter
1 tablespoon milk
2 tablespoons sour cream
chopped fresh chives,
    to garnish

preparation: 10 minutes
cooking: 20 minutes
serves: 4–6

1 Bring a large saucepan of lightly salted water to the boil. Add the potato and parsnip and cook for 20 minutes, or until soft. Drain well.

2 Transfer the potato and parsnip to a bowl, add the butter, milk and sour cream and mash until smooth and fluffy. Season with salt and pepper. Sprinkle with the chives and serve immediately.

nutrition per serve (6)
Protein 5 g; Fat 7 g; Carbohydrate 30 g; Dietary Fibre 5 g; Cholesterol 25 mg; 800 kJ (190 cal)

hint

Sebago, bison, coliban, nicola, pontiac and King Edward are some good all-purpose potatoes that work well in this recipe.

ingredients

2 tablespoons olive oil

2 cloves garlic, sliced

600 g large button
   mushrooms, halved

2 tablespoons chopped
   fresh marjoram

2 tablespoons tomato
   paste

250 g cherry tomatoes,
   halved

1 tablespoon chopped
   fresh oregano leaves

preparation: 15 minutes
cooking: 15 minutes
serves: 4 as a side dish

1 Heat the oil in a saucepan, add the garlic and stir over moderate heat for 1 minute. Do not brown.

2 Add the mushrooms and cook, stirring, for 5 minutes, or until lightly golden.

3 Stir in the marjoram, tomato paste and cherry tomatoes and cook over low heat for 5 minutes, or until the mushrooms are soft. Sprinkle with oregano leaves and season with cracked black pepper.

nutrition per serve
Protein 6 g; Fat 10 g; Carbohydrate 4.5 g; Dietary Fibre 5.3 g; Cholesterol 0 mg; 557 kJ (133 cal)

handy tip...

This dish can be made up to 2 days ahead and is delicious served hot or cold. This 'saucy' dish can be served with mashed potato or soft polenta.

ingredients

750 g orange sweet
  potato, chopped
45 g butter, chopped
1 clove garlic, crushed
2 teaspoons grated fresh
  ginger
1½ tablespoons chopped
  fresh coriander leaves
2 teaspoons soy sauce
fresh coriander sprigs,
  to garnish

preparation: 15 minutes
cooking: 20 minutes
serves: 4

1 Bring a large saucepan of lightly salted water to the boil. Add the orange sweet potato and cook for 10–15 minutes, or until tender. Drain well.

2 Melt the butter in a small saucepan, add the garlic and ginger and cook over low heat, stirring, for 1 minute, or until fragrant.

3 Mash the orange sweet potato until almost smooth. Stir in the garlic mixture, coriander and soy sauce. Garnish with sprigs of coriander and serve immediately.

nutrition per serve
Protein 4 g; Fat 9.5 g; Carbohydrate 27 g; Dietary Fibre 3.5 g; Cholesterol 30 mg; 865 kJ (205 cal)

hint

Orange sweet potato is sweeter than regular potato, with a texture between potato and pumpkin. This mash goes well with pork, chicken, beef or lamb.

ingredients

4 fennel bulbs,
    cut into wedges
1 clove garlic, crushed
1/2 lemon, sliced
2 tablespoons olive oil
60 g butter, melted
3 tablespoons grated
    pecorino pepato
    cheese

preparation: 15 minutes
cooking: 25 minutes
serves: 4

1 Place the fennel in a saucepan with the garlic, lemon, olive oil and 1 teaspoon salt. Pour in enough water to cover the fennel and bring to the boil. Reduce the heat, then simmer for 20 minutes, or until just tender. Drain well.

2 Place the fennel in a heatproof dish, then drizzle with the melted butter. Sprinkle with the cheese and season to taste with salt and freshly ground black pepper.

3 Place under a hot grill until the cheese has browned and melted. Serve immediately.

nutrition per serve
Protein 5.5 g; Fat 24 g; Carbohydrate 6 g; Dietary Fibre 5 g; Cholesterol 45 mg; 1108 kJ (265 cal)

handy tip...

Pecorino pepato is a hard cheese (made from sheep's milk), is studded with black peppercorns and has a mild peppery flavour. If it is not available, use Parmesan instead.

nutrition per serve
Protein 10 g; Fat 20 g; Carbohydrate
35 g; Dietary Fibre 4.7 g; Cholesterol
9.5 mg; 1525 kJ (365 cal)

ingredients

1 kg potatoes,
cut into 2 cm cubes
⅓ cup (80 ml) olive oil
2 rashers bacon,
chopped
1 onion, chopped
2 spring onions, sliced
1 tablespoon fresh thyme,
finely chopped
1 clove garlic, crushed

preparation: 15 minutes
cooking: 35 minutes
serves: 4

1 Bring a large saucepan of water to the boil. Add the potato and cook for 5 minutes, or until just tender. Drain well and dry on a clean tea towel.

2 Heat the oil in a large non-stick frying pan. Add the bacon, onion and spring onion and cook for 5 minutes. Add the potato and cook over low heat, shaking the pan occasionally, for 20 minutes, or until tender. Turn frequently to prevent sticking. Partially cover the pan halfway through cooking. The steam will help cook the potato.

3 Add the thyme and garlic, and season to taste with salt and pepper in the last few minutes of cooking. Increase the heat to crisp the potato, if necessary.

hint

The potatoes can be cooked ahead of time and reheated in a lightly oiled frying pan. Use fresh rosemary instead of thyme, if desired.

ingredients

4 slices white bread,
    crusts removed,
    cut into cubes
3 rashers bacon, chopped
1 cos lettuce
½ cup (125 g) whole-egg
    mayonnaise
4 anchovies, finely
    chopped
1 clove garlic, chopped
1 tablespoon lemon juice
½ cup (50 g) shaved
    Parmesan

preparation: 15 minutes
cooking: 15 minutes
serves: 4

1 Preheat the oven to hot 210°C (415°F/Gas 6–7). Spread the bread evenly on a baking tray and bake for 15 minutes, or until lightly golden. Fry the bacon in a frying pan until crisp, then drain on paper towels. Tear the lettuce leaves into bite-sized pieces.

2 To make the dressing, place the mayonnaise, anchovies, garlic and lemon juice in a small bowl and mix together well.

3 Place the lettuce, bread cubes, Parmesan and bacon in a serving bowl, add the dressing and toss until combined. Serve immediately.

nutrition per serve
Protein 15 g; Fat 17 g; Carbohydrate 21 g; Dietary Fibre 2.5 g; Cholesterol 40 mg; 1236 kJ (295 cal)

handy tip...

The bread cubes can be baked a day in advance, then stored in an airtight container. The dressing can also be made a day in advance, stored in an airtight container in the refrigerator. Assemble the salad just before serving.

ingredients

4 rashers bacon

1.5 kg small Desiree potatoes (or other small, waxy, red-skinned potatoes)

4 spring onions, sliced

¼ cup (7 g) chopped fresh flat-leaf parsley

Dressing

½ cup (125 ml) extra virgin olive oil

1 tablespoon Dijon mustard

⅓ cup (80 ml) white wine vinegar

preparation: 15 minutes
cooking: 20 minutes
serves: 6–8

1 Cook the bacon under a hot grill until crisp. Chop into small pieces.

2 Bring a large saucepan of lightly salted water to the boil. Add the potatoes, reduce the heat and simmer for 10 minutes, or until just tender, trying not to let the skins break away too much. Drain and cool slightly.

3 To make the dressing, place the oil, mustard and vinegar in a jug and whisk together until well blended.

4 When cool enough to handle, cut the potatoes into quarters and place in a large bowl with the spring onion, parsley and half the bacon. Season to taste with salt and freshly ground black pepper. Pour half the dressing over the salad and toss gently to coat the potato and bacon.

5 Transfer to a serving bowl, drizzle with the remaining dressing and sprinkle with the remaining bacon pieces.

nutrition per serve (8)
Protein 8 g; Fat 20 g; Carbohydrate 25 g; Dietary Fibre 3 g; Cholesterol 10 mg; 1365 kJ (325 cal)

hint

Waxy potatoes have a high moisture content and are ideal for salads. Other waxy potatoes include the kipfler, roseval, pink fir apple and jersey royals.

ingredients

15 anchovy fillets
90 g butter
2 large onions, thinly sliced
5 potatoes, cut into
    matchsticks
2 cups (500 ml) cream

preparation: 15 minutes
cooking: 1 hour 5 minutes
serves: 4

1 Preheat the oven to moderately hot 200°C (400°F/Gas 6). Place the anchovy fillets in a bowl of water or milk and soak for 5 minutes to reduce their saltiness. Rinse and drain well.

2 Melt half the butter in a frying pan and cook the onion over medium heat for 5 minutes, or until golden. Chop the remaining butter into small cubes.

3 Spread half the potato over the base of a shallow ovenproof dish, top with the anchovies and onion, then with the remaining potato.

4 Pour half the cream over the potato and scatter the butter cubes on top. Bake for 20 minutes, or until golden. Pour the remaining cream over the top and cook for another 40 minutes, or until the potato is tender.

nutrition per serve
Protein 11 g; Fat 70 g; Carbohydrate 30 g; Dietary Fibre 4 g; Cholesterol 240 mg; 3360 kJ (800 cal)

handy tip...

A traditional Swedish dish, thought to have tempted a religious man from his vow to give up earthly pleasures of the flesh. Often served at the end of a party when it is supposed to tempt guests to stay longer.

ingredients

30 g butter
1 onion, sliced into
    thin rings
750 g waxy or all-purpose
    potatoes, thinly sliced
1½ cups (375 ml) cream
1 cup (125 g) grated
    Cheddar

preparation: 15 minutes
cooking: 45 minutes
serves: 4–6

1 Preheat the oven to moderate 180°C (350°F/Gas 4). Heat the butter in a frying pan, add the onion and cook for 5 minutes, or until soft and translucent.

2 Place the potato slices, onion rings, cream and half the cheese in a large bowl. Season with salt and pepper and mix together well.

3 Spread the potato mixture into a greased 1 litre ovenproof dish and flatten down with clean hands. Sprinkle the remaining cheese over the top, then bake for 40 minutes, or until the potato is tender, the cheese has melted and the top is golden brown.

nutrition per serve (6)
Protein 9 g; Fat 40 g; Carbohydrate 19 g; Dietary Fibre 2.5 g; Cholesterol 120 mg; 1955 kJ (435 cal)

hint

A gratin is any dish topped with cheese and/or breadcrumbs and cooked until browned. There are many versions of gratin, some are creamy, others less so.
If you prefer a lighter texture, you could use some vegetable or chicken stock in place of the cream. Waxy or all-purpose potatoes are the best varieties to use as they hold their shape better when slow-cooked in this way. This gratin is also delicious made with half potato and half orange sweet potato.

ingredients

155 g asparagus
2 tablespoons peanut oil
3 teaspoons sesame oil
1 tablespoon red wine
    vinegar
½ teaspoon sugar
200 g snow peas
1 tablespoon sesame
    seeds

preparation: 15 minutes
cooking: 3 minutes
serves: 4–6

1 Cut the asparagus in half diagonally. Place in a saucepan of boiling water for 1 minute, then drain and plunge into iced water. Drain well.

2 To make the dressing, place the peanut and sesame oils, vinegar and sugar in a small bowl and whisk together well. Place the asparagus and snow peas in a serving bowl. Pour on the dressing and toss well.

3 Place the sesame seeds in a dry frying pan. Cook over medium heat for 1–2 minutes, or until lightly golden. Sprinkle over the salad and serve immediately.

nutrition per serve (6)
Protein 3.5 g; Fat 8.5 g; Carbohydrate 3.5 g; Dietary Fibre 2.5 g; Cholesterol 0 mg; 428 kJ (100 cal)

handy tip...

The vegetables may be prepared up to four hours in advance and the dressing may be added up to one hour in advance.
Any spring vegetables are suitable for this recipe—try sugar snap peas, zucchini and peas.

ingredients

250 g cherry tomatoes, halved
4 bocconcini, quartered
1 clove garlic, crushed
1 tablespoon olive oil
24 cm oval focaccia
1/3 cup (90 g) purchased pizza sauce
2 teaspoons fresh oregano leaves
1 teaspoon fresh rosemary sprigs

preparation: 15 minutes
cooking: 20 minutes
serves: 2

1 Preheat the oven to hot 210°C (415°F/Gas 6-7). Place the tomato, bocconcini, garlic and oil in a bowl and mix well.

2 Place the focaccia on a baking tray, spread with the pizza sauce and bake for 5 minutes. Top with the tomato and bocconcini mixture. Season to taste with salt and pepper. Bake for 20 minutes, or until the focaccia is crunchy and the cheese has melted. Sprinkle with the oregano and rosemary. Cut into wedges and serve.

nutrition per serve
Protein 18 g; Fat 22 g; Carbohydrate 26 g; Dietary Fibre 4 g; Cholesterol 32 mg; 1559 kJ (372 cal)

hint

Any prepared pizza base is suitable for this recipe, fresh or frozen. If you are looking for a healthy alternative, try rounds of Lebanese bread.

ingredients

2 carrots, sliced
   diagonally
30 g butter
2 teaspoons honey
chopped fresh chives,
   to serve

preparation: 5 minutes
cooking: 15 minutes
serves: 4

1 Steam the carrots in a saucepan for 5–10 minutes, or until tender.

2 Place the butter and honey in a small saucepan and stir over low heat until melted.

3 Pour the butter and honey mixture over the carrots and toss to combine. Sprinkle the chives over the top and serve hot.

nutrition per serve
Protein 1 g; Fat 5 g; Carbohydrate 4 g; Dietary Fibre 2 g; Cholesterol 20 mg; 310 kJ (75 cal)

handy tip...

To make this in the microwave, place 1 tablespoon water and the carrots in a microwave-safe bowl. Cover and cook on High (100%) for 6–8 minutes. Drain. Cook the butter and honey in a microwave-safe bowl on High (100%) for 45 seconds, or until melted. Pour over the carrots, toss to coat and sprinkle with chives.

ingredients

80 g butter

3/4 cup (185 g) whole-egg
    mayonnaise

2 tablespoons horseradish
    cream

1 small onion, grated

1/4 teaspoon dry mustard

pinch of paprika

1 large head fresh
    broccoli

1 tablespoon lemon juice

preparation: 5 minutes +
    chilling
cooking: 10 minutes
serves: 6

1 Put 60 g butter in a small saucepan and stir over low heat until melted. Place in a bowl with the mayonnaise, horseradish, onion, mustard and paprika and mix together well. Season to taste with salt and black pepper. Chill.

2 Cut the broccoli into florets and bring a saucepan of water to the boil. Drop the florets into the boiling water and cook for 6–8 minutes. Refresh under cold running water and drain well.

3 Return the broccoli to the pan, add the lemon juice and remaining butter. Serve drizzled with the horseradish sauce.

nutrition per serve
Protein 2 g; Fat 22 g; Carbohydrate 8 g; Dietary Fibre 1.5 g; Cholesterol 45 mg; 970 kJ (232 cal)

hint

For a delicious, tangy sauce that's lower in kilojoules, substitute 1/2 cup (125 g) plain low-fat yoghurt for 1/2 cup (125 g) of the whole-egg mayonnaise.

nutrition per serve
Protein 9.5 g; Fat 10 g; Carbohydrate 3.5 g; Dietary Fibre 5.5 g; Cholesterol 30 mg; 600 kJ (144 cal)

ingredients

30 g butter

3 spring onions, finely chopped

2 rashers bacon, chopped

500 g Brussels sprouts

2 tablespoons slivered almonds

preparation: 10 minutes
cooking: 15 minutes
serves: 4

1 Melt the butter in a small saucepan. Add the spring onion and bacon and cook over medium heat for 5 minutes, or until the spring onion is soft but not brown.

2 Remove the outer leaves from the Brussels sprouts and trim the bases if necessary. Place the sprouts in a saucepan of salted boiling water. Cook, covered, for 5 minutes, or until just tender. Drain. Place in a shallow 1.25 litre heatproof dish.

3 Scatter the spring onion and bacon over the sprouts and season with freshly ground black pepper. Sprinkle with the slivered almonds. Cook under a hot grill for 5–7 minutes, or until the sprouts are hot and the almonds are golden. Serve immediately.

handy tip...

Small Brussels sprouts have the best flavour. Although the name suggests that sprouts originated in Belgium, the Belgians themselves believe they were brought to their country by the Romans.

500 g cauliflower,
  cut into florets
30 g butter
¼ cup (30 g) plain flour
1¼ cups (315 ml) warm
  milk
1 teaspoon Dijon mustard
½ cup (50 g) grated
  Parmesan
¾ cup (90 g) grated
  Cheddar
2 tablespoons fresh
  breadcrumbs

preparation: 15 minutes
cooking: 20 minutes
serves: 4

1 Grease a 1.5 litre heatproof dish. Cook the cauliflower in a saucepan of lightly salted boiling water until just tender. Drain, then place in the prepared dish and keep warm.

2 Melt the butter in a saucepan. Add the flour and cook for 1 minute, or until golden and bubbling. Remove from the heat, then whisk in the milk and mustard. Return to the heat and bring to the boil, stirring constantly. Cook, stirring, over low heat for 2 minutes. Remove from the heat. Add the Parmesan and ½ cup (60 g) of the Cheddar and stir until melted. Season to taste with salt and pepper and pour over the cauliflower.

3 Combine the breadcrumbs and remaining Cheddar and sprinkle over the sauce. Cook under a hot grill until the top is browned and bubbling.

nutrition per serve
Protein 17 g; Fat 20 g; Carbohydrate 15 g; Dietary Fibre 2.5 g; Cholesterol 64 mg; 1325 kJ (315 cal)

hint

For a slightly different and simple creamy mustard sauce, combine ½ cup (125 ml) mayonnaise, 1 cup (250 g) cream and 1 tablespoon wholegrain mustard. Pour over the cauliflower, sprinkle with grated cheese and grill until golden brown.

ingredients

310 g can cannellini
  beans, drained
2 tablespoons lemon juice
¼ cup (60 ml) olive oil
1 clove garlic, crushed
150 g fresh green beans

preparation: 15 minutes
cooking: 5 minutes
serves: 6

1 Place the cannellini beans in a food processor. Using the pulse action, process for 1 minute, or until the mixture is smooth.

2 Place the lemon juice, oil and garlic in a small jar. Screw the top on tightly and shake vigorously for 1 minute, or until combined. Add 2 teaspoons of the dressing to the bean purée and process briefly to combine. Refrigerate, covered, until required.

3 Top and tail the green beans. Place in a saucepan and cover with water. Bring to the boil and cook for 3 minutes, or until tender. Plunge into cold water, then drain. Pat dry with paper towels. Place the beans in a bowl and toss with the remaining dressing. To serve, pile the green beans on serving plates, then spoon over the bean purée. Serve with lamb cutlets, if desired.

nutrition per serve
Protein 4 g; Fat 10 g; Carbohydrate 6 g; Dietary Fibre 4 g; Cholesterol 0 mg; 540 kJ (130 cal)

handy tip...

The cannellini bean purée can be made one day ahead and stored in the refrigerator. Cook the green beans just before serving.

ingredients

4 egg yolks

185 g butter, melted

2 tablespoons lemon juice

310 g fresh asparagus

preparation: 10 minutes
cooking: 10 minutes
serves: 4–6

1 Place the egg yolks in a food processor and process for 20 seconds. With the motor running, pour the melted butter in a thin, steady stream into the food processer and process until thick and creamy. Add the lemon juice and ½ teaspoon cracked black pepper and season with salt.

2 Cut any thick, woody ends from the asparagus and discard. Place the asparagus in a saucepan of boiling water and cook for 2–3 minutes, or until bright green and tender. Drain quickly.

3 Place the asparagus on serving plates and spoon the hollandaise sauce over the top. Serve immediately.

nutrition per serve (6)
Protein 3 g; Fat 30 g; Carbohydrate 1 g; Dietary Fibre 1 g; Cholesterol 200 mg; 1135 kJ (270 cal)

hint

The hollandaise may be kept warm in a bowl over a saucepan of simmering water while the asparagus cooks. Do not overheat it, however, or the sauce will split.

ingredients

2 cups (500 ml) vegetable
  stock
750 g butternut pumpkin,
  cut into 1.5 cm cubes
2 onions, chopped
2 cloves garlic, halved
¼ teaspoon ground
  nutmeg
50 ml cream

preparation: 15 minutes
cooking: 20 minutes
serves: 4

1 Put the stock and 2 cups (500 ml) water into a large saucepan and bring to the boil over high heat. Add the pumpkin, onion and garlic to the stock and return to the boil. Reduce the heat slightly and cook for 15 minutes, or until the pumpkin is soft.

2 Drain the vegetables through a colander, reserving the liquid. Purée the pumpkin mixture in a blender until smooth (you may need to add some of the reserved liquid). Return the pumpkin purée to the pan and stir through enough of the reserved liquid for it to reach the desired consistency. Add the nutmeg and season to taste.

3 Divide among four warm bowls. Pour a little cream into each bowl to create a swirl pattern on the top. Serve with warm crusty bread.

nutrition per serve
Protein 5 g; Fat 6.5 g; Carbohydrate 15 g; Dietary Fibre 3.5 g; Cholesterol 17 mg; 605 kJ (145 cal)

handy tip...

To make a sweeter, nuttier pumpkin soup, roast the pumpkin pieces in a hot 210°C (415°F/Gas 6–7) oven until tender. Blend with ¼ cup (40 g) roasted cashews and swirl through sour cream. For a slightly spicy soup, add 2 teaspoons curry powder when cooking the onion.

12 ripe Roma tomatoes
1 tablespoon olive oil
1 large onion, finely chopped
3 cloves garlic, crushed
1.5 litres vegetable stock
4 fresh thyme sprigs
3 tablespoons tomato paste
2 tablespoons shredded fresh basil

preparation: 15 minutes
cooking: 20 minutes
serves: 4

1 Score a cross in the base of each tomato, place in a heatproof bowl and cover with boiling water. Leave for 30 seconds then transfer to a bowl of cold water. Peel the skin away from the cross and roughly chop the tomatoes.

2 Heat the oil in a saucepan and add the onion and garlic. Cook over medium heat for 3 minutes, or until the onion is soft. Meanwhile, place the stock in a separate saucepan and bring to the boil.

3 Add the tomato and thyme to the onion mixture. Cover and cook for 4 minutes, or until the tomato has softened slightly. Add the stock and tomato paste and bring to the boil. Reduce the heat and simmer, covered, for 10 minutes, or until the onion and tomato are soft. Remove the thyme sprigs.

4 Transfer the soup to a blender or food processor and blend in batches until smooth. Reheat gently, and stir in the shredded basil. Season to taste with salt and freshly ground black pepper. Divide the soup among four soup bowls and garnish with the fresh thyme sprigs. Serve with herb bread.

nutrition per serve
Protein 3.5 g; Fat 5 g; Carbohydrate 8.5 g; Dietary Fibre 8.5 g; Cholesterol 0 mg; 405 kJ (95 cal)

hint

If ripe tomatoes are not available, use 800 g can peeled tomatoes and reduce the stock to 1 litre. If the soup is lacking flavour, add a little sugar when seasoning.

ingredients

4 leeks, trimmed and cut
  into 4 lengthways
30 g butter
3 floury potatoes,
  chopped
3 cups (750 ml) vegetable
  stock
1 cup (250 ml) milk
¼ teaspoon ground
  nutmeg
¼ cup (60 ml) cream,
  to garnish
spring onions, chopped,
  to garnish

preparation: 15 minutes
cooking: 30 minutes
serves: 4

1 Wash the leeks thoroughly in cold water, then cut into small chunks. Heat the butter in a large saucepan. Add the leek and cook for 3–4 minutes, stirring frequently, until softened. Add the potato and stock. Bring slowly to the boil, then reduce the heat and simmer for 20 minutes, or until the vegetables are tender.

2 Cool the mixture slightly, then transfer to a blender or food processor and purée in batches. Return to the pan, stir in the milk and nutmeg, and season well with salt and cracked black pepper. Reheat gently and serve garnished with a swirl of cream and a scattering of spring onion.

nutrition per serve
Protein 4 g; Fat 15 g; Carbohydrate 20 g; Dietary Fibre 4 g; Cholesterol 48 mg; 1006 kJ (240 cal)

handy tip...

Leek and potato soup is also known as Vichyssoise and is delicious served hot or cold. Old floury potatoes such as sebago will give you the best results for this dish.

ingredients

2 tablespoons oil

4 tablespoons Tikka Masala curry paste

350 g waxy potatoes, cut into 2 cm cubes

350 g pumpkin, cut into 2 cm cubes

400 g can chopped tomatoes

1 cup (155 g) frozen peas

300 g firm tofu, cubed

½ cup (80 g) toasted cashews, chopped

preparation: 10 minutes
cooking: 45 minutes
serves: 4

1 Heat the oil in a saucepan. Add the paste and cook over low heat for 2 minutes, or until fragrant.

2 Add the potato and pumpkin and stir until well combined, then add the tomato and 1 cup (250 ml) water. Bring to the boil, then reduce the heat and simmer, partially covered, for 30 minutes, or until the vegetables are tender.

3 Add the peas and tofu and cook for a further 5 minutes. Scatter with the cashews and serve with rice.

nutrition per serve
Protein 15 g; Fat 23 g; Carbohydrate 25 g; Dietary Fibre 7 g; Cholesterol 1 mg; 1638 kJ (390 cal)

hint

Any vegetables may be used in this recipe—carrots, spinach, cauliflower, zucchini and capsicum would be delicious. Any curry paste is suitable, though you may only need to use 1–2 tablespoons as Tikka Masala is very mild.

ingredients

1¼ cups (310 g) red
  lentils
2 tablespoons ghee
1 onion, finely chopped
2 cloves garlic, crushed
1 tablespoon grated fresh
  ginger
1 teaspoon garam masala
1 teaspoon ground
  turmeric
2 tablespoons chopped
  fresh mint

preparation: 15 minutes
cooking: 20 minutes
serves: 4–6

1 Place the lentils in a large bowl and cover with cold water. Leave for 5 minutes, then remove any scum and drain well.

2 Melt the ghee in a saucepan. Add the onion and cook over medium heat for 3 minutes, or until soft and golden. Add the garlic, ginger and spices and cook until fragrant.

3 Add the lentils and 2 cups (500 ml) water and bring to the boil. Reduce the heat and simmer for 15 minutes, or until nearly all the liquid has been absorbed and the dhal is thick. Stir in the chopped mint and serve with plenty of naan bread.

nutrition per serve (6)
Protein 13 g; Fat 6.5 g; Carbohydrate 20 g; Dietary Fibre 7 g; Cholesterol 15 mg; 799 kJ (190 cal)

handy tip...

This Indian dish has a consistency similar to porridge and can be eaten on its own, served with boiled rice or Indian breads, or as an accompaniment to a meat dish.

ingredients

30 g butter
1 leek, finely sliced
340 g can asparagus
   cuts, drained
2 tablespoons chopped
   sun-dried tomatoes
5 eggs
½ cup (125 ml) cream

preparation: 10 minutes
cooking: 35 minutes
serves: 4

1 Preheat the oven to moderate 180°C (350°F/Gas 4). Lightly grease a 23 cm pie plate or flan dish.

2 Melt the butter in a frying pan. Add the leek and cook, stirring, over medium heat for 2 minutes, or until softened. Drain on paper towels.

3 Place the leek, asparagus and sun-dried tomato in a bowl and stir together well. Spread the mixture evenly into the prepared dish. Whisk together the eggs and cream, and season to taste with salt and freshly ground black pepper. Pour over the vegetables and bake for 30 minutes, or until golden brown.

nutrition per serve
Protein 11 g; Fat 25 g; Carbohydrate 3 g; Dietary Fibre 2 g; Cholesterol 287 mg; 1193 kJ (285 cal)

hint

Sun-dried tomatoes are available from supermarkets and delicatessens.
If preferred, this recipe can be adapted to make individual frittatas. Divide the mixture among a 12-hole non-stick muffin tray and bake in a moderate 180°C (350°F/Gas 4) oven for 20–25 minutes, or until set.

chunky minestrone

Heat 1 tablespoon oil in a large saucepan. Add 1 chopped onion and cook over medium heat for 3 minutes, or until golden. Add 2 cups (310 g) mixed frozen vegetables, 400 g can drained kidney beans, 400 g can chopped tomatoes and 1 litre chicken stock. Bring to the boil then add 1 cup (155 g) macaroni. Cook for 30 minutes, or until the macaroni is tender. Season well with salt and pepper and serve topped with grated Parmesan.

serves 4

From left to right: Chunky minestrone; Spicy sausage pasta sauce; Hearty lamb and bean stew; Speedy fish provençale; In-a flash cannelloni; Mussels in tomato and white wine.

spicy sausage pasta sauce

Heat 1 tablespoon oil in a large frying pan. Add 2 crushed cloves garlic and 1 chopped onion, and cook over medium heat for 3 minutes, or until golden. Add 300 g chopped sliced Hungarian salami or ciabi and cook for 3 minutes, or until browned. Stir in a 400 g can peeled tomatoes and ½ cup (125 ml) red wine, then bring to boil. Boil for 10 minutes, or until slightly thickened. Add a few drops of Tabasco sauce and season with salt and freshly ground black pepper. Stir in 1 tablespoon finely shredded basil before serving.

serves 6

hearty lamb and bean stew

Preheat the oven to moderately hot 180°C (350°F/Gas 4). Heat 1 tablespoon oil in a large ovenproof casserole dish and cook 1 kg lamb neck chops in batches until browned on both sides. Add 1 red onion cut into wedges, 1 cup (250 ml) white wine, 300 g can cannellini beans, 800 g can chopped tomatoes and 1 bay leaf. Bake, covered, for 1 hour 30 minutes, or until the lamb is tender and starting to fall off the bone.

serves 4–6

speedy fish provençale

Melt 30 g butter in a large frying pan. Add 1 onion cut into wedges and 1 chopped red capsicum. Cook over medium heat for 3 minutes, or until soft. Add a 400 g can chopped tomatoes, 1 bouquet garni (1 bay leaf, sprig of thyme and 3 sprigs of parsley tied together with string) and bring to the boil. Add 1 tablespoon chopped fresh oregano and 800 g cubed firm white fish fillets, then simmer, covered, for 10 minutes, or until the fish is tender. Season to taste and serve with rice.

serves 4

in-a-flash cannelloni

Preheat the oven to moderately hot 200°C (400°F/Gas 6). Cut 3 fresh lasagne sheets into rectangles large enough to enclose a chevapi or skinless sausage and wrap 10 sausages. Place the cannelloni in a lightly greased ovenproof dish. Pour in two 400 g cans chopped tomatoes, spread 300 g sour cream over the top and sprinkle with 1 cup (100 g) grated Parmesan. Bake for 45 minutes, or until golden and bubbling.

serves 3–4

mussels in tomato and white wine

Heat 1 tablespoon oil in a large saucepan. Add 2 crushed cloves garlic and 1 chopped onion and cook for 3 minutes, or until golden. Add 400 g can chopped tomatoes, 1/2 cup (125 ml) white wine, a pinch of saffron and 1 cup (250 ml) fish stock. Bring to the boil, then reduce the heat and simmer for 10 minutes, or until slightly thickened. Scrub 500 g mussels and remove the hairy beards—discard any mussels that are open. Add the mussels to the pan. Cook, covered, for 5–10 minutes, or until all the mussels have opened—discard any that do not open. Sprinkle with 2 tablespoons chopped fresh parsley and serve with crusty French bread.

serves 4

snacks

ingredients

1 small French bread stick
   (about 30 cm long)
¼ cup (60 ml) olive oil
1 clove garlic, crushed
1 tablespoon tomato paste
1 tablespoon mashed
   anchovies
100 g bocconcini,
   thinly sliced
fresh basil leaves, to serve

preparation: 15 minutes
cooking: 10 minutes
makes: 20

1 Preheat the oven to moderate 180°C (350°F/Gas 4). Cut the bread stick into 1.5 cm slices. Place the slices in a single layer on a baking tray and bake for 5 minutes, or until just crisp and dry.

2 Place the oil and garlic in a small bowl, mix together and brush onto the bread. Place the tomato paste and anchovies in a small bowl and mix together, then spread on the bread. Top with the bocconcini.

3 Return the bread slices to the oven for 3 minutes, or until the cheese has melted. Garnish each slice with a basil leaf before serving.

nutrition per crostini
Protein 2 g; Fat 4 g; Carbohydrate 2 g; Dietary Fibre 0 g; Cholesterol 4 mg; 220 kJ (53 cal)

handy tip...

Bocconcini is fresh mozzarella and comes in small round balls stored in whey. If bocconcini is not available, use grated mozzarella.
For a vegetarian alternative, remove the anchovies and assemble as instructed.

ingredients

250 g mixed nuts
  (almonds, Brazil nuts,
  peanuts, walnuts)
125 g pepitas *(see hint)*
125 g sunflower seeds
125 g cashews
125 g macadamia nuts
½ cup (125 ml) tamari

preparation: 5 minutes +
  10 minutes standing
cooking: 25 minutes
serves: 10–12

1 Preheat the oven to very slow 140°C (275°F/Gas 1). Lightly grease two large baking trays.

2 Place the mixed nuts, pepitas, sunflower seeds, cashews and macadamia nuts in a large bowl. Pour the tamari over the nuts and seeds and toss together well, coating them evenly in the tamari. Stand for 10 minutes.

3 Spread the nut and seed mixture evenly over the prepared baking trays and bake for 20–25 minutes, or until dry roasted. Let the mixture cool completely before serving.

nutrition per serve (12)
Protein 11.5 g; Fat 36 g; Carbohydrate 4 g; Dietary Fibre 5 g; Cholesterol 0 mg; 1604 kJ (383 cal)

hint

Pepitas are peeled pumpkin seeds—they are available at most supermarkets and health food stores.

The nut mixture may be stored in an airtight container for up to 2 weeks. However, once stored, it may become soft. If it does, lay the nuts out flat on a baking tray and bake in a slow (150°C/300°F/Gas 2) oven for 5–10 minutes.

ingredients

2 French bread sticks
   (about 35 cm long)

olive oil

4 ripe tomatoes, finely
   chopped

½ cup (30 g) shredded
   fresh basil

1 clove garlic, crushed

2 tablespoons extra virgin
   olive oil

preparation: 10 minutes
cooking: 15 minutes
makes: 30

1 Cut the bread sticks into 1 cm slices and brush with olive oil. Place each slice under a hot grill or on a baking tray in a moderately hot 200°C (400°F/Gas 6) oven, until golden on both sides, turning as needed.

2 Place the tomato, basil, garlic and extra virgin olive oil in a bowl and mix together. Season well with salt and pepper. Top the toasted bread slices with the tomato mixture and serve.

nutrition per bruschetta
Protein 0.5 g; Fat 2.5 g; Carbohydrate 3 g; Dietary Fibre 0.5 g; Cholesterol 0 mg; 170 kJ (40 cal)

handy tip...

Try these topping variations. Olive, mozzarella and tomato: Combine 300 g chopped pitted marinated Kalamata olives, 100 g diced mozzarella and 1 diced tomato. Spoon on the toasted bread slices. Tapenade and Parmesan: Spread the bruschetta with olive tapenade and top with shaved Parmesan.

ingredients

1 tablespoon olive oil

400 g flat mushrooms, finely chopped

2 cloves garlic, crushed

1 tablespoon chopped fresh parsley

¾ cup (185 g) thick Greek-style yoghurt

¾ cup (185 g) sour cream

2 spring onions, finely chopped

1 tablespoon lemon juice, or to taste

preparation: 15 minutes
cooking: 8 minutes
serves: 8

1 Heat the oil in a frying pan. Add the mushrooms and ½ teaspoon salt and cook over medium heat for 8 minutes, or until very soft and all the liquid has evaporated. Leave the mixture to cool.

2 Place the mushrooms, garlic, parsley, yoghurt, sour cream, spring onion and lemon juice in a bowl and mix together well. Season to taste with salt and freshly ground black pepper. Serve with crackers or savoury toasts.

nutrition per serve
Protein 14 g; Fat 50 g; Carbohydrate 11 g; Dietary Fibre 6 g; Cholesterol 136 mg; 2313 kJ (552 cal)

hint

Use flat or cap mushrooms in this recipe as they have a stronger flavour than button mushrooms.
This dip can be made 2–3 days ahead. Store in an airtight container in the refrigerator. Return to room temperature before serving.

nutrition per serve
Protein 50 g; Fat 27 g; Carbohydrate 43 g; Dietary Fibre 3 g; Cholesterol 144 mg; 2570 kJ (614 cal)

ingredients

2 flour tortillas
⅓ cup (80 g) taco sauce
1 cup (175 g) shredded barbecued chicken
1 cup (125 g) grated Cheddar or mozzarella
2 spring onions, finely chopped
sour cream, to serve
paprika, to serve

preparation: 15 minutes
cooking: 5 minutes
serves: 2

1 Heat a frying pan and place one tortilla in the base. Spread lightly with taco sauce and cook over medium heat for 2–3 minutes, or until heated through.

2 Arrange the shredded chicken evenly over the tortilla, then sprinkle with the grated cheese and spring onion. Place the remaining tortilla on top and cook for 2 minutes, or until lightly brown.

3 Place a plate over the pan, turn the quesadilla out, then slide it back into the pan with the cooked tortilla on top. Cook the other side until the cheese has melted and the quesadilla is heated through. Remove from the pan. Cut the quesadilla into wedges and serve with a dollop of sour cream and a sprinkling of paprika.

handy tip...

Tortillas are thin, round flatbreads made from wheat flour or cornmeal. For a spicy quesadilla, add 1–2 thinly sliced jalapeño chillies.
Shredded beef or refried beans can also be used instead of the chicken.

ingredients

Tartare sauce
1 cup (250 g) whole-egg
    mayonnaise
1½ tablespoons pickled
    capers, finely chopped
2 gherkins, finely chopped

800 g firm white fish fillets,
    boned
2 eggs
½ cup (60 g) plain flour
1½ cups (150 g) dry
    breadcrumbs
light olive oil,
    for deep-frying

preparation: 15 minutes
cooking: 10 minutes
serves: 4

1 To make the tartare sauce, place the mayonnaise, capers and gherkins in a bowl and mix well. Cover and set aside.

2 Cut the fish fillets into strips (2.5 x 10 cm). Place the eggs and 1 tablespoon water in a shallow dish and lightly beat together.

3 Dip each fish strip into the flour and shake off the excess. Dip into the egg mixture, then coat in the breadcrumbs, pressing the crumbs on firmly with your fingers.

4 Fill a deep heavy-based saucepan one third full of oil. Heat the oil to 180°C (350°F), or until a cube of bread dropped in the oil browns in 15 seconds. Deep-fry the fish fingers in two batches, for 3–5 minutes each batch, or until golden brown all over and cooked through. Drain the fish fingers on paper towels and serve immediately with the tartare sauce.

nutrition per serve
Protein 50 g; Fat 39 g; Carbohydrate 40 g; Dietary Fibre 2 g; Cholesterol 250 mg; 2972 kJ (710 cal)

hint

Fish is valued for its low cholesterol count, and its high protein content.
Fresh fish deteriorates quickly and should be stored in the refrigerator and used within 2–3 days. Fresh fish can also be frozen in a single layer. However, defrost completely overnight in the refrigerator before using.

ingredients

4 chicken breast fillets
(about 200 g each),
trimmed
plain flour, to coat
2 eggs, lightly beaten
cornflake crumbs, to coat
½ cup (125 g) whole-egg
mayonnaise
1 tablespoon each
wholegrain and Dijon
mustard
1 tablespoon honey
oil, for deep-frying

preparation: 15 minutes +
15 minutes refrigeration
cooking: 16 minutes
serves: 4

1 Cut each fillet into bite-sized pieces, then pat dry with paper towels. Coat each piece of chicken in the flour, shaking off any excess, dip in the egg and coat with the cornflake crumbs. Cover and refrigerate for 15 minutes.

2 Place the mayonnaise, mustards, honey and ¼ cup (60 ml) water in a bowl and mix together well.

3 Fill a deep heavy-based saucepan one third full of oil. Heat the oil to 180°C (350°F), or until a cube of bread dropped into the oil browns in 15 seconds. Cook the chicken in 3–4 batches for 4 minutes each batch, or until golden brown all over and cooked through. Drain on paper towels and serve hot with the honey mustard sauce.

nutrition per serve
Protein 50 g; Fat 25 g; Carbohydrate 20 g; Dietary Fibre 0.5 g; Cholesterol 200 mg; 2140 kJ (510 cal)

handy tip...

Use plain dry breadcrumbs instead of cornflake crumbs, if desired.
The chicken pieces can be crumbed ahead of time and frozen. Thaw completely before deep-frying.

ingredients

1 avocado, mashed
½ small red onion, finely
  chopped
1 tablespoon lemon juice
2 Roma tomatoes, diced
200 g packet corn
  chips
300 g jar tomato salsa
420 g can red kidney
  beans, rinsed and
  drained
1 cup (125 g) grated
  Cheddar

preparation: 10 minutes
cooking: 8 minutes
serves: 4

1 Place the avocado, onion, lemon juice and tomato in a small bowl and mix together well.

2 Preheat the oven to moderate 180°C (350°F/Gas 4). Arrange the corn chips on a large ovenproof serving platter.

3 Place the salsa and kidney beans in a small saucepan and stir over medium heat until warmed through. Pour the bean mixture over the corn chips and scatter the Cheddar over the top. Bake for 5 minutes, or until the cheese has melted and is golden.

4 Top with the avocado mixture and serve with sour cream, if desired. Serve immediately.

nutrition per serve
Protein 15 g; Fat 40 g; Carbohydrate 30 g; Dietary Fibre 8 g; Cholesterol 30 mg; 2158 kJ (515 cal)

hint

For a 'meaty' version, add 400 g lean beef mince to a frying pan in batches, breaking up any lumps with a fork. Remove from the pan. Fry 1 chopped onion for 2–3 minutes, then return the mince to the pan. Stir in the jar of tomato salsa, and kidney beans if desired, and simmer for 5–10 minutes. Pour over the corn chips, scatter with cheese and bake.

ingredients

4 large potatoes
⅓ cup (90 g) sour cream
½ cup (60 g) grated
  Cheddar
95 g can tuna, drained
130 g can corn kernels,
  drained
2 tablespoons chopped
  fresh chives

preparation: 15 minutes
cooking: 1 hour 30 minutes
serves: 4

1 Preheat the oven to moderately hot 190°C (375°F/Gas 5). Wash and scrub the potatoes clean. Pat dry with paper towels and pierce the skin all over with a fork or skewer.

2 Place the potatoes directly on the oven shelf. Bake for 1 hour 15 minutes, or until cooked through.

3 Cut a lid off the top of each potato and spoon out the flesh, leaving a thick border. Place the flesh in a bowl and mash with a potato masher. Add the sour cream,

cheese, tuna, corn and chives and season well with salt and freshly ground black pepper. Mix until roughly combined.

4 Place the potato shells on a baking tray. Divide the mixture evenly among the potatoes, piling the mixture high. Replace the lids at an angle and return to the oven. Bake for a further 15 minutes and serve hot.

nutrition per serve
Protein 14 g; Fat 15 g; Carbohydrate 26 g; Dietary Fibre 3.5 g; Cholesterol 57 mg; 1250 kJ (300 cal)

handy tip...

For a different kind of baked potato topping, try hummus and tabbouleh—put a spoonful of hummus into a baked potato and top with tabbouleh. For an extra creamy potato, add a spoonful of sour cream as well.

ingredients

2 tablespoons olive oil
2 slender eggplant,
    quartered lengthways
1 large red capsicum,
    cut into 1 cm strips
4 large lavash breads
200 g purchased hummus
1 red onion, finely
    chopped
2 tablespoons chopped
    fresh flat-leaf parsley
1 large tomato, chopped

preparation: 15 minutes +
    cooling time
cooking: 8 minutes
serves: 4

1 Heat the oil in a large frying pan. Add the eggplant and capsicum and cook for 6–8 minutes, or until tender. Drain well on paper towels. Leave to cool, then roughly chop.

2 Lay the lavash breads on a clean flat surface. Spread with the hummus, then sprinkle evenly with the onion and parsley. On the lower half of the long side of the lavash, arrange the eggplant, capsicum and tomato, and season. Roll each bread up firmly from the long side. Cut each roll in half diagonally and serve.

nutrition per serve
Protein 17 g; Fat 20 g; Carbohydrate 67 g; Dietary Fibre 10 g; Cholesterol 0 mg; 2190 kJ (523 cal)

hint

Wrap-ups can be made one hour ahead. If so, wrap each roll firmly in plastic wrap and refrigerate before cutting. This recipe is also delicious with a selection of marinated vegetables, available from delicatessens.

ingredients

Spicy tomato sauce
30 g butter
1 small onion, finely
    chopped
1 teaspoon curry powder
1/2 lemon
2/3 cup (170 ml) tomato
    sauce
2 teaspoons soft brown
    sugar

4 continental frankfurts
4 hot dog rolls

preparation: 15 minutes
cooking: 15 minutes
serves: 4

1 Preheat the oven to moderate 180°C (350°F/Gas 4).

2 To make the spicy tomato sauce, melt the butter in a small saucepan over medium heat. Add the onion and curry powder and cook for 3 minutes, or until the onion is softened. Add 1/2 teaspoon grated lemon rind, 1 tablespoon lemon juice, the tomato sauce, sugar and 2 tablespoons water. Simmer for 2 minutes, or until heated through.

3 Bring a saucepan of water to the boil. Reduce the heat to simmer. Add the frankfurts and cook for 3 minutes, or until heated through.

4 Place the rolls in the oven for 5 minutes, or until warmed. Cut lengthways, leaving one side attached. Drain the frankfurts well. Place a frankfurt in the hot roll and serve with the spicy tomato sauce.

nutrition per serve
Protein 17 g; Fat 20 g; Carbohydrate 60 g; Dietary Fibre 5.5 g; Cholesterol 48 mg; 2022 kJ (483 cal)

handy tip...

Use mini dinner rolls and cocktail frankfurts to make small hot dogs. These are great for kids' parties or to have with drinks.

4 English muffins, split
1/3 cup (90 g) tomato
    paste
1 cup (125 g) firmly
    packed grated
    Cheddar
16 thin slices salami,
    cut into strips
1/2 green capsicum,
    finely chopped
12 pitted black olives,
    sliced

preparation: 10 minutes
cooking: 10 minutes
serves: 4

1 Place the muffins, cut-side-down, on a baking tray and grill under a moderately hot grill until lightly toasted.

2 Spread the cut side of the muffins with the tomato paste and season to taste with salt and freshly ground black pepper. Top with the cheese, salami, capsicum and olives.

3 Return the muffins to the grill for 3–5 minutes, or until the cheese has melted.

nutrition per serve
Protein 20 g; Fat 18 g; Carbohydrate 33 g; Dietary Fibre 3.5 g; Cholesterol 48 mg; 1582 kJ (378 cal)

hint

For a different topping, try ham and pineapple. Replace the salami and olives with 8 slices ham and 1 cup (160 g) drained canned pineapple pieces.

ingredients

1 kg chicken mince
1 cup (80 g) fresh
    breadcrumbs
4 spring onions, sliced
1 tablespoon ground
    coriander
1 cup (50 g) chopped
    fresh coriander leaves
3 tablespoons sweet
    chilli sauce
1–2 tablespoons lemon
    juice
oil, for frying

preparation: 15 minutes
cooking: 40 minutes
serves: 6

1 Preheat the oven to moderately hot 200°C (400°F/Gas 6). Place the mince and breadcrumbs in a bowl and mix together well.

2 Add the spring onion, ground and fresh coriander, chilli sauce and lemon juice and mix together well. Using damp hands, form the mixture into evenly shaped balls that are small enough to eat with your fingers.

3 Heat the oil in a deep frying pan, and shallow-fry the chicken balls in batches over high heat until browned all over. Place them on a baking tray and bake for 5 minutes, or until cooked through.

nutrition per serve
Protein 40 g; Fat 8 g; Carbohydrate 10 g; Dietary Fibre 1 g; Cholesterol 85 mg; 1160 kJ (275 cal)

handy tip...

This mixture can be formed into burger patties. For this size, bake for 10–15 minutes, or until the mixture is cooked through.
This mixture is suitable for beef mince and also makes a delicious filling for sausage rolls.

ingredients

2 tablespoons hazelnuts, roasted

400 g can artichoke hearts, drained

1 clove garlic, chopped

¼ cup (25 g) finely grated Parmesan

¼ cup (60 ml) extra virgin olive oil

2 tablespoons chopped fresh flat-leaf parsley

preparation: 15 minutes
cooking: nil
serves: 6

1 Place the hazelnuts in a food processor and process until finely chopped. Add the artichoke hearts, garlic and Parmesan. Process until smooth. With the motor running, add the oil in a thin stream.

2 Stir in the parsley and spoon into a serving dish. Serve with herb and garlic pitta chips or crisp lavash bread.

nutrition per serve
Protein 4 g; Fat 15 g; Carbohydrate 1 g; Dietary Fibre 2.5 g; Cholesterol 4 mg; 650 kJ (155 cal)

hint

To add extra flavour to the dip, use marinated artichokes instead of canned, and reserve the marinade. Substitute the extra virgin olive oil for the reserved marinade.

ingredients

500 g boneless fish fillets
1 nori sheet
1 tablespoon tempura
    flour

Tempura batter
1 cup (250 ml) iced water
2 cups (250 g) tempura
    flour
oil, for deep-frying

preparation: 10 minutes
cooking: 20 minutes
makes: 24

1 Cut the fish into 24 bite-sized pieces and set aside. Using scissors, cut the nori into tiny squares and combine on a plate with the tempura flour.

2 To make the batter, quickly mix the iced water with the tempura flour. Do not overmix—it should be slightly lumpy. If it is too thick, add more water. Fill a heavy-based saucepan one third full of oil and heat to 180°C (350°F). The oil is ready when ¼ teaspoon of batter dropped into the oil keeps its shape, sizzles and rises to the top. Make sure the oil stays at the same temperature and does not get too hot. The fish should cook through as well as brown.

3 Dip the fish in batches into the nori and flour, then in the batter. Deep-fry until golden, then drain on crumpled paper towels. Season with salt and keep warm in a very slow 120°C (250°F/Gas ½) oven.

nutrition per piece
Protein 5 g; Fat 2 g; Carbohydrate 7.5 g; Dietary Fibre 0.5 g; Cholesterol 14 mg; 300 kJ (72 cal)

handy tip...

This very light, thin batter is made with iced water to ensure that it puffs up as soon as it hits the oil. Tempura flour is available at Asian supermarkets. If unavailable, substitute with 1½ cups (185 g) plain flour and ½ cup (90 g) rice flour. This batter recipe is also suitable for chicken or vegetable pieces.

ingredients

1 kg orange sweet potato, unpeeled

2 tablespoons vegetable oil

chilli powder, to taste

300 g sour cream

2 tablespoons sweet chilli sauce

2 spring onions, finely chopped

1 tablespoon chopped fresh coriander leaves

preparation: 10 minutes
cooking: 50 minutes
serves: 4

1 Preheat the oven to moderately hot 190°C (375°F/Gas 5). Scrub the sweet potato well and pat dry with paper towels. Cut the potatoes into 8–10 cm wedges. Place in a bowl with the oil and toss gently to coat.

2 Place the wedges in a single layer on a large baking tray and sprinkle lightly with chilli powder and salt. Bake for 40–50 minutes, or until tender and lightly browned on the edges.

3 To make the dipping sauce, place the sour cream, sweet chilli sauce, spring onion and coriander in a bowl, mix together and season. Cover and refrigerate.

4 Serve the hot wedges with the dipping sauce.

nutrition per serve
Protein 7 g; Fat 40 g; Carbohydrate 40 g; Dietary Fibre 5 g; Cholesterol 98 mg; 2256 kJ (539 cal)

hint

Wedges can also be made using plain potatoes. Floury potatoes such as idaho, sebago and spunta are the best to use. Scrub 6 large potatoes, cut each into about ten wedges and soak in cold water for 10 minutes. Preheat the oven to hot 200°C (400°F/Gas 6). Drain the wedges on paper towels and toss in 2 tablespoons olive oil. Tip into a shallow baking dish in a single layer and bake for 40–50 minutes, or until golden and crisp, turning occasionally. Drain on paper towels and season. Sprinkle with finely grated Parmesan.

quick feta and spinach freeform pie

Preheat the oven to moderate 180°C (350°F/Gas 4). Combine 300 g thawed frozen spinach, drained well, 5 chopped spring onions, 2 lightly beaten eggs, 200 g crumbled feta and 200 g cream-style cottage cheese in a bowl. Line a 23 cm pie plate with a sheet of filo pastry, brush lightly with melted butter and keep layering another nine layers with melted butter. Spoon in the filling and fold the pastry over loosely, but do not cover all the filling in the centre. Bake for 35–40 minutes, or until the pastry is golden brown.

serves 4–6

olive and tomato tarts

Preheat the oven to moderately hot 200°C (400°F/Gas 6). Place a 22 cm purchased shortcrust pastry shell on an oven tray and bake for 10 minutes, or until golden brown. Heat 1 tablespoon oil in a frying pan, add 400 g can chopped tomatoes, 2 teaspoons chopped fresh thyme and 1 teaspoon sugar. Bring to the boil and cook over high heat for 15 minutes, or until very thick. Stir in ¼ cup (25 g) grated Parmesan. Spoon the mixture into the pastry shell, top with 8 anchovy fillets and ⅔ cup (100 g) pitted Kalamata olives, and bake for 15 minutes.

serves 4

prosciutto-wrapped chicken fillets

Preheat the oven to moderate 180°C (350°F/Gas 4). Wrap 4 lightly pounded chicken fillets with 4–6 wafer thin slices of prosciutto and a sprig of rosemary. Heat 1 tablespoon oil in a large frying pan and cook the fillets in batches, for 5–7 minutes on each side, or until browned. Transfer to an oven tray and bake for 15 minutes, or until tender. Serve with bottled tomato relish.

serves 4

grilled haloumi bruschetta

Cut 300 g haloumi into thick slices and place in a shallow glass dish. Add 2 tablespoons extra virgin olive oil, 2 crushed cloves garlic and 2 tablespoons balsamic vinegar, then cover and marinate in the refrigerator for 30 minutes. Drain the haloumi and reserve the marinade. Place the haloumi on a baking tray and cook under a hot grill for 3 minutes on each side, or until golden brown. Cut a French baguette into thick slices on the diagonal and toast under the grill until golden on both sides, then top with a slice of haloumi. Combine 2 chopped Roma tomatoes, 2 tablespoons drained baby capers and 1 finely chopped red onion. Spoon on top of the haloumi and drizzle with the reserved marinade.

makes 15

speedy caesar salad

Tear 1 cos lettuce into large bite-sized pieces and place in a large salad bowl. Add 1½ cups (150 g) grated Parmesan, 4 quartered hard-boiled eggs, 1 cup (30 g) purchased croutons, 6 chopped anchovy fillets and 6 rashers bacon cooked until crisp then broken into large pieces. Toss gently, then drizzle with 1 cup (250 ml) bottled caesar salad dressing.

serves 4

simple salami and bocconcini pizzas

Preheat the oven to hot 220°C (425°F/Gas 7). Spread 2 tablespoons tomato paste over a 30 cm purchased pizza base and top with 50 g thinly sliced spicy salami, 100 g thinly sliced drained baby bocconcini and 150 g halved cherry tomatoes. Sprinkle with ¼ cup (25 g) grated fresh Parmesan and bake for 30 minutes, or until crisp and bubbling. Sprinkle with finely shredded basil just before serving.

serves 4

From left to right: Quick feta and spinach free-form pie; Olive and tomato tarts; Prosciutto-wrapped chicken fillets; Grilled haloumi bruschetta; Speedy Caesar salad; Simple salami and bocconcini pizzas.

ingredients

Herbed aïoli
1 cup (250 g) whole-egg
  mayonnaise
2 cloves garlic, crushed
2 tablespoons chopped
  fresh mixed herbs
  (parsley, chives and
  tarragon)

4 large onions
1 cup (125 g) plain flour
1 egg, lightly beaten
1 cup (250 ml) milk
olive oil, for deep-frying

preparation: 15 minutes
cooking: 10 minutes
serves: 4

1 To make the herbed aïoli, place the mayonnaise, garlic and herbs in a bowl and mix together well. Season with salt and freshly ground black pepper. Cover and set aside.

2 Cut 1.5 cm from the ends of each onion and discard. Cut the onions into 7 mm slices and separate into rings (use the smaller centre rings for another purpose).

3 Sift the flour into a bowl and make a well in the centre. Combine the egg and the milk and gradually add to the flour, stirring to make a smooth batter. Season well with salt and freshly ground black pepper. Heat a large, deep saucepan one third full with oil to 180°C (350°F), or until a cube of bread dropped in the oil browns in 15 seconds.

4 Dip the onion rings separately into the batter and drain off any excess. Deep-fry in the hot oil in batches for 2 minutes each batch, or until golden brown, turning once. Drain on paper towels and serve with the herbed aïoli.

nutrition per serve
Protein 10 g; Fat 33 g; Carbohydrate 45 g; Dietary Fibre 4 g; Cholesterol 72 mg; 2140 kJ (512 cal)

handy tip...

Onion rings make a great alternative to potato chips. Aïoli is a garlic mayonnaise from France. In Marseilles it is said that aïoli should contain at least two garlic cloves per serving. It is used over fish, meat and cold boiled potatoes. It is also added to soup.

8 flat field mushrooms
  (about 8 cm wide)
1 tablespoon olive oil
250 g English spinach
  leaves, cooked
250 g ricotta, well drained
2 tablespoons chopped
  fresh basil
2 tablespoons pine nuts
½ cup (50 g) freshly
  grated Parmesan

preparation: 15 minutes
cooking: 20 minutes
serves: 4

1 Preheat the oven to moderate 180°C (350°F/Gas 4). Trim the mushroom stalks level with the caps. Brush the rounded side of the mushrooms with the oil and arrange rounded-side down on a baking tray.

2 Squeeze any excess liquid from the cooked spinach and roughly chop the leaves. Place the spinach in a bowl and add the ricotta and basil. Season with salt and freshly ground black pepper and mix together well. Divide the filling among the mushrooms, and sprinkle with the pine nuts and grated Parmesan.

3 Bake for 15–20 minutes, or until the mushrooms are tender and the cheese begins to brown. Serve immediately.

nutrition per serve
Protein 8 g; Fat 15 g; Carbohydrate 1 g; Dietary Fibre 2.5 g; Cholesterol 12 mg; 752 kJ (180 cal)

hint

Ricotta is a smooth, moist, white cheese with a bland, sweet flavour. It is traditionally made from whey. Skim or full-cream milk is sometimes added, giving the cheese a creamier consistency and a fuller flavour. It is suitable for sweet and savoury dishes.

ingredients

4 slices bread, crusts
    removed
45 g can anchovy fillets
    in oil, drained
2 teaspoons lemon juice
60 g butter, softened
3 eggs, lightly beaten
½ cup (125 ml) cream
1 tablespoon finely
    chopped fresh parsley
pinch of cayenne pepper

preparation: 15 minutes
cooking: 25 minutes
serves: 4

1 Preheat the oven to moderate 180°C (350°F/Gas 4). Cut the bread diagonally in half. Arrange the triangles on an ungreased 30 x 28 cm baking tray and bake for 20 minutes, or until crisp and golden. Remove from the oven and allow to cool.

2 Place the anchovies and lemon juice in a bowl and mash with a fork to form a paste. Gradually blend in all but 1 teaspoon butter and stir until smooth.

3 Spread the anchovy mixture on the toasted triangles. Arrange 2 triangles on each serving plate.

4 Place the egg, cream, parsley and cayenne pepper in a bowl and whisk together well. Heat the remaining butter in a saucepan. Add the egg mixture and stir with a wooden spoon over low heat for 4 minutes, or until just cooked. Spoon the mixture over the anchovy toasts. Serve immediately.

nutrition per serve
Protein 11 g; Fat 30 g; Carbohydrate 14 g; Dietary Fibre 1 g; Cholesterol 225 mg; 1570 kJ (375 cal)

handy tip...

The egg mixture for this dish may also be cooked over boiling water in a double boiler for a smoother, creamier texture. This will take longer than the 4 minutes specified in this recipe. Cook the eggs just before serving. If the strong, salty taste of anchovies does not appeal, sardines may be substituted.

ingredients

2 sheets frozen puff pastry

300 g goats cheese, sliced

2 cooking apples, unpeeled

2 tablespoons extra virgin olive oil

1 tablespoon chopped fresh lemon thyme

preparation: 10 minutes
cooking: 25 minutes
makes: 32

1 Preheat the oven to hot 210°C (415°F/Gas 6–7). While the pastry is still frozen, cut each sheet into four squares and then each square into quarters. Place slightly apart on a lightly greased baking tray. Set aside for a few minutes to thaw and then lay the cheese over the centre of each square of pastry, leaving a small border.

2 Core the apples and slice them thinly. Overlap several slices on the pastry, making sure the cheese is covered completely. Lightly brush the apples with oil and sprinkle with lemon thyme and a little salt and pepper to taste.

3 Bake the tarts for 20–25 minutes, or until the pastry is cooked through and golden brown at the edges. Serve immediately.

nutrition per tart
Protein 2 g; Fat 5.75 g; Carbohydrate 5 g; Dietary Fibre 0.5 g; Cholesterol 9 mg; 335 kJ (80 cal)

hint
The pastry can be topped with cheese, covered and refrigerated overnight.
Top with the apple just before cooking.
Sliced pear may also be used instead of the apple.

500 g potatoes, cut into
   1 cm cubes
1 carrot, cut into
   1 cm cubes
1 parsnip, cut into
   1 cm cubes
1½ cups (115 g) chopped
   cabbage
½ cup (80 g) frozen peas
1 tablespoon chopped
   fresh chives
45 g butter

preparation: 15 minutes
cooking: 30 minutes
serves: 4

1 Bring a large saucepan of lightly salted water to the boil. Add the potato, carrot and parsnip and return to the boil. Reduce the heat, cover and simmer for 8 minutes, or until almost tender. Add the cabbage and peas, return to the boil and cook, covered, for 3 minutes. Drain the vegetables very well, then mash roughly with a potato masher. Add the chives and season with salt and pepper.

2 Melt the butter in a large frying pan, then add 4 lightly greased egg rings. Spoon half the vegetable mixture into the rings and press down firmly. Cook over medium heat for 4–5 minutes on each side, or until lightly browned. Remove carefully from the egg rings and repeat with the remaining mixture. Serve hot with toast.

nutrition per serve
Protein 5.5 g; Fat 9.5 g; Carbohydrate 23 g; Dietary Fibre 6 g; Cholesterol 30 mg; 850 kJ (205 cal)

handy tip...

'Bubble and Squeak' is a great way to use up leftover roasted or cooked vegetables. Add some pieces of crispy bacon to the mashed vegetables, if desired.

ingredients

4 flour tortillas
25 g butter, melted
1 teaspoon olive oil
1 chorizo sausage, peeled
    and finely chopped
25 g butter
5 eggs, lightly beaten
3 tablespoons milk
1 tablespoon chopped
    fresh coriander,
    to garnish

preparation: 15 minutes
cooking: 10 minutes
makes: 28

1 To make the tostadas, preheat the oven to moderately hot 200°C (400°F/Gas 6). Line two baking trays with baking paper. Cut the tortillas into 28 rounds with a 6 cm cutter and place on the baking tray. Brush with the melted butter. Bake for 5–6 minutes, or until golden and crisp, taking care not to burn. Transfer to a serving platter.

2 Meanwhile, heat the oil in a small saucepan and cook the chorizo until crispy. Drain on paper towels. Wipe out the pan with paper towels and gently melt the butter. Combine the eggs and milk in a small bowl, add to the pan and cook gently over low heat, stirring constantly, for 4 minutes, or until soft and creamy.

3 Remove from the heat and spoon the mixture into a warm bowl. (This is to stop the eggs from cooking further.) Fold in the chorizo and season to taste with salt and freshly ground pepper. Pile 2–3 teaspoons of the egg and chorizo mixture onto each tostada. Scatter with the fresh coriander and serve immediately.

nutrition per tostada
Protein 3 g; Fat 3.5 g; Carbohydrate 7.5 g; Dietary Fibre 0.5 g; Cholesterol 40 mg; 301 kJ (72 cal)

hint

You can cook the tostadas ahead of time. Just before serving, wrap them in foil and warm them in the oven for a few minutes. You will have to cook the egg and chorizo at the last minute.

desserts

ingredients

3 oranges
200 g raspberries
200 g blueberries
4 tablespoons caster
    sugar
mascarpone, to serve

preparation: 20 minutes +
    30 minutes refrigeration
cooking: 10 minutes
serves: 4–6

1 Cut a 2 cm-wide slice from the ends of each orange. Remove the rind in wide strips, including the pith and white membrane. Remove the pith from the rind with a sharp knife. Cut the rind into thin strips.

2 Separate the orange segments by carefully cutting between the membrane and the flesh. Place the orange segments and the berries in a bowl, sprinkle with 2 tablespoons of the sugar and toss lightly. Cover and refrigerate for 30 minutes.

3 Place the remaining sugar and $1/3$ cup (80 ml) water in a saucepan. Stir over low heat, without boiling, until the sugar has dissolved. Bring to the boil, then reduce the heat and add the orange rind. Simmer for 2 minutes, or until the rind is tender. Cool. Reserve 1 tablespoon of the syrupy rind.

4 Pour the syrup over the berry mixture and gently mix together. Spoon into serving goblets and garnish with the reserved rind and large dollops of mascarpone.

nutrition per serve (6)
Protein 1 g; Fat 0 g; Carbohydrate 24 g; Dietary Fibre 3.5 g; Cholesterol 0 mg; 427 kJ (100 cal)

handy tip...

The fruit may be combined with syrup and refrigerated for up to 4 hours.
For liqueur fruits, add $1/4$ cup (60 ml) Cointreau, or your favourite liqueur, to the fruits. Cover and refrigerate for at least 30 minutes to marinate. Serve with mascarpone or cream.

nutrition per serve
Protein 1.5 g; Fat 22 g; Carbohydrate
32 g; Dietary Fibre 1 g; Cholesterol
68 mg; 1342 kJ (320 cal)

ingredients

400 g packet frozen
  mango
½ cup (125 g) caster
  sugar
¼ cup (60 ml) mango or
  apricot nectar
300 ml cream
mango slices, to garnish
fresh mint sprigs,
  to garnish

preparation: 10 minutes +
  freezing
cooking: nil
serves: 6

1 Defrost the mango until it is soft enough to mash but still icy. Place the mango in a large bowl and add the sugar and mango nectar. Stir for 1–2 minutes, or until the sugar has dissolved.

2 Beat the cream in a bowl until stiff peaks form. Gently fold the cream through the mango mixture.

3 Spoon the mixture into a lamington tray or plastic container, cover and freeze for 1 hour 30 minutes, or until half-frozen. Quickly spoon the mixture into a food processor. Process for 30 seconds, or until smooth. Return to the tray, cover and freeze completely.

4 Remove the ice cream from the freezer for 15 minutes before serving, to allow it to soften a little. Serve the ice cream in scoops and garnish with the mango slices and sprigs of mint.

hint

The ice cream should be frozen for at least eight hours before serving and can be kept frozen for up to three weeks. When available, use fresh mangoes. Purée the flesh of 3–4 large mangoes in a food processor.

nutrition per serve
Protein 5 g; Fat 14 g; Carbohydrate 20 g; Dietary Fibre 2.5 g; Cholesterol 40 mg; 1017 kJ (245 cal)

ingredients

425 g can peach halves

415 g can apricot halves

⅓ cup (80 ml) Cointreau

2 tablespoons soft brown sugar

250 g mascarpone

preparation: 5 minutes
cooking: 8 minutes
serves: 6

1 Drain the peach and apricot halves and reserve the syrup. Place the apricots and peaches in an ovenproof dish and pour over half the reserved syrup.

2 Sprinkle the fruit with the Cointreau, then the sugar. Cook under a medium grill for 5 minutes, or until the fruit is soft and a golden glaze has formed on top.

3 Serve immediately with a dollop of mascarpone and dust with ground nutmeg, if desired.

handy tip...

Any liqueur or sweet wine may be used for this recipe such as Grand Marnier. Use fresh peaches and apricots when available.

¼ cup (90 g) honey
2 large green apples,
    peeled, cored and
    cut into eighths
2 large firm ripe pears,
    peeled, cored and
    cut into eighths
8 purchased waffles
2 x 200 g tubs honey-
    flavoured yoghurt

preparation: 15 minutes
cooking: 10 minutes
serves: 4

1 Place the honey and 1 cup (250 ml) water in a large saucepan and bring to the boil. Add the fruit, then reduce the heat, cover and simmer, stirring occasionally, for 8 minutes, or until tender.

2 To serve, warm the waffles in the oven or microwave according to the packet instructions.

3 Place two waffles on each plate. Spoon some apple and pear mixture on the waffles, then pour on the cooking syrup. Top with a dollop of honey-flavoured yoghurt and serve immediately.

nutrition per serve
Protein 5 g; Fat 4.5 g; Carbohydrate 45 g; Dietary Fibre 2.5 g; Cholesterol 15 mg; 1324 kJ (300 cal)

hint

Waffles are sold in the freezer cabinet and can be reheated in a toaster. For a special occasion, purchase fresh Belgian waffles from the deli section and reheat by warming in the oven.

ingredients

300 ml cream
300 g packet frozen
  raspberries, thawed
18 small meringues
2 x 30 g flaky chocolate
  bars, roughly broken

preparation: 15 minutes
cooking: nil
serves: 6

1 Place the cream in a large bowl and, using electric beaters, beat until soft peaks form. Fold the raspberries through the cream until just combined.

2 Divide the meringues among the serving plates. Spoon the raspberry cream into the shells and sprinkle with the chocolate shards. Serve immediately.

nutrition per serve
Protein 4 g; Fat 26 g; Carbohydrate 78 g; Dietary Fibre 3 g; Cholesterol 68 mg; 2276 kJ (544 cal)

handy tip...

For a banana and passionfruit quick pavlova, fold 2 thickly sliced bananas and the pulp of 2 passionfruit through the cream. Spoon into the pavlova shells and drizzle with extra passionfruit. Alternatively, use chopped, fresh strawberries or drained canned fruit.

ingredients

Strawberry sauce
300 g fresh or thawed
    frozen strawberries
1/2 cup (160 g) strawberry
    jam

2 eggs
2 tablespoons oil
1/3 cup (90 g) caster sugar
1 3/4 cups (215 g)
    self-raising flour, sifted
oil, for deep-frying
3/4 cup (185 g) caster
    sugar, extra, to coat

preparation: 15 minutes
cooking: 6 minutes
serves: 4–6

1 To make the sauce, place the strawberries and the jam in a food processor and process until smooth.

2 Place the eggs, oil, sugar and 2 tablespoons water in a bowl and mix together until smooth. Stir in the flour and mix to a soft dough. Roll 2 teaspoons of the mixture into a ball with floured hands. Repeat with the remaining mixture.

3 Fill a deep, heavy-based saucepan one third full of oil and heat to moderately hot 190°C (375°F), or until a cube of bread dropped into the oil browns in 10 seconds. Cook the doughnut balls in three batches for 1–2 minutes each batch, or until cooked through and lightly browned all over. While still hot, roll in the extra sugar. Serve immediately with the strawberry sauce, and if desired, ice cream and fresh strawberries.

nutrition per serve (6)
Protein 6.5 g; Fat 15 g; Carbohydrate 90 g; Dietary Fibre 3 g; Cholesterol 60 mg; 2133 kJ (510 cal)

hint

Use a good-quality vegetable oil for deep-frying the doughnuts. Do not use olive or grapeseed oil as the flavour will overpower the doughnuts.

ingredients

2 cups (250 g) self-raising flour, sifted

125 g butter, roughly chopped

2 tablespoons caster sugar

50 ml milk

2/3 cup (210 g) raspberry jam

1 tablespoon milk, extra

preparation: 20 minutes
cooking: 35 minutes
serves: 4

1 Preheat the oven to moderate 180°C (350°F/Gas 4). Line a baking tray with baking paper. Sift the flour into a large mixing bowl and add the butter. Rub the butter into the flour with your fingertips until the mixture resembles fine breadcrumbs. Stir in the sugar.

2 Add the milk and 50 ml water, and stir with a flat-bladed knife to form a dough. Turn out onto a lightly floured surface and gather together to form a smooth dough.

3 On a large sheet of non-stick baking paper, roll out the dough into a rectangle (33 x 23 cm) about 5 mm thick. Spread with the raspberry jam, leaving a 5 mm border around the edge.

4 Roll up lengthways like a Swiss roll and place on the tray seam-side-down. Brush with the extra milk and bake for 35 minutes, or until golden and cooked through. Leave to stand for a few minutes, then cut into thick slices using a serrated knife. Serve warm with custard or cream.

nutrition per serve
Protein 7 g; Fat 25 g; Carbohydrate 73 g; Dietary Fibre 3 g; Cholesterol 80 mg; 2330 kJ (555 cal)

handy tip...

Any flavoured jam can be used for this recipe. Apricot, fruits of the forest, rhubarb and ginger, or lime marmalade are all delicious substitutes.

ingredients

1½ cups (375 ml) strongly brewed espresso coffee

¾ cup (185 ml) Kahlua or Tia Maria

500 g mascarpone

2 tablespoons caster sugar

½ cup (125 ml) cream, lightly whipped

260 g thin sponge finger biscuits

¼ cup (30 g) cocoa powder

preparation: 15 minutes + overnight chilling

cooking: nil

serves: 8

1 Place the coffee and ½ cup (125 ml) of the Kahlua in a shallow dish and stir together. Set aside.

2 Place the mascarpone, sugar and remaining Kahlua in a large bowl and mix together well. Gently fold in the cream.

3 Quickly dip half the sponge finger biscuits into the coffee mixture (it is important to do this quickly so they do not take up too much liquid and go soggy), and place them in a single layer on the bottom of a 2 litre ceramic dish.

4 Spread half of the mascarpone mixture over the biscuits and dust liberally with half of the cocoa, using a fine sieve. Dunk the remaining biscuits in the coffee and lay them on top, then spread with the remaining mascarpone mixture. Dust with the remaining cocoa, then cover and refrigerate overnight.

nutrition per serve
Protein 9 g; Fat 26 g; Carbohydrate 64 g; Dietary Fibre 1 g; Cholesterol 82 mg; 2142 kJ (512 cal)

hint

Tiramisu means 'pick-me-up' in Italian. Sometimes referred to as Italian trifle, tiramisu actually has a much lighter texture than trifle.

If you would prefer this as an alcohol-free dessert, you can omit the Kahlua or Tia Maria and use ¾ cup (185 ml) more coffee to make up the loss of liquid.

ingredients

1 egg, lightly beaten
2 tablespoons custard
   powder
2 tablespoons sugar
1 cup (250 ml) milk
½ cup (125 ml) cream
4 bananas, thickly sliced
   on the diagonal
2 tablespoons shredded
   coconut, toasted
½ teaspoon ground
   cinnamon

preparation: 15 minutes
cooking: 5 minutes
serves: 4

1 Place the egg, custard powder, sugar, milk and cream in a heatproof bowl and whisk until the mixture is smooth.

2 Place the bowl over a saucepan of simmering water without touching the water. Stir constantly for 5 minutes, or until the custard thickens slightly and coats the back of a wooden spoon.

3 Divide the banana pieces among four serving dishes and drizzle with the custard. Sprinkle with the toasted coconut and ground cinnamon. Garnish with fresh mint, if desired, and serve immediately.

nutrition per serve
Protein 6.5 g; Fat 15 g; Carbohydrate 42 g; Dietary Fibre 3.5 g; Cholesterol 95 mg; 1475 kJ (355 cal)

handy tip...

This will keep for up to 2 days in the refrigerator, if the banana is stirred through the custard.
For variety, the custard may be flavoured with a few drops of almond or vanilla essence.

ingredients

2 cups (500 g) caster
    sugar
5 large peaches
¾ cup (185 ml)
    Champagne
2 egg whites

preparation: 15 minutes +
    freezing
cooking: 20 minutes
serves: 6

1 Place the sugar and 1 litre water in a large saucepan. Stir over medium heat without boiling until the sugar has dissolved. Bring to the boil, add the peaches and simmer for 20 minutes. Remove the peaches from the saucepan with a slotted spoon and cool completely. Reserve 1 cup (250 ml) of the poaching liquid.

2 Remove the skin and stones from the peaches, and cut the flesh into chunks. Place in a food processor and process until smooth. Add the reserved liquid and Champagne and process briefly until combined.

3 Pour the mixture into a shallow metal tray and freeze for 6 hours, or until just firm. Transfer the mixture to a large bowl and beat with electric beaters until smooth.

4 Place the egg whites in a separate bowl and beat with electric beaters until soft peaks form. Gently fold the egg white into the sorbet mixture with a metal spoon. Return the mixture to the metal tray and freeze until firm. Serve the sorbet in scoops, with sliced fresh peaches and dessert wafers, if desired.

nutrition per serve
Protein 2 g; Fat 0 g; Carbohydrate 88 g; Dietary Fibre 1 g; Cholesterol 0 mg; 1535 kJ (365 cal)

hint

Don't be tempted to use cheap Champagne or sparkling wine in this recipe—the difference will be noticeable. Use a wine of the same quality you would choose to drink. Other soft stone fruits, such as nectarines or plums, can be used in this sorbet if you prefer.

ingredients

250 g strawberries, halved
1 banana, peeled and thickly sliced
2 kiwi fruit, peeled, halved and sliced
250 g packet marshmallows
2 apples, cored and cut into 2 cm cubes

Fondue
250 g dark cooking chocolate, chopped
½ cup (125 ml) thick cream
2–3 teaspoons orange-flavoured liqueur

preparation: 15 minutes
cooking: 8 minutes
serves: 6

1 Thread the strawberry, banana, kiwi fruit, marshmallows and apple alternately onto skewers.

2 To make the fondue, place the chocolate and cream in a heatproof bowl. Place over a saucepan of simmering water without touching the water. Stir until melted and smooth. Remove the bowl from the heat.

3 Add the liqueur to the chocolate mixture, then transfer the fondue to a warmed serving bowl. Serve warm with the fruit skewers.

nutrition per serve
Protein 5 g; Fat 24 g; Carbohydrate 54 g; Dietary Fibre 4 g; Cholesterol 30 mg; 1880 kJ (450 cal)

handy tip...

The fondue can be prepared several hours in advance. Reheat gently before serving. White chocolate fondue can easily be made—just use white chocolate instead of the dark chocolate. You may need to add a little more cream if it is too thick.

ingredients

2 x 170 g cans
   passionfruit in syrup
300 g silken tofu, chopped
600 ml buttermilk
2 tablespoons caster
   sugar
1 teaspoon vanilla
   essence
6 teaspoons gelatine
¾ cup (185 g) passionfruit
   pulp
8 strawberries, halved,
   to garnish

preparation: 10 minutes +
   overnight refrigeration
cooking: nil
serves: 8

1 Push the passionfruit in syrup through a sieve. Discard the seeds. Combine the strained syrup with the tofu, buttermilk, caster sugar and vanilla in a blender. Blend for 90 seconds on high, to mix thoroughly. Leave in the blender.

2 Put ⅓ cup (80 ml) water in a small bowl and put the bowl in a slightly larger bowl of boiling water. Sprinkle the gelatine onto the water in the small bowl and stir until dissolved. Leave to cool.

3 Place eight 200 ml dariole moulds in a baking dish. Add the gelatine to the blender and mix on high for 1 minute. Pour into the moulds, cover the dish with plastic wrap and refrigerate overnight.

4 When ready to serve, carefully run a spatula around the edge of each mould and dip the bases into hot water for 2 seconds to make removal easier. Place each on a plate and spoon the passionfruit pulp around the bases. Garnish with fresh strawberries.

nutrition per serve
Protein 8 g; Fat 2.5 g; Carbohydrate 10 g; Dietary Fibre 10 g; Cholesterol 3 mg; 455 kJ (110 cal)

hint

It is important to thoroughly dissolve the gelatine (the liquid will be clear and golden). Don't be tempted to add the gelatine to the passionfruit mixture while it is still warm or it will become lumpy.

ingredients

300 g fresh or frozen
    blueberries
½ cup (125 ml) port
    (or muscat)
1 cinnamon stick,
    broken in half
½ cup (125 g) caster
    sugar
1 tablespoon brandy
500 ml good-quality vanilla
    ice cream

preparation: 15 minutes
cooking: 8 minutes
serves: 4

1 Place the blueberries, port and both halves of the cinnamon stick in a small saucepan. Add the sugar to taste (this will vary depending on the tartness of the berries). Simmer very gently over low heat for 5–8 minutes, or until the berries are tender. Remove from the heat and add the brandy. Allow to cool slightly.

2 Place scoops of ice cream into serving dishes. Top with the simmered blueberries and any juices. Serve with whipped cream, if desired.

nutrition per serve
Protein 5.5 g; Fat 14 g; Carbohydrate 70 g; Dietary Fibre 1.5 g; Cholesterol 35 mg; 1885 kJ (450 cal)

handy tip...

The syrup can be served hot or cold over the ice cream. If allowed to cool, the berries will macerate in the port and absorb more flavour.

ingredients

250 g dark chocolate,
    chopped
3 eggs
¼ cup (60 g) caster sugar
2 teaspoons dark rum
1 cup (250 ml) cream,
    softly whipped

preparation: 15 minutes +
    2 hours chilling
cooking: 5 minutes
serves: 4

1 Place the chocolate in a heatproof bowl. Place the bowl over a saucepan of simmering water without touching the water. Stir occasionally until the chocolate is melted. Remove from the heat and cool.

2 Place the eggs and sugar in a bowl and beat with electric beaters for 5 minutes, or until thick, pale and increased in volume.

3 Add the melted chocolate and rum and beat together until well combined. Gently fold in the cream with a metal spoon until the mixture is just combined.

4 Spoon the mousse into four 1 cup (250 ml) dessert glasses. Refrigerate for 2 hours, or until set. Decorate with chocolate leaves, if desired.

nutrition per serve
Protein 9 g; Fat 50 g; Carbohydrate 60 g; Dietary Fibre 1 g; Cholesterol 220 mg; 2900 kJ (685 cal)

hint

The chocolate must be allowed to cool before you add the cream or the mixture will go lumpy.
If you are melting the chocolate in the microwave, chop it into pieces. Stir to test after cooking to ensure it melts completely, as chocolate will hold its shape.

ingredients

250 g strawberries,
  hulled and halved
200 g blueberries
425 g can pitted black
  cherries, strained,
  reserving ½ cup
  (125 ml) juice
½ teaspoon cornflour
1 tablespoon icing sugar,
  sifted

Topping
90 g butter
¼ cup (90 g) golden syrup
2 cups (200 g) rolled oats

preparation: 10 minutes
cooking: 15 minutes
serves: 6

1 Preheat the oven to moderate 180°C (350°F/Gas 4). Place the fruit in an ovenproof dish and mix together well. Place the cornflour with the reserved cherry juice in a small bowl and blend together until smooth. Pour over the fruit, then sprinkle the icing sugar over the top.

2 To make the topping, place the butter and golden syrup in a small saucepan and stir over low heat until melted. Remove from the heat and stir in the rolled oats.

3 Spoon the topping evenly over the berries. Bake for 15 minutes, or until the topping is golden and crunchy. Delicious served hot with whipped cream or ice cream.

nutrition per serve
Protein 5 g; Fat 15 g; Carbohydrate 52 g; Dietary Fibre 5 g; Cholesterol 38 mg; 1522 kJ (365 cal)

handy tip...

For extra flavour, add blanched slivered almonds to the topping.
Try muesli as an alternative to rolled oats.

ingredients

400–500 g fresh
strawberries
1 cup (250 g) caster sugar

preparation: 15 minutes +
freezing
cooking: 5 minutes
serves: 2

1 Place the strawberries in a food processor or blender and purée until smooth—you will need 2 cups (500 ml) of purée.

2 Place the sugar and 1 cup (250 ml) water in a saucepan and stir over low heat until the sugar has dissolved. Remove from the heat and allow to cool.

3 Add the strawberry purée to the cooled sugar syrup, mix together well and pour into a metal freezer tray. Freeze for 3–4 hours, or until the mixture begins to set around the edges.

4 Place the mixture in a bowl and beat with electric beaters until smooth. Return to the metal tray and refreeze until set. Serve with fresh strawberries and whipped cream, if desired.

nutrition per serve
Protein 8.5 g; Fat 0 g; Carbohydrate 264 g; Dietary Fibre 11 g; Cholesterol 0 mg; 4405 kJ (1052 cal)

hint

It is important to freeze the sorbet in a shallow metal tray—it will freeze more quickly and evenly. The process of freezing, beating and refreezing will give you smaller ice crystals.

ingredients

1½ cups (375 g) sugar
1 tablespoon finely
   shredded fresh ginger
1 stem lemon grass,
   bruised *(see tip)*
4 firm ripe beurre bosc
   pears, peeled, halved
   and cored
lemon sorbet, to serve
mint leaves, to garnish

preparation: 10 minutes
cooking: 20 minutes
serves: 4

1 Place 2 cups (500 ml) water in a saucepan and bring to the boil. Add the sugar and stir together until it has completely dissolved. Add the ginger and lemon grass, bring to the boil, then reduce the heat and simmer for 5 minutes.

2 Gently lower the pear halves into the syrup and poach over low heat for 10 minutes, or until tender, turning occasionally. Remove the lemon grass.

3 Divide the pears among the serving dishes and spoon on a little syrup. Serve warm with the lemon sorbet and garnish with the mint.

nutrition per serve
Protein 0.5 g; Fat 0 g; Carbohydrate 112 g; Dietary Fibre 3.5 g; Cholesterol 0 mg; 1800 kJ (430 cal)

handy tip...

Bruising the stem of lemon grass enables you to get the full flavour. Cut the stem into 5 cm lengths. Using the back of a chef's knife, firmly press down on the lemon grass to crush the coarse outer skin.

ingredients

½ cup (45 g) flaked almonds

250 g packet jam rollettes (mini jam swiss rolls)

⅓ cup (80 ml) medium dry sherry

2 fresh mangoes or 2 fresh peaches, chopped

2½ cups (600 ml) ready-made custard

300 ml cream

preparation: 15 minutes
cooking: 8 minutes
serves: 6

1 Preheat the oven to moderate 180°C (350°F/Gas 4). Scatter the flaked almonds over a baking tray and toast in the oven for 6–8 minutes, or until golden. Cut the jam rollettes into 1 cm slices and place half on the base of a 2.5 litre glass serving bowl.

2 Sprinkle with half the sherry, then add half the mango. Top with half the custard. Repeat the layers, finishing with the custard, then refrigerate until cold.

3 Whip the cream until stiff peaks form, then spread over the custard. Scatter with the toasted almonds and serve.

nutrition per serve
Protein 9 g; Fat 27 g; Carbohydrate 45 g; Dietary Fibre 1.5 g; Cholesterol 130 mg; 1920 kJ (460 cal)

hint

If possible, use fresh fruit. If you can't buy fresh fruit, use a 425 g can of drained mango or peach slices.
This trifle doesn't have jelly. If you would like to add jelly, prepare it according to the packet instructions and allow it to set. Cut into pieces and layer it in the trifle.

ingredients

3 large mangoes, peeled
3/4 cup (185 ml) cream
2 tablespoons soft brown
 sugar
1 tablespoon caster sugar

preparation: 15 minutes
cooking: 5 minutes
serves: 6

1 Cut the mango flesh into thin slices and arrange in six 3/4 cup (185 ml) ramekin dishes. Pour the cream evenly into each dish, then sprinkle with the sugars.

2 Place under a hot grill for 5 minutes, or until the sugar has caramelised and the mango is warm. Serve immediately, with a wafer biscuit or tuille.

nutrition per serve
Protein 1.5 g; Fat 13 g; Carbohydrate 20 g; Dietary Fibre 1 g; Cholesterol 42 mg; 845 kJ (200 cal)

handy tip...

Make this dish just before serving.
This recipe can also be made using bananas or peaches.
For a richer dessert, add a few drops of Grand Marnier to the cream.

ingredients

150 g mixed nuts
(almonds, brazil nuts,
cashews, hazelnuts,
pecans)
1/3 cup (90 g) caster sugar
2 tablespoons cream
250 g mascarpone
2 tablespoons soft brown
sugar
1/2 cup (125 ml) cream,
extra
1 teaspoon vanilla
essence
18 cm ready-made
cooked shortcrust
pastry flan

preparation: 20 minutes
cooking: 8 minutes
serves: 4

1 Preheat the oven to moderate 180°C (350°F/Gas 4). Spread the nuts on a baking tray and roast in the oven for 5 minutes, or until lightly golden. Allow to cool.

2 Meanwhile, place the caster sugar in a small saucepan and stir over medium heat for 2–3 minutes, or until the sugar dissolves and turns golden. Remove from the heat and stir in the cream—be careful as it will spit a little. Stir until smooth and well combined. Allow to cool.

3 Place the mascarpone, brown sugar, extra cream and vanilla in a bowl and beat with electric beaters until combined—be careful not to overmix or it will curdle.

4 Spoon the mixture evenly into the pastry flan. Arrange the nuts evenly over the surface. Drizzle the toffee sauce over the nuts in a zigzag pattern. Chill until ready to serve.

nutrition per serve
Protein 14 g; Fat 73 g; Carbohydrate 56 g; Dietary Fibre 4 g; Cholesterol 129 mg; 3846 kJ (919 cal)

hint

The toffee sauce has to cool before you drizzle it over the nuts, otherwise it will melt the mascarpone filling. The sauce should have a thick consistency suitable to drizzle.

ingredients

3 eggs
1/2 cup (95 g) soft brown
  sugar
1 1/2 cups (375 ml) milk
1/2 cup (125 ml) cream
1 teaspoon vanilla
  essence
ground nutmeg, for
  dusting

preparation: 5 minutes
cooking: 35 minutes
serves: 4

1 Preheat the oven to moderate 180°C (350°F/Gas 4). Grease a 1 litre ovenproof dish.

2 Place the eggs, sugar, milk, cream and vanilla in a bowl and whisk together for 1 minute. Pour the custard mixture into the prepared dish.

3 Place the dish in a shallow baking tin and pour enough hot water into the tin to come halfway up the side. Sprinkle the nutmeg over the top of the custard and bake for 15 minutes. Reduce the heat to warm 160°C (315°F/Gas 2–3) and bake for a further 20 minutes, or until the custard is set and a sharp knife comes out clean when inserted in the centre. Remove the dish from the water immediately. Serve warm or cold with fresh or canned fruit.

nutrition per serve
Protein 8.5 g; Fat 20 g; Carbohydrate 30 g; Dietary Fibre 0 g; Cholesterol 190 mg; 1364 kJ (326 cal)

handy tip...

The mixture can be prepared several hours in advance. If serving warm, cook just before serving. If serving cold, the custard can be cooked a day in advance, and stored, covered, in the refrigerator.

ingredients

¾ cup (90 g) self-raising flour
1 tablespoon cocoa powder
½ cup (125 g) caster sugar
1 egg, lightly beaten
¼ cup (60 ml) milk
60 g butter, melted
⅓ cup (60 g) soft brown sugar
3 teaspoons cocoa powder, extra

preparation: 10 minutes
cooking: 20 minutes
serves: 4

1 Preheat the oven to moderate 180°C (350°F/Gas 4). Grease four ½ cup (125 ml) ramekins.

2 Sift the flour and cocoa into a bowl and stir in the sugar. Add the combined egg, milk and butter and stir together well.

3 Spoon the mixture evenly among the ramekins. Sprinkle with the combined sugar and extra cocoa powder. Carefully pour ¼ cup (60 ml) boiling water onto each pudding, then place on a baking tray. Bake for 15–20 minutes, or until a skewer comes out clean when inserted in the centre of the pudding. Dust with icing sugar, if desired, then serve immediately with cream or ice cream.

nutrition per serve
Protein 6 g; Fat 16 g; Carbohydrate 65 g; Dietary Fibre 1.25 g; Cholesterol 85 mg; 1731 kJ (413 cal)

hint

When testing whether the puddings are ready, insert the skewer at an angle. This way there is a larger area checked for doneness.

black forest dessert

Drain 425 g can black cherries. Cut a 550 g purchased chocolate cake into three equal layers using a serrated knife. Whip 300 ml cream until soft peaks form. Brush the bottom layer of the cake with 2 tablespoons cherry jam. Top with half the cherries and half the whipped cream, then repeat the layers, finishing with the cake. Dust with icing sugar and serve with chocolate ice cream.

serves 6

two-fruit strudel

Preheat the oven to hot 220°C (425°F/Gas 7). Place drained 425 g can two-fruits, ½ teaspoon ground cinnamon, 2 tablespoons soft brown sugar and 1 teaspoon vanilla essence in a bowl. Spoon the mixture onto the edge of 1 thawed sheet of ready-rolled puff pastry. Fold in the edges and roll into a strudel shape. Trim the ends to prevent the filling from falling out. Place on a non-stick baking tray, brush with 1 lightly beaten egg and sprinkle with raw sugar. Bake for 20 minutes, or until crisp and golden brown.

serves 4

mango and almond trifle

Line the base of a 2 litre glass serving bowl with a single layer of sponge finger biscuits, then drizzle with ¼ cup (60 ml) sherry. Top with drained 425 g can mango slices and 1 cup (250 ml) ready-made custard. Top with another single layer of sponge finger biscuits, drained 425 g can mango slices, 2 tablespoons sherry, 1 cup (250 ml) custard and 300 ml whipped cream. Refrigerate overnight. Just before serving, roughly chop 100 g toasted flaked almonds and sprinkle over the cream.

serves 6–8

pear galette

Preheat the oven to moderately hot 200°C (400°F/Gas 6). Cut 2 thawed sheets of ready-rolled puff pastry into quarters. Drain 800 g can pear halves and pat the pears dry with paper towels. Cut the pears into thin slices, taking care not to cut all the way through at the stem end—this allows the pear to fan out and maintain its shape. Place the pear core-side-down on the pastry and gently fan out the slices. Following the pear shape, cut around the pear, leaving a 2 cm border. Brush the pastry lightly with beaten egg and sprinkle the pear with brown sugar. Place on a non-stick baking tray and bake for 15–20 minutes, or until the pastry is puffed and golden. Serve hot with vanilla ice cream.

makes 8

raspberry and blackberry jelly

Drain 425 g canned raspberries and 425 g canned blackberries, reserving ½ cup (125 ml) of the juice. Combine the reserved juice with enough hot water to make up an 85 g packet of raspberry jelly crystals, according to the packet instructions. Stir the liquid until the jelly crystals have dissolved. Divide the berries among 4–6 champagne glasses, pour in the liquid and chill until set.

serves 4–6

blackberries and plums with streusel topping

Preheat the oven to moderate 180°C (350°F/Gas 4). Drain an 825 g can plums. Cut the plums in half and remove the stones. Place in a 1.5 litre ovenproof dish with a drained 425 g can blackberries. Place ¾ cup (90 g) plain flour, 1 cup (60 g) shredded coconut, 3 tablespoons soft brown sugar, 3 tablespoons rolled oats and 60 g melted butter in a bowl and mix together well. Sprinkle over the top of the fruit and bake for 15–20 minutes, or until golden.

serves 4

From left to right: Black forest dessert; Two-fruit strudel; Mango and almond trifle; Pear galette; Raspberry and blackberry jelly; Blackberries and plums with streusel topping.

1 cup (125 g) self-raising
   flour
40 g cold butter, chopped
1 egg
1 tablespoon milk
1 cup (250 g) sugar
40 g butter, extra
2 tablespoons golden
   syrup
¼ cup (60 ml) lemon juice

preparation: 15 minutes
cooking: 30 minutes
serves: 4

1 Sift the flour into a bowl and add a pinch of salt. Rub the butter into the flour with your fingertips until the mixture resembles fine breadcrumbs, and make a well in the centre. Stir the combined egg and milk into the flour mixture with a flat-bladed knife to form a soft dough.

2 To make the syrup, place 2 cups (500 ml) water in a large saucepan. Add the sugar, butter, golden syrup and lemon juice. Stir over medium heat until combined and the sugar has dissolved.

3 Bring to the boil, then gently drop dessertspoons of the dough into the syrup. Reduce the heat and simmer, covered, for 20 minutes, or until a knife inserted into a dumpling comes out clean.

4 Divide the dumplings among serving bowls, spoon on the syrup, and serve with whipped cream.

nutrition per serve
Protein 5 g; Fat 20 g; Carbohydrate 95 g; Dietary Fibre 1 g; Cholesterol 97 mg; 2327 kJ (555 cal)

handy tip...

For a richer sauce, use brown sugar instead of white sugar. For spiced dumplings, add ½ teaspoon each of ground cinnamon, nutmeg and cloves to the dry ingredients.

ingredients

100 g butter
200 g plain sweet biscuits,
　finely crushed (see hint)
500 g cream cheese,
　at room temperature
2/3 cup (160 g) caster
　sugar
2 eggs, lightly beaten
1/2 teaspoon finely grated
　lemon rind
1 tablespoon lemon juice

preparation: 15 minutes +
overnight refrigeration
cooking: 25 minutes
serves: 6–8

1 Preheat the oven to slow 150°C (300°F/Gas 2). Grease a 20 cm springform tin and line the base with baking paper.

2 Melt the butter in a saucepan. Place the biscuits in a bowl, add the butter and mix together until combined. Press the mixture firmly and evenly onto the base and side of the prepared tin. Place in the freezer while preparing the filling. (It is not necessary to press the crumbs to the top of the tin, as the mixture does not quite fill the tin).

3 Place the cream cheese and sugar in a large bowl and beat with electric beaters until smooth. Gradually add the egg and beat until mixed together well. Stir in the lemon rind and juice.

4 Pour into the prepared tin and smooth the surface. Bake for 25 minutes. Turn the oven off, leave the door open slightly and allow the cheesecake to cool in the oven. Refrigerate overnight.

nutrition per serve (8)
Protein 8 g; Fat 35 g; Carbohydrate 38 g; Dietary Fibre 0.5 g; Cholesterol 140 mg; 2107 kJ (505 cal)

hint

Biscuits are quickly and easily crushed in a food processor. Alternatively, place them into two clean plastic bags and crush them with a rolling pin.
Add extra flavour to the crust by folding through some toasted macadamia nuts.

ingredients

4 eggs, separated
½ cup (125 g) caster sugar
1⅓ cups (340 g) fresh ricotta
¼ cup (35 g) finely chopped pistachio nuts
1 teaspoon grated lemon rind
2 tablespoons lemon juice
1 tablespoon vanilla sugar (see tip)
200 g fresh or frozen raspberries

preparation: 15 minutes
cooking: 25 minutes
serves: 4

1 Preheat the oven to moderate 180°C (350°F/Gas 4). Grease four 1 cup (250 ml) ramekin dishes.

2 Place the egg yolks and sugar in a bowl and beat with electric beaters until thick and pale. Add the ricotta, pistachio nuts, lemon rind and juice and mix together well.

3 In a separate bowl, whisk the egg whites until stiff peaks form. Beat in the vanilla sugar, then fold into the ricotta mixture, stirring gently until just combined.

4 Divide the raspberries among the ramekins and spoon the ricotta filling over the top. Place on a baking tray and bake for 20–25 minutes, or until puffed and lightly browned. Dust with icing sugar.

nutrition per serve
Protein 18 g; Fat 19 g; Carbohydrate 40 g; Dietary Fibre 4 g; Cholesterol 222 mg; 1705 kJ (405 cal)

handy tip...

You can buy vanilla sugar at the supermarket or make your own. Split a whole vanilla bean in half lengthways and place in a jar of caster sugar (about 1 kg). Leave for at least 4 days before using.
Any berries may be used in this recipe—mango is also delicious.

nutrition per serve
Protein 3.5 g; Fat 8 g; Carbohydrate
30 g; Dietary Fibre 6 g; Cholesterol
20 mg; 885 kJ (210 cal)

ingredients

600 g rhubarb
2 strips lemon rind
1 tablespoon honey,
    or to taste
2 firm, ripe pears
½ cup (50 g) rolled oats
¼ cup (35 g) wholemeal
    plain flour
⅓ cup (60 g) soft brown
    sugar
50 g butter

preparation: 15 minutes
cooking: 25 minutes
serves: 6

1 Preheat the oven to moderate 180°C (350°F/Gas 4). Trim the rhubarb, wash and cut into 3 cm pieces. Place in a saucepan with the lemon rind and 1 tablespoon water. Cook, covered, over low heat for 10 minutes, or until tender. Cool slightly. Stir in the honey, then remove the lemon rind.

2 Peel, core and cut the pears into 2 cm cubes and combine with the rhubarb. Spoon into a 1.25 litre dish and smooth the surface.

3 To make the topping, place the oats, flour and brown sugar in a bowl and mix together well. Add the butter and rub in with your fingertips until the mixture resembles breadcrumbs. Spread evenly over the fruit. Bake for 15 minutes, or until cooked and golden. Serve warm with whipped cream or custard.

hint

The amount of honey added to the rhubarb will depend on how sweet the fruit is. Sugar can be used instead of honey, if preferred.
Most fruits are suitable for making crumble except citrus fruits such as lemon, lime and grapefruit. Try apple and berry, pear and apricot, or peach, nectarine and apple.

ingredients

800 g can pitted cherries,
very well drained

½ cup (60 g) self-raising
flour, sifted

⅓ cup (90 g) sugar

2 eggs, lightly beaten

1 cup (250 ml) milk

25 g butter, melted

icing sugar, for dusting

preparation: 15 minutes
cooking: 40 minutes
serves: 6–8

1 Preheat the oven to moderate 180°C (350°F/Gas 4). Grease a 23 cm glass or ceramic shallow pie plate. Spread the cherries into the dish in a single layer.

2 Place the flour and sugar in a bowl and make a well in the centre. Pour in the combined eggs, milk and butter gradually and whisk until just combined—do not overbeat.

3 Pour the batter over the cherries and bake for 40 minutes. Dust generously with icing sugar and serve immediately.

nutrition per serve (8)
Protein 4 g; Fat 5 g; Carbohydrate 38 g; Dietary Fibre 2 g; Cholesterol 57 mg; 876 kJ (210 cal)

handy tip...

A clafoutis (pronounced 'clafootee') is a classic French batter pudding. It is traditionally made with cherries, but other berries—blueberries, blackberries, raspberries, or small, well-flavoured strawberries—may be used instead if you prefer. A delicious version can also be made using slices of poached pear.

nutrition per serve
Protein 9 g; Fat 15 g; Carbohydrate
60 g; Dietary Fibre 0 g; Cholesterol
165 mg; 1630 kJ (390 cal)

ingredients

30 g butter, softened

¾ cup (185 g) caster sugar

1 teaspoon grated lemon rind

3 eggs, separated

¼ cup (30 g) plain flour

½ cup (125 ml) lemon juice

1½ cups (375 ml) warm milk

icing sugar, to dust

preparation: 10 minutes
cooking: 40 minutes
serves: 4

1 Preheat the oven to moderate 180°C (350°F/Gas 4). Grease a 1.5 litre ovenproof dish. Place the butter, sugar, rind and egg yolks in a bowl and beat with electric beaters until light and creamy.

2 Fold in the sifted flour in two batches, alternately with the lemon juice and milk. Place the egg whites in a separate clean, dry bowl and beat with electric beaters until soft peaks form. Pour the lemon mixture down the inside of the bowl of the beaten egg whites and fold the whites gently into the mixture with a metal spoon.

3 Pour the combined mixture into the prepared dish and put the dish in a baking tin. Pour in enough warm water to come halfway up the sides of the dish. Bake for 40 minutes, or until puffed and golden. Dust with icing sugar and serve with ice cream.

hint

Try using limes or oranges for a different citrus flavour. It is essential that this dessert is served immediately. If it is left to sit, the sauce will absorb into the cake and it will be dry and gluggy.

1 cup (250 g) sugar

Custard
1 litre milk, warmed
½ cup (125 g) sugar
6 eggs
1½ teaspoons vanilla
  essence

preparation: 15 minutes +
  refrigeration
cooking: 40 minutes
serves: 8

1 Preheat the oven to moderate 180°C (350°F/Gas 4). Grease eight ½ cup (125 ml) ramekins.

2 Place the sugar and ¼ cup (60 ml) water in a saucepan. Stir over low heat until the sugar dissolves. Bring to the boil, then reduce the heat and simmer for 6 minutes, or until the mixture turns golden brown. Remove from the heat. Pour a little of the hot mixture into each ramekin and swirl to cover the base. Set aside.

3 To make the custard, place the milk and sugar in a saucepan and stir gently over low heat until the sugar has dissolved. Place the eggs and vanilla in a bowl and whisk together for 2 minutes, then stir in the warm milk. Strain the mixture into a jug and pour into the ramekins.

4 Place the ramekins in a baking tin, then pour in enough hot water to come halfway up the sides. Bake for 30 minutes, or until the custard is set and a knife comes out clean when inserted. Allow to cool, then refrigerate for at least 6 hours.

5 To unmould, run a knife around the edge of each custard and gently upturn onto a serving plate. Shake gently to remove, if necessary. Serve with whipped cream, fresh fruit and wafers, if desired.

nutrition per serve
Protein 9 g; Fat 8.5 g; Carbohydrate 53 g; Dietary Fibre 0 g; Cholesterol 150 mg; 1315 kJ (314 cal)

handy tip...

This can be made 1 day ahead and stored in the refrigerator. To avoid a burnt flavour in step 2, remove the pan containing the caramel from the heat just before it reaches the desired colour. The mixture will darken further even after cooking has finished.
The custard for Crème Caramel may be flavoured with spices such as cardamom, cinnamon and nutmeg; with lemon or orange rind; or with your favourite spirit or liqueur.

ingredients

75 g caster sugar
rind of 1 orange
3 teaspoons gelatine
2½ cups (600 ml) pink
   Champagne
300 g mixed berries,
   fresh or frozen

preparation: 15 minutes +
  cooling + refrigeration
cooking: 5 minutes
serves: 4–6

1 Place the sugar, orange rind and 1⅓ cups (330 ml) water in a saucepan. Bring to the boil, stirring over low heat until the sugar dissolves. When dissolved, remove the pan from the heat and leave to cool for 1 hour.

2 Strain the rind out of the syrup. Place about ¼ cup (60 ml) syrup in a heatproof bowl, sprinkle the gelatine in an even layer over the top and leave to go spongy. Bring a saucepan filled with about 4 cm water to the boil. When it boils, remove from the heat and carefully lower the gelatine bowl into the water (it should come up halfway), then stir until dissolved. Cool slightly, add to the rest of the syrup and mix. Add the Champagne, then pour a little of the jelly into the base of a 1.25 litre loaf tin and refrigerate until set. Don't leave too long or the next layer will not stick.

3 Arrange the fruit in the tin, pour in a little more jelly to cover the fruit, set in the refrigerator, then pour the rest of the jelly in and set completely. (Setting in layers will ensure a smooth surface on top and stop the fruit floating.)

4 To unmould, wipe the tin with a cloth dipped in hot water then invert the terrine onto a plate. Bring to room temperature before serving—it should not be stiff and should sag very slightly. Serve with cream or ice cream, if desired.

nutrition per serve (6)
Protein 2 g; Fat 2 g; Carbohydrate 17 g; Dietary Fibre 1.5 g; Cholesterol 0 mg; 575 kJ (137 cal)

hint

If you wish to use gelatine sheets, put 6 sheets in a bowl of cold water and leave until floppy. Remove the gelatine, squeeze out any excess water. Add the gelatine to the hot sugar syrup and stir until thoroughly dissolved.

ingredients

125 g fresh or frozen
  raspberries
150 g fresh or frozen
  blueberries
2 tablespoons orange-
  flavoured liqueur
8 brandy snap baskets
8 small scoops strawberry
  swirl ice cream
mint leaves, to garnish

preparation: 20 minutes
cooking: nil
serves: 8

1 Place the raspberries and blueberries in a bowl, pour in the orange-flavoured liqueur and stir gently to combine.

2 Place each brandy basket on a serving plate. Place one small scoop of ice cream in one half of each basket. Add the berries to the other half of the basket. Serve decorated with a few mint leaves.

nutrition per serve
Protein 2.5 g; Fat 11 g; Carbohydrate 35 g; Dietary Fibre 1.5 g; Cholesterol 32 mg; 1067 kJ (255 cal)

handy tip...

Brandy snap baskets are available at supermarkets or delicatessens.
For a delicious variation, try spooning the berries into meringue nests instead of the brandy snap baskets.

ingredients

170 g butter, chopped
3 cups (240 g) coarse fresh breadcrumbs
¾ cup (165 g) firmly packed soft brown sugar
½ teaspoon ground nutmeg
825 g can peaches, drained, chopped
¾ cup (90 g) slivered almonds

preparation: 20 minutes
cooking: 50 minutes
serves: 4

1 Preheat the oven to moderate 180°C (350°F/Gas 4). Grease a 1.25 litre soufflé dish.

2 In a large frying pan, melt 150 g of the butter, add the breadcrumbs and toss over medium heat until the breadcrumbs are golden brown. Place the sugar and nutmeg in a bowl and mix together well.

3 Place one third of the breadcrumb mixture over the base of the prepared dish and top with half of the peaches, a third of the sugar mixture and half of the almonds. Repeat with a second layer of each and top with a final layer of breadcrumbs. Use the back of a spoon to firmly press the mixture down. Sprinkle with the remaining sugar and dot with the remaining butter. Bake for 35–40 minutes, or until golden brown.

nutrition per serve
Protein 15 g; Fat 48 g; Carbohydrate 105 g; Dietary Fibre 7.5 g; Cholesterol 110 mg; 3745 kJ (895 cal)

hint

Any canned fruit is suitable for this recipe. For example, mix canned apples with ½ teaspoon of ground cinnamon and 1 teaspoon vanilla. You could also substitute the almonds with ground hazelnuts, for a slightly different flavour.

praline ice cream terrine with mango coulis

Line the base and sides of a 19 x 10 cm loaf tin with baking paper. Firmly press 2 litres softened French vanilla ice cream into the tin. Smooth the surface and tap gently to release any air pockets. Freeze for 1–2 hours, or until firm. In a non-stick frying pan, heat 1 cup (250 g) sugar, stirring over low heat until dissolved. Bring to the boil and cook until it has turned a light golden colour. Add 30 g slivered almonds, then pour onto a foil-lined baking tray and leave to harden. Process half the praline in a food processor until crushed, and break the remaining praline into large pieces. Place a well-drained 800 g can mango slices, 1 tablespoon icing sugar and 1 tablespoon Cointreau in a blender and process until smooth. Remove the ice cream from the tin and sprinkle the crushed praline over the ice cream. Slice the ice cream to serve and garnish with praline pieces and mango coulis.

serves 4–6

banana and caramel parfait

Place 20 g butter, ½ cup (95 g) soft brown sugar and ½ cup (125 ml) cream in a small saucepan and stir over low heat for 5 minutes, or until the sugar has dissolved. Simmer for 2 minutes. Set aside and allow to cool slightly. Divide 1 thinly sliced banana evenly between two large parfait glasses. Top each banana layer with ¼ cup (60 ml) ready-made custard, a scoop of vanilla ice cream and some caramel sauce. Repeat the layers. Serve with wafers.

serves 2

blueberry ice cream pie

Line the base of a 22 cm round springform tin with baking paper. Place 250 g plain sweet biscuits in a food processor and process until crumbly. Add 125 g melted butter and mix well. Press firmly into the base and side of the prepared tin, then sprinkle 250 g fresh or frozen blueberries or blackberries over the base. Dollop 2 litres of softened berry swirl ice cream carefully over the berries until the base is covered. Smooth over the surface and tap the tin lightly to remove any air pockets. Freeze for 1–2 hours, or until firm. Melt 100 g chocolate and pipe or drizzle over the top to decorate.

serves 6

pecan pie

Finely crush 250 g sweet biscuits in a food processor. Add 185 g melted butter and ½ teaspoon ground cinnamon and stir together well. Press the crumb mix into the base of a 22 cm round fluted flan tin and chill. Soften 1 litre pecan caramel ice cream until just spreadable then evenly spread over the pie base and return to the freezer. Press 50 g whole pecans around the edge and return to the freezer until firm. Drizzle with ½ cup (125 ml) bottled caramel fudge topping and serve immediately.

serves 6

christmas ice cream pudding

Place 1 tablespoon brandy, 150 g mixed dried fruit and ½ teaspoon ground cinnamon in a bowl and allow to stand for 15 minutes. Add 2 litres softened vanilla ice cream and mix together well. Spoon the mixture into six 1 cup (250 ml) dariole moulds or ramekins. Freeze for 1 hour, or until firm. Turn out the ice cream from the moulds using a warm cloth and place onto a baking tray. Return to the freezer for 5–10 minutes. Melt 100 g dark chocolate and drizzle over each pudding. Return to the freezer for 5–10 minutes. Melt 100 g white chocolate and drizzle over the top of the dark chocolate. Return to the freezer for 10 minutes to set firm before serving. Top each pudding with ½ red and green glacé cherry.

serves 6

bombe alaska

Preheat the oven to very hot 230°C (450°F/Gas 8). Drain a 440 g can sliced pineapple and reserve the juice. Cut a 300 g jam roll into six, 2 cm thick slices. Place the jam rolls onto a baking tray and brush lightly with the reserved juice. Top the jam rolls with a slice of pineapple and a scoop of raspberry or strawberry ice cream, then place in the freezer while you make the meringue. Place 2 egg whites in a clean, dry bowl and whisk until soft peaks form. Gradually add ⅓ cup (90 g) caster sugar. Beat until glossy and stiff peaks form. Spread the meringue roughly over the ice cream then bake for 2–3 minutes, or until lightly golden on the outside. Serve immediately.

serves 8

From left to right: Praline ice cream terrine with mango coulis; Banana and caramel parfait; Blueberry ice cream pie; Christmas ice cream pudding; Pecan pie; Bombe Alaska.

nutrition per serve
Protein 5 g; Fat 24 g; Carbohydrate 25 g; Dietary Fibre 0 g; Cholesterol 77 mg; 1378 kJ (330 cal)

ingredients

¼ cup (55 g) short-grain rice
1⅔ cups (410 ml) milk
1½ tablespoons caster sugar
¾ cup (185 ml) cream
¼ teaspoon vanilla essence
¼ teaspoon grated nutmeg
1 bay leaf

preparation: 10 minutes
cooking: 2 hours
serves: 4

1 Preheat the oven to slow 150°C (300°F/Gas 2). Grease a 1 litre ovenproof dish.

2 Place the rice, milk, sugar, cream and vanilla essence in a bowl and mix together. Pour into the greased dish. Dust the surface with the grated nutmeg and float the bay leaf on top.

3 Bake for 2 hours, by which time the rice should have absorbed most of the milk and will have become creamy in texture with a brown skin on top. Remove the bay leaf before serving and serve hot, if desired.

handy tip...

Alternatively, try adding a couple of tablespoons of sultanas. Add grated lemon or orange rind to give the pudding a citrus flavour. Rice pudding is delicious served hot or cold.
For a low-fat version, use skim milk.

ingredients

2 cups (250 g) plain flour
3 eggs, lightly beaten
1 cup (250 ml) milk
60 g butter, melted

Sauce
2 tablespoons butter
3 tablespoons sifted
   cocoa powder
1 cup (185 g) soft brown
   sugar
300 ml cream

preparation: 5 minutes +
   30 minutes standing
cooking: 20 minutes
serves: 4

1 Sift the flour into a large bowl and make a well in the centre. Add the combined egg, milk and ¾ cup (185 ml) water and whisk together to form a smooth batter. Stir in the melted butter. Pour the mixture into a jug and set aside for 30 minutes.

2 Heat a 20 cm crêpe pan or non-stick frying pan and grease lightly with butter. When the pan is hot, pour in ¼ cup (60 ml) of the mixture and tilt the pan to cover. Tip out any excess batter. When the edges begin to curl, gently turn the crêpe over with an egg slice. Cook until lightly browned on both sides, and slide onto a plate. If not serving immediately, keep the crêpes warm in a preheated oven. Cook the remaining batter and stack the crêpes on top of each other with a piece of greaseproof paper between each one.

3 To make the sauce, place the butter, cocoa and sugar in a saucepan and mix well. Add the cream and stir over low heat until it comes to the boil.

4 To serve, fold three crêpes into quarters and put them on a plate. Pour a generous amount of the sauce over the top and add a scoop of vanilla ice cream.

nutrition per serve
Protein 18 g; Fat 60 g; Carbohydrate 99 g; Dietary Fibre 3 g; Cholesterol 300 mg; 4185 kJ (1005 cal)

hint

This dessert can be made ahead of time. The sauce will keep well in the refrigerator for up to a week and the crêpes can be made ahead and frozen. Store the crêpes in between layers of baking paper. Defrost and reheat in the oven.

ingredients

2/3 cup (85 g) self-raising
    flour
2 eggs
1/2 cup (125 ml) milk
60 g butter
1/3 cup (60 g) soft brown
    sugar
3 teaspoons grated
    orange rind
1/4 cup (60 ml) orange
    juice
3 bananas, sliced

preparation: 15 minutes
cooking: 15 minutes
serves: 4

1 Sift the flour into a bowl and make a well in the centre. Place the eggs, milk and 1/4 cup (60 ml) water in a small bowl and whisk until combined, then gradually add to the flour. Stir until the liquid is mixed together well and the batter is free of lumps.

2 Pour 2–3 tablespoons of batter onto a lightly greased 20 cm crêpe pan, swirling evenly over the base. Cook over medium heat for 1 minute, or until the underside is golden. Turn the crêpe over and cook the other side. Transfer to a plate, cover with a tea towel and keep warm. Repeat the process with the remaining batter, greasing the pan when necessary. You will need 8 crêpes for this recipe.

3 Heat the butter in a saucepan, add the brown sugar and stir over low heat until the sugar has dissolved and the mixture is bubbling. Add the rind and juice and bring to the boil. Reduce the heat and simmer for 2 minutes.

Add the banana and simmer for a further minute. Divide the mixture among the 8 crêpes. Fold the crêpes into quarters to enclose, arrange on serving plates and serve.

nutrition per serve
Protein 8 g; Fat 16 g; Carbohydrate 54 g; Dietary Fibre 3 g; Cholesterol 133 mg; 1632 kJ (390 cal)

handy tip...

The batter can be made several hours ahead. Cover the bowl with plastic wrap and refrigerate. Cook the crêpes just before serving. Alternatively, the crêpes can be cooked several hours ahead. Place on a baking tray and cover with aluminium foil. Just before serving, place in a moderate 180°C (350°F/Gas 4) oven for 10 minutes, or until warmed through.

ingredients

1 sheet ready-rolled puff pastry

¼ cup (60 ml) bottled apple sauce

3 medium green apples

20 g butter, melted

2 tablespoons soft brown sugar

¼ teaspoon ground cinnamon

preparation: 15 minutes
cooking: 25 minutes
serves: 6

1 Preheat the oven to moderate 180°C (350°F/Gas 4). Lightly grease a baking tray.

2 Lay out the pastry on a work surface. Using a plate as a guide, cut a 23 cm circle from the pastry and place on the prepared tray. Spread the apple sauce over the pastry, leaving a 2 cm border around the pastry edge.

3 Peel, core and quarter the apples. Slice thinly and arrange decoratively over the apple sauce, fanning out from the centre of the pastry. Brush the melted butter over the apple, then sprinkle with the sugar and cinnamon.

4 Bake for 25 minutes, or until the edge of the pastry is golden brown. Serve hot, with whipped cream, custard or vanilla ice cream, if desired.

nutrition per serve
Protein 2 g; Fat 9 g; Carbohydrate 27 g; Dietary Fibre 2 g; Cholesterol 16 mg; 812 kJ (194 cal)

hint

This dish is best made just before serving.
Granny Smith apples are excellent for cooking as they soften without losing their shape. Tinned fruit is not suitable for this recipe.

ingredients

250 g cream cheese, softened

1 tablespoon lemon juice

3 tablespoons caster sugar

1/3 cup (40 g) sultanas

1/4 cup (30 g) plain flour, sifted

2 sheets ready-rolled puff pastry

2 tablespoons milk

1 tablespoon caster sugar, extra

preparation: 15 minutes
cooking: 25 minutes
serves: 6

1 Preheat the oven to moderate 180°C (350°F/Gas 4). Lightly grease a baking tray.

2 Place the cream cheese, lemon juice and sugar in a bowl and beat with electric beaters until smooth. Add the sultanas and flour and stir with a wooden spoon.

3 Place half the cheese mixture along one side of one of the pastry sheets, about 5 cm in from the edge. Roll up as for a swiss roll and press the ends together to seal. Repeat with the remaining mixture and pastry sheet.

4 Place the rolls on the prepared tray. Lightly brush with the milk and sprinkle with the extra sugar. Bake for 25 minutes, or until golden brown.

nutrition per serve
Protein 7.5 g; Fat 27 g; Carbohydrate 43 g; Dietary Fibre 1 g; Cholesterol 55 mg; 1843 kJ (440 cal)

handy tip...

For something different, try a berry, white chocolate and cream cheese strudel. Instead of the sultanas, fold in 100 g raspberries and 1/4 cup (40 g) grated white chocolate.

ingredients

2 large beurre bosc pears
(about 600 g)
75 ml dry white wine
¼ cup (60 g) caster sugar
225 ml milk
3 eggs
2 teaspoons vanilla
essence
75 g plain flour
icing sugar, to dust

preparation: 15 minutes +
1 hour marinating
cooking: 50 minutes
serves: 4–6

1 Peel and core the pears, and cut them into 12 slices each. Place in a large bowl and pour in the combined wine and sugar. Gently stir, then set aside for 1 hour. (Do not leave for any longer or the pears will turn brown.)

2 Preheat the oven to moderate 180°C (350°F/Gas 4). Grease a shallow, round 1.25 litre ovenproof dish. Drain the pears and reserve the syrup. Spread the pear slices evenly over the base of the dish.

3 Pour the syrup into the bowl of a food processor. With the motor running, add the milk, eggs, vanilla essence and flour. Process until smooth, then pour the mixture over the pears. Bake for 50 minutes, or until the tart is puffed and golden on top. Sprinkle the sifted icing sugar liberally over the top. Serve hot or warm with cream or ice cream, if desired.

nutrition per serve (6)
Protein 6 g; Fat 4 g; Carbohydrate 35 g; Dietary Fibre 3 g; Cholesterol 95 mg; 860 kJ (205 cal)

hint

Apples can be used instead of the pears—firm apples such as Granny Smith or Golden Delicious are best for cooking.

ingredients

50 g dark chocolate
60 g butter, softened
4 egg yolks
1¼ cups (310 ml) cream
2 teaspoons vanilla
2 tablespoons whisky
¼ cup (30 g) dark cocoa,
    for dusting

preparation: 10 minutes +
    3 hours freezing
cooking: nil
serves: 6

1 Line a 21 x 14 x 7 cm loaf tin with plastic wrap.

2 Roughly chop the chocolate. Place in a heatproof bowl and stand over a saucepan of simmering water. Melt the chocolate gently, then allow to cool.

3 Place the butter and egg yolks in a small bowl and beat with electric beaters until thick and creamy, then beat in the cooled chocolate mixture.

4 Place the cream and vanilla in a separate bowl and beat with electric beaters until soft peaks form. Fold in the whisky. Fold the cream and chocolate mixtures together with a metal spoon until they are just combined.

5 Pour the mixture into the prepared tin and freeze for 2–3 hours, or until firm. Remove from the freezer, unmould and carefully peel away the plastic wrap. Smooth out the wrinkles on the surface of the loaf with a flat-bladed knife. Place on a serving plate and dust with cocoa. Cut into slices and serve with extra cream and dessert wafers, if desired.

nutrition per serve
Protein 4 g; Fat 37 g; Carbohydrate 8 g; Dietary Fibre 0.5 g; Cholesterol 215 mg; 1613 kJ (385 cal)

handy tip...

This dish should be served immediately. If not, return it to the freezer until you are ready.
The whisky can be replaced with a coffee liqueur.

ingredients

2 sheets frozen shortcrust
  pastry, thawed
2 x 750 g cans pie apples
pinch ground cloves
½ teaspoon finely grated
  lemon rind
1 sheet frozen puff pastry,
  thawed
2 teaspoons milk
2 teaspoons sugar

preparation: 15 minutes
cooking: 40 minutes
serves: 4

1 Preheat the oven to moderately hot 200°C (400°F/Gas 6). Grease a 20 cm round pie dish. Line the dish with both sheets of shortcrust pastry, trimming the overhanging edges. Line the pastry shell with a piece of crumpled baking paper that is large enough to cover the base and side, and pour in some baking beads or uncooked rice. Bake for 10 minutes. Remove the baking paper and beads, and bake for a further 10 minutes, or until the base is dry and lightly golden.

2 Place the apples, ground cloves and lemon rind in a bowl and mix together. Spoon the apple mixture into the hot pastry shell.

3 Cover the top of the pie with the sheet of puff pastry and use a sharp knife to trim off any excess pastry. Cut a whole in the centre to allow the steam to escape, and decorate with any leftover pastry.

4 Glaze the pastry with the milk and sprinkle with the sugar. Bake for 20 minutes, or until the pastry is golden brown. Serve warm or cold, with whipped cream or ice cream.

nutrition per serve
Protein 8 g; Fat 33 g; Carbohydrate 93 g; Dietary Fibre 4.5 g; Cholesterol 36 mg; 2876 kJ (687 cal)

hint

For an apple and blackberry pie, substitute 300 g of canned apple for frozen or canned blackberries. Drain the canned berries well before adding to the apples.

ingredients

4 egg yolks
¼ cup (60 g) caster sugar
½ cup (125 ml) Marsala,
  sherry or sweet white
  wine
400 g mixed berries
  (eg. raspberries,
  blackberries, mulberries,
  strawberries)

preparation: 15 minutes
cooking: 5 minutes
serves: 4–6

1 Place the egg yolks, sugar and Marsala in a large heatproof bowl and stand over a pan of barely simmering water. Beat with electric beaters for 5 minutes, or until thick, light and foamy.

2 Divide the mixed berries among the serving dishes, pour over the sabayon and serve immediately.

nutrition per serve (6)
Protein 3 g; Fat 3 g; Carbohydrate 16 g; Dietary Fibre 2 g; Cholesterol 120 mg; 522 kJ (125 cal)

handy tip...

Sabayon should be made just before serving time, as the sabayon mixture will separate if it is left to stand. This dish may be grilled until golden brown and served hot.

ingredients

60 g butter
½ cup (95 g) soft brown
    sugar
2 tablespoons lemon juice
1 tablespoon orange
    liqueur
4 firm, ripe bananas,
    sliced in half lengthways

preparation: 5 minutes
cooking: 10 minutes
serves: 4

1 Melt the butter in a frying pan. Add the sugar and mix together well. Simmer for 3 minutes, or until golden and bubbly.

2 Add the lemon juice and orange liqueur and stir gently. Add the bananas to the sauce and simmer for 5 minutes, or until the sauce thickens. Spoon the sauce occasionally over the bananas to baste them.

3 Serve the bananas and sauce with ice cream or with waffles and whipped cream, if desired.

nutrition per serve
Protein 2.5 g; Fat 12 g; Carbohydrate 55 g; Dietary Fibre 3 g; Cholesterol 38 mg; 1427 kJ (340 cal)

hint

This recipe also makes a delicious pancake filling if you chop the bananas instead of halving them.
Try stacking the pancakes between layers of bananas and sauce. Sprinkle with demerara sugar and flash under a grill until toffee-like.

cakes & bakes

140 g unsalted butter

¾ cup (185 g) caster
  sugar

2 eggs, lightly beaten

1 teaspoon vanilla
  essence

2 cups (250 g) self-raising
  flour, sifted

½ cup (125 ml) milk

Lemon glacé icing

1 cup (125 g) icing sugar,
  sifted

3–4 teaspoons lemon juice

preparation: 20 minutes

cooking: 45 minutes

serves: 6–8

1 Preheat the oven to moderate 180°C (350°F/Gas 4). Grease the base and side of a deep 20 cm round cake tin. Line the base with baking paper.

2 Place 125 g of the butter and all the sugar in a large bowl and beat with electric beaters until light and creamy. Add the egg gradually, beating thoroughly after each addition. Add the vanilla essence and beat until combined. Fold in the flour alternately with the milk, using a metal spoon. Stir until just combined and the mixture is almost smooth.

3 Spoon the mixture into the prepared tin and smooth the surface with the back of a spoon. Bake for 45 minutes, or until a skewer comes out clean when inserted in the centre of the cake. Leave in the tin for 10 minutes before turning onto a wire rack to cool.

4 To make the lemon glacé icing, melt the remaining butter. Place the butter, icing sugar and enough lemon juice in a small bowl to form a firm paste. Place the bowl over a saucepan of simmering water, stirring constantly until the icing is smooth and glossy—do not overheat or the icing will be dull and grainy. Remove from the heat. Spread the icing over the cake using a flat-bladed knife and serve.

nutrition per serve (8)
Protein 4.9 g; Fat 16 g; Carbohydrate 61 g; Dietary Fibre 1 g; Cholesterol 90 mg; 1677 kJ (400 cal)

handy tip...

Uniced, the cake can be stored in an airtight container for 1 week or in the freezer for up to 3 months.
Sugar helps in incorporating air into fat, so it is important to use the appropriate sugar to the recipe. Caster sugar is ideal for butter cakes because it is superfine—the finer the crystals, the more numerous the air cells and the lighter the finished cake.

ingredients

1 cup (250 g) caster sugar
1¾ cups (215 g)
    self-raising flour
⅔ cup (85 g) cocoa
    powder
1 teaspoon bicarbonate of
    soda
¼ cup (60 ml) vegetable
    oil
2 eggs
¾ cup (185 g) sour cream

preparation: 15 minutes
cooking: 40 minutes
serves: 6–8

1 Preheat the oven to moderate 180°C (350°F/Gas 4). Grease a deep 20 cm baba or ring tin.

2 Place the sugar, flour, cocoa, bicarbonate of soda, oil, eggs, sour cream and ⅔ cup (170 ml) water in a food processor. Process in short bursts until the mixture is well combined and smooth in texture.

3 Spoon the mixture evenly into the prepared tin. Bake for 35–40 minutes, or until a skewer comes out clean when inserted in the centre of the cake. Leave in the tin for 10 minutes before turning onto a wire rack to cool. Serve with whipped cream and fresh berries, if desired, or drizzle with a rich chocolate icing *(see hint).*

nutrition per serve (8)
Protein 4 g; Fat 13 g; Carbohydrate 24 g; Dietary Fibre 0.5 g; Cholesterol 40 mg; 959 kJ (229 cal)

hint

To make a rich chocolate icing, place 60 g butter, 100 g dark chocolate, chopped and 1 tablespoon cream in a small heatproof bowl. Stand over a saucepan of simmering water and stir until the butter and chocolate have melted and the mixture is smooth. Cool slightly until the mixture is cool enough to drizzle.

ingredients

½ cup (60 g) plain flour
½ cup (60 g)
   self-raising flour
4 eggs, separated
⅔ cup (160 g) caster
   sugar
½ cup (160 g) strawberry
   jam
½ cup (125 ml) cream,
   whipped
icing sugar, to dust

preparation: 15 minutes
cooking: 20 minutes
serves: 8

1 Preheat the oven to moderate 180°C (350°F/Gas 4). Grease two shallow 20 cm sandwich tins and line the base of each tin with baking paper.

2 Sift the flours together three times onto baking paper. Place the egg whites in a large clean, dry bowl. Beat with electric beaters until firm peaks form. Add the sugar gradually, beating constantly until the sugar has dissolved and the mixture is thick and glossy.

3 Add the egg yolks and beat for another 20 seconds. Fold in the flour quickly and lightly with a metal spoon.

4 Pour the mixture into the prepared tins and spread evenly. Bake for 20 minutes, or until lightly golden and springy to touch. Leave in the tins for 5 minutes before turning onto wire racks to cool.

5 Spread the jam evenly onto one of the sponges, then spoon the cream over the jam. Top with the second sponge, and dust with sifted icing sugar before serving.

nutrition per serve
Protein 6.5 g; Fat 10.5 g; Carbohydrate 27 g; Dietary Fibre 0.9 g; Cholesterol 156 mg; 947 kJ (226 cal)

handy tip...

Unfilled sponges can be frozen for up to one month—freeze in separate freezer bags. Thaw sponges at room temperature (for about 20 minutes). A filled sponge is best served immediately. The secret to making a perfect sponge lies in the folding technique. Use only a large metal spoon, working quickly yet gently to incorporate the flour. A beating action, or using a wooden spoon, will cause loss of volume in the egg mixture and will result in a flat, heavy cake.

ingredients

125 g butter
½ cup (125 g) caster sugar
3 eggs, lightly beaten
1¼ cups (155 g)
  self-raising flour, sifted
3 teaspoons caraway
  seeds
2 tablespoons milk
icing sugar, to dust

preparation: 15 minutes
cooking: 40 minutes
serves: 6–8

1 Preheat the oven to moderate 180°C (350°F/Gas 4). Grease a deep 20 cm round cake tin and line the base with baking paper.

2 Place the butter and sugar in a bowl and beat with electric beaters until light and creamy. Add the egg gradually, beating thoroughly after each addition. Using a metal spoon, gently fold in the flour and caraway seeds alternately with the milk.

3 Spoon into the prepared tin and smooth the surface. Bake for 40 minutes, or until a skewer comes out clean when inserted in the centre of the cake. Leave in the tin for 20 minutes before turning onto a wire rack to cool. Dust with icing sugar.

nutrition per serve (8)
Protein 7 g; Fat 24 g; Carbohydrate 43 g; Dietary Fibre 1 g; Cholesterol 72 mg; 1705 kJ (408 cal)

hint

Seed cake is a traditional English cake made to celebrate the end of spring sowing of the crop.
This cake will store well for up to one week in an airtight container, or up to three months in the freezer.

ingredients

1½ cups (280 g) fruit medley *(see tip)*

½ cup (60 g) raisins

1 cup (70 g) processed bran

½ cup (95 g) soft brown sugar

1½ cups (375 ml) milk

1½ cups (185 g) self-raising flour, sifted

whole blanched almonds, to decorate

preparation: 15 minutes + 15 minutes soaking
cooking: 50 minutes
serves: 6–8

1 Preheat the oven to moderate 180°C (350°F/Gas 4). Lightly grease a 23 x 13 x 7 cm loaf tin. Line the base with baking paper.

2 Place the fruit medley, raisins, bran, sugar and milk in a bowl and mix together well. Leave to soak for at least 15 minutes.

3 Add the flour to the mixture and mix together well. Spoon into the prepared tin, smooth the surface and decorate with the almonds. Bake for 45–50 minutes, or until a skewer comes out clean when inserted in the centre of the cake. Leave in the tin for 5 minutes, then turn onto a wire rack to cool. Serve plain, sliced with butter or toasted.

nutrition per serve (8)
Protein 7.5 g; Fat 3 g; Carbohydrate 52.5 g; Dietary Fibre 10.5 g; Cholesterol 6 mg; 1100 kJ (263 cal)

handy tip...

Use any combination of chopped dried fruits—apricots, pears, apples, peaches and sultanas. Make sure you finely chop the fruit before soaking. This loaf is delicious toasted and served for breakfast.

1½ cups (185 g)
    self-raising flour
½ cup (60 g) plain flour
185 g unsalted butter
⅔ cup (160 g) caster
    sugar
3 eggs, lightly beaten
⅓ cup (80 ml) milk
1 cup (220 g) pie apples
2 tablespoons golden
    syrup

preparation: 20 minutes
cooking: 1 hour 5 minutes
serves: 8–10

1 Preheat the oven to moderate 180°C (375°F/Gas 4). Grease a deep 23 cm round cake tin. Line the base with baking paper.

2 Sift the flours into a large mixing bowl and make a well in the centre.

3 Place the butter and sugar in a small saucepan and stir over low heat for 5 minutes, or until the sugar has dissolved. Remove from the heat. Place the egg and milk in a bowl and whisk together well.

4 Add the butter and egg mixtures to the flour and stir with a wooden spoon until just combined—do not overbeat.

5 Pour half the mixture into the prepared tin. Smooth the surface. Top with the pie apples and drizzle with the golden syrup. Spoon in the remaining cake mixture and smooth the surface. Bake for 50–60 minutes, or until a skewer comes out clean when inserted in the centre of the cake. Dust with icing sugar and serve with cream.

nutrition per serve (10)
Protein 4.5 g; Fat 17 g; Carbohydrate 44 g; Dietary Fibre 1 g; Cholesterol 102 mg; 1448 kJ (346 cal)

hint

Use 1 cup of freshly cooked apple instead of the pie apples, if desired. Add a clove or a pinch of cinnamon to the apple for extra flavour. Canned chopped two-fruits may be used to replace the apple. Drain well before using.

ingredients

3 cups (375 g) plain flour
1 tablespoon baking
powder
1 cup (185 g) soft brown
sugar
125 g butter, melted
2 eggs, lightly beaten
1 cup (250 ml) milk
1⅓ cups (205 g) fresh or
thawed frozen
blueberries

preparation: 20 minutes
cooking: 20 minutes
makes: 12 muffins

1 Preheat the oven to hot 210°C (415°F/Gas 6–7). Grease two trays of six ½ cup (125 ml) muffin holes.

2 Sift the flour and baking powder into a large bowl. Stir in the sugar and make a well in the centre. Add the combined melted butter, egg and milk all at once, and fold until just combined. (Do not overmix, the batter should look quite lumpy.)

3 Gently fold in the blueberries, then spoon the batter into the prepared tins. Bake for 20 minutes, or until golden brown. Cool on a wire rack.

nutrition per muffin
Protein 7 g; Fat 12 g; Carbohydrate 40 g; Dietary Fibre 1.5 g; Cholesterol 65 mg; 1240 kJ (300 cal)

handy tip...

If using frozen blueberries, drain the liquid once they have thawed before using. To make chocolate chip muffins replace the blueberries with chocolate chips.

ingredients

80 g butter
½ cup (125 g) caster sugar
1 egg, lightly beaten
¾ cup (90 g) self-raising flour, sifted
¼ cup (30 g) plain flour, sifted
½ cup (125 ml) milk
1 tablespoon caster sugar, extra
1 teaspoon ground cinnamon

preparation: 20 minutes
cooking: 30 minutes
serves: 6–8

1 Preheat the oven to 180°C (350°F/Gas 4). Grease a round 20 cm cake tin and line the base with baking paper.

2 Place the butter and sugar in a bowl and beat with electric beaters until light and creamy. Add the egg gradually, beating well after each addition.

3 Transfer the mixture to a large bowl. Using a metal spoon, fold in the sifted flours, alternately with milk. Stir until smooth. Spoon into the prepared tin and smooth the surface. Bake for 30 minutes or until a skewer comes out clean when inserted into the centre of the cake. Leave the cake in the tin for 5 minutes before turning out onto a wire rack to cool.

4 Combine the cinnamon and extra sugar in a small bowl. Brush the cake with a little melted butter while still warm, then sprinkle with the cinnamon sugar.

nutrition per serve (8)
Protein 3 g; Fat 7.5 g; Carbohydrate 31 g; Dietary Fibre 0.6 g; Cholesterol 44 mg; 848 kJ (203 cal)

hint

Cinnamon is the dried bark of the cinnamon tree. A native to Sri Lanka, it is sold ground and in the form of a quill—a stick of cinnamon in the shape of a scroll.

ingredients

150 g butter
200 g dark chocolate, chopped
3/4 cup (185 g) caster sugar
3 eggs
1 teaspoon vanilla essence
1 cup (125 g) plain flour, sifted

preparation: 10 minutes + cooling
cooking: 40 minutes
makes: 16

1 Preheat the oven to moderate 180°C (350°F/Gas 4). Grease a 20 cm square cake tin and line the base with baking paper.

2 Place the butter, chocolate and sugar in a heatproof bowl, then place over a small saucepan of simmering water. Stir occasionally, until the chocolate has melted and the mixture is smooth. Remove from the heat. Allow to cool.

3 Beat in the eggs and vanilla essence, then fold in the flour. Pour into the prepared tin and bake for 35 minutes, or until firm. Cool in the tin before turning out.

nutrition per brownie
Protein 2.5 g; Fat 12 g; Carbohydrate 25 g; Dietary Fibre 0.5 g; Cholesterol 60 mg; 910 kJ (217 cal)

handy tip...

For chocolate fudge walnut brownies, fold 1/2 cup (60 g) roughly chopped walnuts into the mixture.
To make rum and raisin brownies, soak 1/2 cup (60 g) raisins in 3 tablespoons rum for 10 minutes or until plump. Fold through the mixture.

ingredients

2 cups (250 g)
  self-raising flour, sifted
30 g butter, chopped
½ cup (125 ml) milk
milk, extra, for glazing

preparation: 20 minutes
cooking: 12 minutes
makes: 12

1 Preheat the oven to hot 210°C (415°F/Gas 6–7). Lightly grease a baking tray.

2 Place the flour and a pinch of salt into a bowl. Add the butter and rub in lightly using your fingertips until fine and crumbly.

3 Make a well in the centre of the flour. Combine the milk and ⅓ cup (80 ml) water and add almost all the liquid. Mix with a flat-bladed knife, until the dough comes together in clumps. Use the remaining liquid if necessary.

4 With floured hands, gently gather the dough together, lift out onto a lightly floured surface and pat into a smooth ball. Do not knead the dough or the scones will be tough. Pat the dough out to a 2 cm thickness. Using a 5 cm cutter, cut into rounds. Gather the dough trimmings together and, without handling too much, cut out more rounds.

5 Place the scones close together on the prepared baking tray and glaze with the extra milk. Bake for 10–12 minutes, or until golden brown. Serve warm with jam and whipped cream.

nutrition per scone
Protein 2.5 g; Fat 2.5 g; Carbohydrate 15 g; Dietary Fibre 0.5 g; Cholesterol 8 mg; 405 kJ (96 cal)

hint

It is worth adding a pinch of salt to your scones, even the sweet ones. Salt acts as a flavour enhancer and will not be tasted in the cooked scones.

melted caramel choc bar

Chop two 60 g chocolate-covered caramel nougat bars and place in a saucepan. Add ½ cup (125 ml) cream and stir over low heat until the chocolate melts. Drizzle the icing over a chocolate cake and allow to cool. Serve with ice cream or cream.

covers 1 round cake

citrus cream cheese

Place 250 g softened cream cheese, 60 g softened butter, 1 teaspoon grated lemon, lime or orange rind and 1 cup (125 g) icing sugar in a bowl and beat until thick and smooth. Spread over slices or cakes.

covers 12 muffins

From left to right: Melted caramel choc bar; Citrus cream cheese; Coffee cream; Marshmallow topping; Passionfruit glacé topping; Toffee syrup topping.

coffee cream

Place 250 g softened unsalted butter, 1 cup (125 g) sifted icing sugar, 1 tablespoon coffee essence or liqueur and 2 teaspoons milk in a bowl and beat until thick and pale.

covers 1 loaf cake

marshmallow topping

Place ½ cup (60 g) sifted icing sugar, 30 g softened butter and 1 tablespoon boiling water in a heatproof bowl and beat until smooth. Add 50 g chopped marshmallows. Place the bowl over a saucepan of simmering water and stir for 3–5 minutes, or until the marshmallows have melted. Allow to cool, then spread over homemade or purchased plain biscuits.

covers 20 small oval biscuits

passionfruit glacé topping

Place 1¼ cups (155 g) sifted icing sugar and 2 tablespoons fresh passionfruit pulp in a heatproof bowl. Place the bowl over a saucepan of simmering water and stir for 5 minutes, or until smooth and glossy. Spread over biscuits, slices or cream sponges.

covers 24 cup cakes

toffee syrup topping

Place ¾ cup (140 g) soft brown sugar, 1 cup (250 ml) cream and 60 g butter in a saucepan and stir until the sugar dissolves. Bring to the boil, then reduce the heat and simmer for 2 minutes, or until the sauce has slightly thickened. Serve over date loaf or banana cake.

covers 1 small loaf cake

2 cups (250 g) self-raising
   flour
1 cup (150 g) oat bran
3/4 cup (185 g) caster
   sugar
60 g butter, melted
3/4 cup (185 ml) milk
2 eggs, lightly beaten
1 cup (240 g) mashed,
   ripe banana
   (2 medium bananas)

preparation: 15 minutes
cooking: 15 minutes
makes: 12

1 Preheat the oven to hot 210°C (415°F/Gas 6-7). Grease twelve 1/2 cup (125 ml) muffin holes.

2 Sift the flour into a large bowl, then add the oat bran and sugar. Make a well in the centre. Whisk together the butter, milk, egg and banana and add to the dry ingredients all at once. Stir with a wooden spoon until just mixed—do not over beat as the batter should remain lumpy.

3 Spoon the mixture into the prepared holes. Bake for 15 minutes, or until puffed and brown. Transfer the muffins to a wire rack to cool.

nutrition per muffin
Protein 6 g; Fat 6.5 g; Carbohydrate 40 g; Dietary Fibre 3 g; Cholesterol 45 mg; 984 kJ (235 cal)

handy tip...

For muffins with a difference, beat 100 g cream cheese, 2 tablespoons icing sugar and 2 teaspoons lemon juice with electric beaters until light and creamy. Spread over the muffins and top with dried banana slices.

150 g unsalted butter, softened

2 teaspoons grated orange rind

1 teaspoon grated lemon rind

¾ cup (185 g) caster sugar

2 eggs, lightly beaten

⅓ cup (60 g) ground almonds

1⅔ cups (210 g) self-raising flour, sifted

¾ cup (185 g) plain yoghurt

preparation: 10 minutes
cooking: 40 minutes
serves: 8–10

1 Preheat the oven to moderate 180°C (350°F/Gas 4). Lightly grease a 23 cm ring or baba tin.

2 Place the butter, orange and lemon rinds and sugar in a bowl and beat with electric beaters until light and creamy. Add the egg gradually, beating thoroughly after each addition. Add the ground almonds, flour and yoghurt and beat on low speed for 1 minute, or until well combined.

3 Spoon the mixture into the prepared tin. Bake for 40 minutes, or until a skewer comes out clean when inserted into the centre of the cake. Turn out onto a wire rack to cool. Serve with cream or an orange glacé *(see hint)*, if desired.

nutrition per serve (10)
Protein 5.4 g; Fat 17 g; Carbohydrate 35 g; Dietary Fibre 1.4 g; Cholesterol 77 mg; 1312 kJ (314 cal)

hint

To make an orange glacé icing, combine 1 cup (125 g) sifted icing sugar, 1 teaspoon finely grated lemon rind, 10 g unsalted butter and 1–2 tablespoons orange juice in a small heatproof bowl to form a paste. Stand over a saucepan of simmering water and stir until the icing is smooth and glossy.

ingredients

250 g plain chocolate
    biscuits
1 tablespoon drinking
    chocolate
1½ cups (150 g) pecans
185 g butter, melted

Caramel topping
½ cup (90 g) lightly
    packed soft brown
    sugar
60 g butter
400 g can sweetened
    condensed milk

preparation: 15 minutes +
    chilling
cooking: 35 minutes
makes: 16 pieces

1 Preheat the oven to moderate 180°C (350°F/Gas 4). Lightly grease a shallow 18 x 28 cm cake tin and line with baking paper, over-hanging two opposite sides.

2 Place the biscuits, drinking chocolate and a third of the pecans in a food processor and process until finely crushed. Transfer to a bowl and add the melted butter. Mix well, then press into the tin. Press the rest of the pecans gently over the top.

3 To make the caramel topping, place the brown sugar and butter in a saucepan over low heat, until the butter melts and the sugar dissolves. Remove from the heat, stir in the condensed milk, then pour over the biscuit base.

4 Bake for 25–30 minutes, or until the caramel is firm and golden—the edges will bubble and darken.

Cool, then refrigerate for at least 3 hours.

5 Trim off the crusty edges and cut the slice into squares. If desired, before serving, hold a piece of paper over one half of each piece and sprinkle the other half with icing sugar, then sprinkle the other side with drinking chocolate.

nutrition per square
Protein 4 g; Fat 25 g; Carbohydrate 35 g; Dietary Fibre 1 g; Cholesterol 50 mg; 1614 kJ (385 cal)

handy tip...

Pecans are a smooth-shelled nut containing a ridged kernel, similar in appearance to a walnut. They are native to America, particularly the south central area.
Unshelled nuts can be stored in a cool dry place for up to 6 months—shelled pecans should be stored in an airtight container for up to 3 months.

ingredients

200 g dark chocolate, chopped
2 cups (60 g) cornflakes
½ cup (60 g) sultanas
½ cup (80 g) roasted unsalted peanuts
½ cup (100 g) red glacé cherries, halved
¼ cup (30 g) currants
1 tablespoon chopped mixed peel
⅔ cup (210 g) sweetened condensed milk

preparation: 15 minutes + chilling
cooking: 15 minutes
makes: 24 pieces

1 Preheat the oven to moderate 180°C (350°F/Gas 4). Line a shallow 18 x 28 cm cake tin with foil and lightly grease.

2 Put the chocolate in a heatproof bowl over a small saucepan of simmering water. Stir until melted and smooth. Spread the chocolate evenly into the tin and refrigerate for 15 minutes, or until set.

3 Place the cornflakes, sultanas, peanuts, glacé cherries, currants, mixed peel and condensed milk in a bowl. Mix together until all the ingredients are well coated with the condensed milk—try not to crush the cornflakes too much while mixing. Spread the mixture evenly over the chocolate, then bake for 12 minutes, or until the top is lightly golden.

4 Allow to cool, then refrigerate for 15 minutes to set the chocolate before cutting into squares.

nutrition per square
Protein 2 g; Fat 5 g; Carbohydrate 15 g; Dietary Fibre 0.5 g; Cholesterol 3 mg; 450 kJ (110 cal)

hint

This slice is a variation on the traditional Florentine biscuits—biscuits with plenty of dried fruits, mixed peel and nuts, and coated with melted chocolate on one side.
This slice can be stored in the fridge for up to two weeks.

ingredients

125 g butter
½ cup (125 g) caster sugar
2 eggs, lightly beaten
1 teaspoon vanilla essence
1½ cups (360 g) mashed, ripe banana (3 medium bananas)
1 teaspoon bicarbonate of soda
½ cup (125 ml) milk
2 cups (250 g) self-raising flour

preparation: 20 minutes
cooking: 1 hour
serves: 6–8

1 Preheat the oven to moderate 180°C (350°F/Gas 4). Grease a 20 cm round cake tin and line the base with baking paper.

2 Place the butter and sugar in a bowl and beat with electric beaters until light and creamy. Add the egg gradually, beating thoroughly after each addition. Add the vanilla essence and mashed banana and beat until well combined.

3 Transfer the mixture to a large bowl. Dissolve the bicarbonate of soda in the milk. Using a metal spoon, fold in the sifted flour alternately with the milk mixture. Stir until all the ingredients are just combined and the mixture is smooth.

4 Spoon into the prepared tin and smooth the surface. Bake for 1 hour, or until a skewer comes out clean when inserted into the centre of the cake. Leave the cake in the tin for 10 minutes before turning onto a wire rack. Delicious on its on or top with butter frosting and toasted flaked coconut.

nutrition per serve (8)
Protein 6 g; Fat 15 g; Carbohydrate 47.5 g; Dietary Fibre 2 g; Cholesterol 87 mg; 1443 kJ (345 cal)

handy tip...

To make a butter frosting, beat together 125 g butter, ¾ cup (90 g) icing sugar and 1 tablespoon lemon juice until smooth and creamy. Spread onto the cooled cake. This is also delicious with the citrus cream cheese icing on page 282.

ingredients

1¼ cups (155 g)
   self-raising flour
125 g unsalted butter,
   chopped
⅔ cup (160 g) caster
   sugar
3 eggs, lightly beaten
⅓ cup (80 ml) buttermilk
2 teaspoons finely grated
   orange rind

preparation: 15 minutes
cooking: 50 minutes
serves: 6–8

1 Preheat the oven to moderate 180°C (350°F/Gas 4). Grease a 21 x 14 x 7 cm loaf tin. Line the base and sides with baking paper.

2 Place the flour, butter and sugar in a food processor and, using the pulse button, process the dry ingredients for 20 seconds, or until the mixture is fine and crumbly. Add the combined egg, buttermilk and orange rind and process for 10 seconds, or until the mixture is smooth.

3 Spoon the mixture into the prepared tin and smooth the surface with the back of a spoon. Bake for 50 minutes, or until a skewer comes out clean when inserted into the centre of the cake. Leave the cake in the tin for 5 minutes before turning out onto a wire rack to cool.

nutrition per serve (8)
Protein 5 g; Fat 15 g; Carbohydrate 35 g; Dietary Fibre 0.75 g; Cholesterol 108 mg; 1211 kJ (289 cal)

hint

Yoghurt, sour cream or milk can be used instead of buttermilk in this recipe. Decorate with an orange or lemon butter frosting (such as the one suggested in the 'handy tip' on page 288) and purchased orange sweets, if desired.

ingredients

340 g packet Golden Buttercake cake mix
½ cup (95 g) finely chopped fresh pitted dates
1 teaspoon ground mixed spice
1 egg, lightly beaten
½ cup (125 ml) buttermilk
¼ cup (90 g) honey
20 g unsalted butter

preparation: 10 minutes
cooking: 35 minutes
serves: 6–8

1 Preheat the oven to moderate 180°C (350°F/Gas 4). Grease a shallow 20 cm round cake tin. Line the base and side with baking paper.

2 Place the cake mix, dates, mixed spice, egg and buttermilk in a bowl and beat with electric beaters on low speed for 1 minute, or until the ingredients are just combined. Beat on medium speed for 2 minutes, or until the mixture is smooth.

3 Spoon the mixture into the prepared tin. Bake for 35 minutes, or until a skewer comes out clean when inserted into the centre of the cake. Leave the cake in the tin for 10 minutes before carefully turning out onto a wire rack.

4 Combine the honey, butter and 1 tablespoon water in a small saucepan. Stir over low heat for 1 minute, or until the butter has just melted. Brush over the warm cake and serve with custard or ice cream, if desired.

nutrition per serve (8)
Protein 5 g; Fat 37 g; Carbohydrate 12 g; Dietary Fibre 2.5 g; Cholesterol 89 mg; 1659 kJ (396 cal)

handy tip...

Decorate the cake with sifted icing sugar, if desired.
This cake is delicious served warm as a dessert.

ingredients

200 g whole hazelnuts
185 g butter
6 egg whites
1¼ cups (155 g)
    plain flour
¼ cup (30 g) cocoa
    powder
2 cups (250 g) icing sugar
icing sugar, extra, to dust

preparation: 20 minutes
cooking: 40 minutes
makes: 12

1 Preheat the oven to moderately hot 200°C (400°F/Gas 6). Grease twelve ½ cup (125 ml) friand or muffin holes.

2 Spread the hazelnuts out on a baking tray and bake for 8–10 minutes, or until fragrant (take care not to burn). Place in a clean tea towel and rub vigorously to loosen the skins. Discard the skins. Cool, then process in a food processor until finely ground.

3 Place the butter in a small saucepan and melt over medium heat, then cook for 3–4 minutes, or until it turns a deep golden colour. Allow to cool slightly.

4 Lightly whisk the egg whites in a bowl until frothy but not firm. Sift the flour, cocoa powder and icing sugar into a large bowl and stir in the ground hazelnuts. Make a well in the centre and add the egg whites and butter and mix until combined.

5 Spoon the mixture into the friand holes until three-quarters filled. Bake for 20–25 minutes, or until a skewer comes out clean when inserted into the centre of each friand. Leave in the tin for a few minutes, then cool on a wire rack. Dust with icing sugar, to serve.

nutrition per friand
Protein 5.5 g; Fat 25 g; Carbohydrate 30 g; Dietary Fibre 2.5 g; Cholesterol 40 mg; 1475 kJ (355 cal)

hint

Friands will keep for up to 4 days in an airtight container. The hazelnuts can be substituted with ground almonds or pistachios. Roast the nuts before grinding to bring out the flavour.

ingredients

750 g mixed dried fruit
1/2 cup (125 ml) brandy
250 g butter
1 cup (185 g) soft brown sugar
5 eggs
2¾ cups (350 g) plain flour
1 tablespoon mixed spice
1 teaspoon baking powder

preparation: 15 minutes
cooking: 2 hours 30 minutes
serves: 8–10

1 Preheat the oven to slow 150°C (300°F/Gas 2). Grease a deep 20 cm cake tin and line the base and side with two layers of baking paper.

2 Place the mixed fruit in a large bowl, add the brandy and mix together well.

3 Place the butter and sugar in a bowl and beat with electric beaters until combined. Gradually add the eggs one at a time, beating well after each addition. Sift the flour, mixed spice and baking powder together and fold half of the dry ingredients into the mixture. Stir in the mixed fruit and brandy then mix in the remaining dry ingredients.

4 Spoon into the prepared tin and smooth the surface. Bake for 2 hours 30 minutes, or until a skewer comes out clean when inserted into the centre of the cake. Cover the cake with aluminium foil and leave to cool in the tin.

nutrition per serve (10)
Protein 8.5 g; Fat 3.5 g; Carbohydrate 123 g; Dietary Fibre 5.5 g; Cholesterol 90 mg; 2385 kJ (570 cal)

handy tip...

Light fruit cake is not as dense as your average fruit cake, therefore will not last as long. Stored in an airtight container, in the cupboard or refrigerator, it will keep for three weeks.

ingredients

1 large orange
2 eggs, lightly beaten
2 cups (310 g) grated
  carrot
2/3 cup (85 g) chopped
  pecans
1/2 teaspoon ground
  cinnamon
1/2 cup (125 ml) oil
2/3 cup (160 g) caster
  sugar
1 1/3 cups (165 g)
  self-raising flour

preparation: 15 minutes
cooking: 45 minutes
serves: 6–8

1 Preheat the oven to moderate 180°C (350°F/Gas 4). Grease a shallow 20 cm square cake tin and line the base with baking paper. Finely grate 2 teaspoons of orange rind and squeeze 1/3 cup (80 ml) of juice.

2 Place the eggs, carrot, orange rind and juice, pecans, cinnamon, oil and sugar in a large bowl and mix together with a wooden spoon.

3 Sift the flour into the bowl and mix together with a wooden spoon for 1 minute, or until the mixture is thick and the ingredients are well combined.

4 Spoon the mixture evenly into the prepared tin and smooth the surface. Bake for 45 minutes, or until a skewer comes out clean when inserted into the centre of the cake. Turn out onto a wire rack to cool. Serve warm or cold. Top with a cream cheese icing *(see hint)* and chopped pecans, if desired.

nutrition per serve (8)
Protein 5 g; Fat 24 g; Carbohydrate 38 g; Dietary Fibre 2.9 g; Cholesterol 45 mg; 1604 kJ (383 cal)

hint

To make a cream cheese icing, place 100 g cream cheese and 3/4 cup (90 g) sifted icing sugar in a bowl and beat until light and creamy. Add 1–2 tablespoons finely grated lemon or orange rind and beat for a further 2 minutes, or until the mixture is smooth and fluffy.
Walnuts can be used instead of pecans, if desired.

recipe developers:

Alison Adams, Laura Ammons, Roslyn Anderson, Wendy Berecry, Anna Beaumont, Janelle Bloom, Rosey Brian, Wendy Brodhurst, Janene Brooks, Anna Paola Boyd, Kerrie Carr, Glynn Christian, Rebecca Clancy, Judy Clarke, Amanda Cooper, Anne Creber, Jane Croswell-Jones, Rosemary De Santis, Alex Diblasi, Michelle Earl, Sheryle Eastwood, Stephanie Elias, Susan Geraghty, Gabrielle Gibson, Joanne Glynn, Wendy Goggin, Jenny Grainger, Alex Grant-Mitchell, Lulu Grimes, Margaret Harris, Donna Hay, Eva Katz, Coral Kingston, Kathy Knudsen, Jane Lawson, Michelle Lawton, Michaela Le Compte, Barbara Lowery, Peter Oszko, Rachel Mackey, Voula Mantzouridis, Tracey Meharg, Rosemary Mellish, Jean Miles, Kerrie Mullins, Denise Munro, Kate Murdoch, Angela Nahas, Liz Nolan, Sally Parker, Jackie Passmore, Rosemary Penman, Jennene Plummer, Justine Poole, Tracey Port, Wendy Quisumbing, Zoe Radze, Kerrie Ray, Jo Richardson, Tracy Rutherford, Alison Turner, Maria Sampsonis, Chris Sheppard, Deborah Solomon, Stephanie Souvlis, Dimitra Stais, Beverly Sutherland Smith, Jody Vassallo, Maria Villegas, Lovoni Welch.

home economists:

Frances Abdallaoui, Alison Adams, Laura Ammons, Roslyn Anderson, Anna Beaumont, Anna Paola Boyd, Wendy Brodhurst, Kerry Carr, Rebecca Clancy, Alex Diblasi, Michelle Earl, Jenny Fanshaw, Leanne Field, Jo Forrest, Maria Gargas, Susan Geraghty, Joanne Glynn, Wendy Goggin, Alex Grant-Mitchell, Michelle Lawton, Michaela Le Compte, Melanie McDermott, Rachel Mackey, Voula Mantzouridis, Ben Masters, Tracey Meharg, Beth Mitchell, Kerrie Mullins, Kate Murdoch, Angela Nahas, Bridget O'Connor, Peter Oszko, Justine Poole, Zoe Radze, Kerrie Ray, Jo Richardson, Tracy Rutherford, Maria Sampsonis, Clare Simmonds, Margot Smithyman, Michelle Thrift, Angela Tregonning, Alison Turner, Maria Villegas.

photographers:

Jon Bader, Paul Clarke, Cris Cordeiro, Craig Cranko, Ben Dearnley, Andrew Elton, Joe Filshie, Roberto Jean Francois, Andrew Furlong, Phil Hayley, Chris Jones, Ray Joyce, Tony Lyon, Andre Martin, Luis Martin, Andrew Payne, Peter Scott, Warren Web, Damien Wood.

food stylists:

Wendy Berecry, Anna-Marie Bruechert, Marie-Hélène Clauzon, Amanda Cooper, Rosemary De Santis, Georgina Dolling, Carolyn Fienberg, Kay Francis, Mary Harris, Di Kirby, Vicki Liley, Rosemary Mellish, Lucy Mortensen, Michelle Noerianto, Anna Phillips, Hans Schlupp, Suzie Smith.

food preparation:

Alison Adams, Ann Bollard, Bronwyn Clark, Michelle Earl, Jo Forrest, Wendy Goggin, Christine Sheppard, Cherise Koch, Tatjana Lakajev, Michelle Lawton, Melanie McDermott, Kerrie Mullins, Liz Nolan, Sally Parker, Justine Poole, Tracey Port, Kerrie Ray, Jo Richardson, Tracy Rutherford, Stephanie Souvlis, Dimitra Stais, Alison Turner, Maria Villegas.

The publisher wishes to thank the following for their assistance in the photography for this book:
Country Road
Dulux Paints
Porters Paints
Regeneration tiles
Studio Ramsay
Wheel & Barrow
Witchery

USEFUL INFORMATION

The recipes in this book were developed using a tablespoon measure of 20 ml. In some other countries the tablespoon is 15 ml. For most recipes this difference will not be noticeable but, for recipes using baking powder, gelatine, bicarbonate of soda, small amounts of flour and cornflour, we suggest that, if you are using the smaller tablespoon, you add an extra teaspoon for each tablespoon.

The recipes in this book are written using convenient cup measurements. You can buy special measuring cups in the supermarket or use an ordinary household cup: first you need to check it holds 250 ml (8 fl oz) by filling it with water and measuring the water (pour it into a measuring jug or even an empty yoghurt carton). This cup can then be used for both liquid and dry cup measurements.

Liquid cup measures

1/4 cup	60 ml	2 fluid oz
1/3 cup	80 ml	2 1/2 fluid oz
1/2 cup	125 ml	4 fluid oz
3/4 cup	180 ml	6 fluid oz
1 cup	250 ml	8 fluid oz

Spoon measures

1/4 teaspoon	1.25 ml
1/2 teaspoon	2.5 ml
1 teaspoon	5 ml
1 tablespoon	20 ml

Nutritional information

The nutritional information given for each recipe does not include any garnishes or accompaniments, such as rice or pasta, unless they are included in specific quantities in the ingredients list. The nutritional values are approximations and can be affected by biological and seasonal variations in foods, the unknown composition of some manufactured foods and uncertainty in the dietary database. Nutrient data given are derived primarily from the NUTTAB95 database produced by the Australian New Zealand Food Authority.

Oven Temperatures
You may find cooking times vary depending on the oven you are using. For fan-forced ovens, as a general rule, set oven temperature to 20°C lower than indicated in the recipe.

Note: Those who might be at risk from the effects of salmonella food poisoning (the elderly, pregnant women, young children and those suffering from immune deficiency diseases) should consult their GP with any concerns about eating raw eggs.

Alternative names

bicarbonate of soda	—	baking soda
capsicum	—	red or green (bell) pepper
chickpeas	—	garbanzo beans
cornflour	—	cornstarch
fresh coriander	—	cilantro
cream	—	single cream
eggplant	—	aubergine
flat-leaf parsley	—	Italian parsley
hazelnut	—	filbert
plain flour	—	all-purpose flour
prawns	—	shrimp
sambal oelek	—	chilli paste
snow pea	—	mange tout
spring onion	—	scallion
thick cream	—	double/heavy cream
tomato paste (US/Aus.)	—	tomato purée (UK)
kettle barbecue	—	Kettle grill/Covered barbecue
zucchini	—	courgette

Weight

10 g	1/4 oz	220 g	7 oz	425 g	14 oz
30 g	1 oz	250 g	8 oz	475 g	15 oz
60 g	2 oz	275 g	9 oz	500 g	1 lb
90 g	3 oz	300 g	10 oz	600 g	1 1/4 lb
125 g	4 oz	330 g	11 oz	650 g	1 lb 5 oz
150 g	5 oz	375 g	12 oz	750 g	1 1/2 lb
185 g	6 oz	400 g	13 oz	1 kg	2 lb

Published by Murdoch Books®, a division of Murdoch Magazines Pty Limited, GPO Box 1203, Sydney NSW 1045.
This edition published in 2000 for Index Books Ltd, Henson Way, Kettering, Northamptonshire, NN16 8PX, United Kingdom.
Editor: Stephanie Kistner **Designer:** Michelle Cutler **CEO & Publisher:** Anne Wilson

A catalogue record of this book is available from the British Library.
ISBN 1 897730 77 2
First printed in 2000. This edition first printed 2000.
Printed by Tien Wah Press, Singapore. PRINTED IN SINGAPORE.